ELITES, ENTERPRISE AND THE MAKING OF THE
BRITISH OVERSEAS EMPIRE, 1688–1775

Also by H. V. Bowen

A DEAR AND NOBLE BOY: THE LIFE AND LETTERS OF
LOUIS STOKES, 1897–1916 (*editor with R. A. Barlow*)

REVENUE AND REFORM: THE INDIAN PROBLEM IN BRITISH
POLITICS, 1757–1773

Elites, Enterprise and the Making of the British Overseas Empire 1688–1775

H. V. Bowen

Lecturer in Economic and Social History
University of Leicester

First published by
MACMILLAN PRESS LTD
Houndmills, Basingstoke, Hampshire RG21 6XS
and London
Companies and representatives
throughout the world

ISBN 0–333–62208–1

A catalogue record for this book is available
from the British Library.

This book is printed on paper suitable for recycling and made from fully managed and sustained forest sources.

Transferred to digital printing 2000

Printed in Great Britain by
Antony Rowe Ltd, Chippenham,Wiltshire

In memory of Philip Lawson

Contents

Preface   xi

PART ONE   CONTEXTS AND CONTOURS

1   Historians and the Eighteenth-Century Empire   3

2   The Dynamics of Expansion   22

PART TWO   METROPOLITAN ELITES AND THE
           OVERSEAS EMPIRE

3   Gentlemen and Entrepreneurs: Landowners,
    Merchants and Bankers   47

4   Investment in Empire   79

PART THREE   OVERSEAS ELITES IN THE BRITISH
             EMPIRE

5   Imperial Ties and the Anglicization of the
    Overseas Empire   103

6   Merchants, Planters and the Gentlemanly Ideal   125

PART FOUR   A NEW IMPERIAL ORDER, 1750–75

7   The End of the English Empire   149

8   Enterprise and Expansion: Drawing a Line   171

Afterword   194

Notes   197

Bibliography   237

Index   252

Preface

This book does not aspire to offer comprehensive coverage and explanation of British imperial expansion during the eighteenth century. The aim is altogether more modest. This work of synthesis, based upon secondary sources, endeavours to trace the development of the forces and influences exerted by elites which served to give the empire much of its shape, coherence and direction before it was shaken by the upheavals of the 1770s. Accordingly, discussion is located in a thematic rather than strictly chronological framework of organization. Of course, there is an obvious danger in doing this, because imperialism represented a complex interaction of many forces and influences, and to focus on only one major theme invariably means that others appear to have been neglected or marginalized. Nevertheless, by concentrating attention on one central element which lay at the very heart of the development of the British empire, it is hoped that several important strands in recent historical writing can be drawn together and brought to bear on the question of how, and why, the eighteenth-century empire acquired its form. At the same time, it must also be stressed that this book does not seek to place developments within a framework of interpretation shaped by the need to trace and explain either the causes of the American Revolution or the dissolution of what used to be referred to as the 'first British empire'. Attention is devoted to the cultural, economic and social dimensions of the British imperial experience, and an implicit assumption within the book is that analysis of political and constitutional issues serves to highlight aspects of crisis and short-term change within the empire but often tends to obscure important underlying changes and continuities. It is these underlying changes and, above all, continuities that are to be found at the core of the book.

In the past, historical analysis of the eighteenth-century British empire was often set within terms of reference defined by constitutional, military or political developments. In recent years, however, the scope of debate has broadened to include consideration of other important, but less formal, imperial sinews or bonds which held the empire together. Thus, the

British Atlantic empire before 1775 has been variously described as an 'empire of goods' and an 'empire of paper'. That empire is also increasingly being seen as an entity in which the position of, and government by, elites was reinforced and legitimized by adherence to a set of common cultural values and assumptions, both in Britain and overseas. By drawing on these wider definitions of the imperial tie, and by considering the implications of developments taking place within the domestic economy and society, this book attempts to place eighteenth-century British imperialism in a broad historiographical context. This allows the empire to be seen not as a series of discrete geographical areas or units scattered across the globe, but rather as a commercial, cultural and social body of reasonably sharp definition which had its roots very firmly planted in metropolitan society. It also helps with the identification of central characteristics which brought great inner strength and flexibility to the empire and allowed it to make successful adaptations to new circumstances and situations. Indeed, with one eye on the future, it is argued that it was these characteristics that eventually played a considerable part in helping Britain to survive as an imperial nation after the loss of the American colonies in 1782.

Part One, comprising two chapters, establishes the general context for the subsequent discussion. Chapter 1 marks out some key areas of debate by reviewing the recent historiography of the eighteenth-century empire, while Chapter 2 identifies some of the principal dynamic processes that contributed to the expansion of British overseas activity during the eighteenth century. The two chapters in Part Two are devoted to an assessment of how the domestic elite shaped and, in turn, were shaped by the imperial process before 1775. Chapter 3 considers the different elites who played a leading role in the activities that contributed to the expansion of the empire. These were the individuals and groups who controlled the levers of political, commercial and financial power within Britain, and their attitudes, assumptions and general outlook exerted a profound influence on the development of the metropolitan economy, society and culture. In particular, many of them were committed to a wide range of economic activities based upon innovation and improvement and they played the leading part in helping to create and sustain the enterprise culture that emerged at the end of the seventeenth century. As an important part of this new business environment, the expansion of British overseas interests offered an ever-increasing range of financial and commercial opportunities to the metropolitan investor, and individuals from all elites were to be found acquiring their own personal stake in the empire. At the same time, the extent to which imperialism represented an important agent of economic and social change in Britain is examined. The relationships and interactions between elite groups are assessed, and consideration is given to the way in which an interest in, and commitment to, the empire affected elite culture and attitudes in Britain. In Chapter 4, the extent to which the elite held a financial stake in the overseas empire is established. Through a wide range of investments, individuals from all the elites are shown to have been deeply implicated in the various imperial processes and it is argued that, from a metropolitan perspective, this provided the single most important link or tie between the core and the periphery of the empire.

In Part Three, the focus shifts to the wider world in an attempt to define the part played within the imperial process by the emergence of different elites in Britain's overseas possessions. The aim here is to consider the extent to which the British overseas presence was shaped and defined through local elites whose ideals, assumptions and modes of behaviour closely resembled those of the metropolitan elite. Chapter 5 identifies the way in which, from an overseas perspective, various cultural and economic ties bound the periphery to the imperial core. These imperial ties played an important role in reinforcing the position of particular overseas elites within a broader transoceanic elite. This theme is explored further in Chapter 6 through an examination of the extent to which adherence to a gentlemanly ideal enabled overseas elites to adopt lifestyles that were modelled on those of their counterparts in the mother country and which also helped their members to define their place and position within emerging local hierarchies. In all quarters of the globe, this process served to give the eighteenth-century empire at least some degree of the social order and structure that had been developed at home.

Lest it be thought that the preceding chapters have granted too sharp a sense of unity, common purpose and identity to the transoceanic imperial elite, Part Four seeks to explore two important areas of change in the mid-eighteenth-century empire. Both areas illustrate the extent to which relationships within, and between, different elites were in a semi-permanent state of redefinition. In Chapter 7, the changing composition of British overseas communities is sketched against a general background in which the Englishness of the empire was being diluted, both at the core and the periphery, by the emergence of new and powerful ethnic and cultural forces. This was a reflection of the fact that an expanding empire, based upon enterprise and opportunity, offered prospects of advancement and profit to individuals from across Britain and Europe. Diversity and cosmopolitanism had become two of the dominant characteristics of the empire and this was seen quite clearly in the membership of some overseas elites. This did not necessarily weaken the empire but it illustrated the extent to which the central defining features of eighteenth-century British imperialism were sufficiently flexible and adaptable to allow different cultures, languages, religions and traditions to find a prominent place in British territories in the wider world. If cosmopolitanism did not by itself serve to weaken the empire, Chapter 8 considers other ways in which an unfettered expansionist process, based upon a vigorous and innovative enterprise culture, had begun to present new problems and difficulties to the authorities. In particular, territorial expansion prompted a metropolitan reappraisal of the basic principles underpinning imperial activity and, as this occurred, domestic elites and the overseas elite increasingly began to move out of step with one another on a wide range of issues. As those in Britain reassessed the importance of empire, so those at the periphery found some of their commercial and business ambitions becoming more restricted by the metropolitan authorities. This caused misunderstanding and tension within imperial relationships and had significant repercussions in both North America and India which fed into the general imperial crisis of the period between 1765 and 1775. Finally, brief concluding remarks address the important question of continuity within the empire by suggesting ways in which the general characteristics of the imperialism that had been developing during the eighteenth century enabled Britain to survive at a time when her very future as an imperial nation was being threatened by political crisis and military disaster.

Because the study of imperial history has long been bedev-illed by problems associated with definition, it is perhaps nec-essary at the outset to consider a few of the terms used in this book. Britain came into being in 1707 following the Act of Union between England and Scotland. I have thus taken care to refer to England, Scotland and Wales when examining de-velopments located in a specific geographical context and to Britain when discussing matters relating to the greater polity that emerged after 1707. When discussing the period before the Act of Union, the empire is referred to as the English empire, and after 1707 it becomes the British empire. The overseas empire is, in the main, the territory and possessions brought under formal British control in India, North America and the West Indies. Accordingly, the 'core' of the empire is taken to be mainland Britain and the 'periphery' is British territory in the wider world. Ireland is something of a special case in the sense that it might be regarded quite legitimately as part of either the core or the periphery of the British empire. Contemporaries debated the question of Ireland's status at great length and historians have continued that discussion ever since. For the sake of convenience, I have regarded Ireland as representing, in the words of one distinguished historian, a 'kingdom and colony', but in the commentary that follows I have not defined it as belonging to the overseas empire.

I am most grateful to Philip Cottrell, P.J. Marshall and P.D.G. Thomas for their careful reading of early drafts of chapters. In their different ways, they each made many helpful comments and suggestions, and their criticism was always constructive and thought-provoking. Needless to say, of course, they bear no responsibility for what follows. I also owe a large debt to Tony Hopkins. We have not always agreed with one another, but he has been a source of great encouragement and advice as I have attempted to examine 'gentlemanly capitalism' in its eighteenth-century context. Most of all, thanks go to my family who have again offered patient and good-humoured support while a book was being written.

This book is dedicated to the memory of Phil Lawson. For me, as for many students of eighteenth-century history, his work, enthusiasm and friendship were sources of inspiration and great strength.

Part One
Contexts and Contours

1 Historians and the Eighteenth-Century Empire

Between 1688 and 1775 Britain's scattered imperial possessions around the world grew in both number and size. The extent to which these territories, forts and trading posts ever constituted an integrated and clearly defined empire is, perhaps, a matter for debate. This has arisen because a diverse and seemingly unconnected range of British overseas activities were located within two quite distinct geographical contexts: factors behind developments in the North Atlantic empire appear to have had little in common with those which determined the growth of commercial influence and political power in Asia. Yet, although few direct links and comparisons can be made between the outward form, structure and development of Britain's Atlantic empire and her north Indian empire, both empires shared several important characteristics. During the years before 1775, threats from rival European and indigenous powers were gradually removed, political and administrative control was secured, and economic hegemony was firmly established. These common traits manifested themselves in general expansionist tendencies which often occurred simultaneously in quite separate and far-distant spheres of overseas activity. By the 1760s, territorial advances were occurring on two broad geographical fronts, in North America and India, and the parallel economic expansion was reflected in increased levels of British business, commercial and investment activity at the periphery of the empire. Until the great imperial crisis of the 1770s, spatial expansion and business growth lay at the heart of the British imperial experience.[1]

Although expansion and growth were the central features of British imperialism before 1775, the forces promoting the extension of overseas interests and territory were uncoordinated and unplanned. In particular, they were subjected to little effective formal control from the centre of an empire whose political and administrative contours were shaped by poor communications and slow and ineffective decision-making processes. Yet, in the absence of any clearly defined and consciously implemented imperial design, Britain succeeded in establishing an increasingly formidable presence in the wider world. Dramatic reverses of fortune occurred from time to time, but by the 1760s the North American colonies had been consolidated and extended, supremacy had been achieved in the West Indies, and economic and political hegemony had been established over several north Indian provinces. Beyond the frontiers of British possessions, merchants and traders had developed networks of far-ranging commercial connections and associations. All these features had in different ways served to enhance the nation's economic fortunes and, more generally, they had helped to elevate Britain to great-power status. Of course, events in India and North America were soon to demonstrate that the British hold on their possessions was a tenuous one, and no one could deny that France still posed a very real long-term threat, but by the 1760s Britain stood in the very first rank of the world's imperial powers.

In view of her limited success in the field of warfare before the early years of the eighteenth century, the mid-century position represented a considerable change of fortune, and the transformation was all the more dramatic for the great victories and advances of the 1750s and 1760s having been startling and unexpected in both their size and scale. The successful use of military force and naval power had been of paramount importance in the expansion of the empire, but informed observers could also reflect on developments in trade, finance and politics that had allowed the state and private individuals to harness and deploy considerable human and capital resources on a global scale. It did not pass unnoticed by informed contemporaries, including George III, that Britain's rise to military and imperial supremacy was underpinned by, and dependent upon, the creation of a relatively stable domestic economic and political framework. These structures helped to give the nation's businessmen and entrepreneurs a competitive edge over their main rivals and competitors in the wider world.[2] Innovation and enterprise at home, it could be argued, had led to achievement and success abroad, and nowhere was this more clearly illustrated than in the expanding number of wealthy British financiers and merchants whose personal business empires represented in miniature the geography of the British empire as a whole.

As successive generations of historians have endeavoured to describe and explain the improvement of Britain's imperial fortunes between 1688 and 1775, they have, like imperial historians of other periods, tended to use biography, regional case study or the examination of specific imperial problems in domestic politics as the main vehicles for the advancement of understanding of the imperial process. As a result of this, a rich and erudite scholarly tradition has been established, but at the same time this has bestowed an atomized inheritance which almost defies a comparative and broad analytical approach. The lines of inquiry pursued by historians of British India often seem to have little in common with those developed by scholars in a North American context and, yet, if we are attempting to develop a broad overview of the imperial process, there is a need to try and explain and link closely related historical trends, even though they were separated by thousands of miles and occurred in quite different local conditions. In recent years, several historians have commented on the retreat of British imperial history into narrow specialization and they have drawn attention to the failure of historians to apply ideas and interpretations developed in fields of inquiry parallel to one another. Indeed, one can only agree with the observation that 'it seems doubtful, for example, that historians of British Canada regularly read histories of the British West Indies.'[3] This, of course, is not surprising because of the great volume of academic work generated by historians of each sector of British imperial activity, but the point is still an important and valid one: comparative approaches or what is sometimes rather contemptuously dismissed as the 'broad sweep' have become unfashionable beyond the context provided by textbooks and general chronological surveys.

A NEW IMPERIAL HISTORY

Over the last forty years or so, American scholars have been at the forefront of those seeking to re-examine eighteenth-century British imperialism. Previous generations of scholars tended to define imperial relationships in rather narrow

constitutional, military and political terms, but much important recent work on colonial North America and the broader
English-speaking world bordering the Atlantic Ocean has been
devoted to a reassessment of the cultural and economic links
between the core and the periphery of the British empire.
Many of these historians have adopted what has been called an
'Atlantic perspective' which seeks to explore the interactions
between cultural, political and social processes occurring simultaneously on both sides of the Ocean. At the same time, in
a closely related commercial context, attention has recently
been drawn to the growing level of economic interdepend-
ence between different parts of the eighteenth-century Atlantic trading world.[4] Indeed, such has been the range and diversity
of the recent work devoted to these themes that some historians have been bold enough to hail the arrival of a 'new' form
of imperial history.[5]

Many of the historians involved in this new imperial history
have acknowledged the important advances made in recent
years towards the incorporation of the Irish, Scottish and Welsh
dimensions of economic and social development into the
mainstream of British historical writing. Moreover, they have
recognized the way in which redefinitions of Britishness and
national identity, recently given shape and coherence by the
work of Linda Colley,[6] have had important implications for
the study of colonial and imperial history. Although there is
much that remains to be done in this field, the progress
already made has reshaped scholarly attitudes towards the
advance and development of British overseas influence during
the course of the eighteenth century. Just as the nature of the
relationship between the metropole, provinces and peripheries of mainland Britain has been reassessed, so the shaping of
the overseas empire has also been linked to the same forces
and influences that helped to forge a British identity, national
unity and the modern state. Some parts of Ireland, Scotland
and Wales were brought into the British state by processes of
'anglicization' or cultural assimilation, as well as by political
and economic union, and in similar fashion Britain's overseas
possessions also found their identity being shaped by metropolitan values and ideas in addition to the realities of military
and political subordination. As John Clive and Bernard Bailyn
remarked in their brief, but path-breaking, essay published in

1954, the 'direct transfers of goods, persons, books, and ideas reflect the profound fact that Scotland and America were provinces, cultural as well as political and economic, of the English-speaking world whose center was London.'[7] As scholars have moved away from the search for evidence of the existence of a distinctly 'American' form of culture during the colonial period, some have emphatically affirmed their belief that the colonies were firmly located within what one historian has described as an 'Anglo-American cultural system'.[8] This was based upon shared values and ideas, as well as material goods, and its central features found clear expression in all quarters of the English-speaking world.

The essay written forty years ago by Clive and Bailyn played an important part in helping to point historians towards rich and hitherto unexploited seams of historical inquiry. Partly as a consequence of this, perceptions of eighteenth-century British imperialism have been quite profoundly altered over the last few decades. In particular, the nature of the relationship and imperial ties between Britain and her overseas dependencies has been reassessed and re-examined, and this revisionism has manifested itself in several quite different contexts. Thus, for example, some historians have engaged in vigorous exchanges about the extent to which British armed force and 'garrison government' were key elements in defining the administrative features of the North Atlantic empire.[9] A large number of other scholars have focused attention on the way in which the eighteenth-century empire developed within a material, commercial and cultural framework provided by the goods, information, news and fashions supplied to the periphery by the mother country.[10] Whatever differences of interpretation may exist, most scholars now agree that overseas possessions and colonies, particularly those in the Atlantic world, should no longer be seen as distant outposts loosely connected to an exploiting metropole, but rather they are increasingly identified as being integrated elements within a greater organic whole. Their histories and development are no longer treated in splendid historiographical isolation. British overseas territories are seen as extensions, modifications and reflections of the way in which metropolitan society developed. Colonies are now deemed to have an important place of their own in the various interactive cultural, economic and political processes which gave the empire shape, coherence and identity. Indeed, through the adoption of a comparative approach and by seeking out similarities rather than diversities, one leading American authority has been able to draw together the threads of much modern scholarship and illustrate the extent to which 'the several regions of overseas settlement in Britain's early modern empire exhibited a similar pattern of social development'.[11] In turn, this pattern of development at the periphery was similar in many ways to that evident in metropolitan society.

There are signs that historians of Hanoverian Britain, following the lead given by their American counterparts, are also beginning to develop a fuller transoceanic perspective or framework of reference for their analyses of continuity and change in the eighteenth century. Important recent research and work in progress related to a diverse range issues such as identity, cultural interaction and the nature of economic development reflects a recognition that the metropolis, provinces and imperial periphery all need to be woven into any analysis of how the modern British state and its empire emerged.[12] The work of Colley, already cited, acknowledges more fully than most the part played by imperialism and overseas activity in helping to forge a sense of British identity.[13] In a different field of endeavour, J.C.D. Clark adopted a transatlantic perspective during the course of a recent analysis of Anglo-American relations during the eighteenth century. Clark made the important point that there is a need to relate the sense of common identity, created from material culture within the broad English-speaking world, to the various forms of consciousness, based upon the influences of religion and law, which led to both conflict and unity, alliance and antagonism, within that transatlantic world.[14] Such general approaches have much to commend them, for they help to locate some of the developments occurring in mainland Britain within a broader set of interactive cultural, political and religious processes taking place across the wider Atlantic empire. In other words, if one moves beyond the obvious commercial and material benefits stemming from imperial activity, the possession of an expanding empire is now more widely acknowledged as having had an important part to play in determining the course taken by metropolitan society during the the eighteenth century.

For all the importance of the steps that have been taken towards reinterpretation of the causes, nature and consequences of eighteenth-century British imperial development, expansion is still not often afforded a great deal of attention as a process which occurred on a global scale. Of course, the fact that British interests were expanding in several different sectors of activity is often acknowledged by those concentrating on only one geographical dimension of imperial history.[15] However, scholarly endeavour has tended to have been weighted heavily in favour of analyses of British imperialism defined within Atlantic terms of reference. There are, of course, many sound reasons as to why this should be the case, not least of which is the fact that contemporaries afforded much more importance to the Atlantic empire than they did to any other area of imperial activity. Nevertheless, a focus of attention which concentrates on the Atlantic sphere of British overseas activity limits understanding of eighteenth-century imperialism. In particular, it distorts the way in which Britons viewed the wider world and their place in it. Most important of all, concentration on the Atlantic empire indicates a failure to take any new approach to British imperialism to its logical conclusion. Although any approach to imperial history that adopts a transoceanic, pluralist and multicultural perspective will help to shed new light on the development of the British empire, a failure to give due weight and attention to the Asian sphere of British activity is to be regretted.[16] The boundaries of the British imperial experience must not be too narrowly drawn. The Atlantic Empire was not *the* English or British Empire, but all too often the two labels have been regarded by historians as interchangeable. The burgeoning Oriental empire is often perceived as having its own separate agenda for historical debate, and India, partly because it was not a colony of white settlement like North America and the West Indies, is seen as representing something of a 'special case'. Yet, as has recently been observed with regard to British India in the nineteenth century,[17] there can be no room for special cases in interpretations of imperialism, particularly if they are intended to offer general explanations for the processes of overseas expansion.

There are some signs that a broader approach towards eighteenth-century British trade and empire is emerging as scholars adopt a view from the centre which stresses close connections between British activities in different parts of the world. Rather than concentrating exclusively on the Atlantic trading world or the empire of the east, a number of historians are now beginning to emphasize the extent to which Britons traded simultaneously with different quarters of the globe. As merchants and businessmen diversified their activities and extended their commercial and investment networks,[18] perceptions of British power and national interest began to change. By the 1760s, when the complex implications of the East India Company's territorial expansion in India were beginning to manifest themselves for all to see, politicians and commentators were seeking to draw together some hitherto loose imperial threads in an attempt to bring a greater sense of order and coherence to Britain's overseas possessions and colonies. Specific imperial and commercial problems could no longer be treated in isolation from one another. Not only did the conduct of policy in one sector often bear directly on affairs in another sector, but a view was coalescing which saw the empire depicted as being a greater integrated whole rather than as simply a series of separate unconnected areas of British activity.[19] With more historians now willing and prepared to make such connections, important aspects of the development of the empire can be examined in a new light.

BARRIERS AND BOUNDARIES IN EIGHTEENTH-CENTURY IMPERIAL HISTORIOGRAPHY

Within the British historiographical tradition, the various economic, cultural and political forces that shaped the overseas empire before 1775 have rarely been considered to have been connected to the same general process. Similarly, the influences exerted by Britons in different fields of endeavour in the wider world have seldom been seen as having any common thread or purpose. There appears to have been no dominant central theme embracing west and east, thus linking the empire of settlement with the Asian trading empire. It is partly because of this that the eighteenth-century dimension has not often been incorporated into scholarly debate on imperial theory in its broadest sense. Rather, imperial historians seeking to advance general explanations for expansion have tended

to concentrate their attention on major nineteenth-century
themes and issues. Until recently, few serious attempts have
been made to integrate the main features of eighteenth-century
imperialism into any framework of interpretation designed to
explain the long-term development of Britain's overseas empire.

Part of the reason for the eighteenth century sitting somewhat uncomfortably within general imperial historiography
stems from there having been little agreement among scholars
about how the early Hanoverian empire should be regarded in
relation to its nineteenth-century successor. Because of uncertainties over this important issue, the eighteenth century often
provides no more than general background material for imperial historians discussing the period after 1815. Indeed,
few historians have attempted to bridge the difficult gap that
exists between the 1780s and the 1820s, and few continuities
are perceived to link the two dates.[20] This is not surprising, because in 1775 Britain entered a prolonged period of imperial
and military crisis, first suffering the loss of America and then
embarking on a long and exhausting struggle with France. As
a result, the scope and form of the empire of 1820 seems, on
first inspection, to bear little resemblance to that of 1770. A
great deal of scholarly endeavour over the last thirty years or
so has been devoted to debate about whether, and to what
extent, a very different new, or second, British empire emerged
from the ashes of that which was lost in the aftermath of the
Battle of Yorktown in 1781.

The work of Vincent Harlow (which is sometimes represented erroneously as being little more than the development
of a 'swing to the east' theory) has exerted considerable influence on the lines of chronological demarcation that have been
established within eighteenth-century imperial studies. By examining questions of continuity and discontinuity within the
development of the Empire, it has focused considerable attention on the extent to which the years 1763 and 1783 should be
represented as key dates, or points of departure, within the
broad sweep of the imperial process.[21] This provoked a lively
debate about the form and direction taken by British imperial
expansion after 1763.[22] Attention was paid to the trends
which served to connect the years on either side of the War of
American Independence, but this served to create something
of an imbalance within eighteenth-century imperial studies by

concentrating a disproportionate amount of scholarly endeavour in Britain on the developments and upheavals that occurred
during the second half of the century. In turn, this has played
its part in discouraging attempts to identify much longer run
features and influences within the imperial process which gave
continuity, structure and shape to the empire during the early
and middle years of the century. Of course, historians are
always attracted by crisis and change, and after 1775 the empire of George III experienced both of these characteristics in
abundance. However, this alone cannot justify the salutary historiographical neglect bestowed upon the development of the
empire during the reigns of George I and George II. In order
to make sense of the empire created in its broadest terms by
the 1760s, it is necessary that consideration is given to it on its
own terms, before it was subjected to the strains which eventually led to crisis in the 1760s and to its partial dissolution in
the 1780s. Any teleological approach to eighteenth-century
imperial history, seeking to identify the origins of later crises
during the early or middle part of the century, can often ignore,
or lose sight of, the existence of many strong expansionist
dynamics within British society. These were not only present
from the 1680s onwards, but persisted into the nineteenth century and so provided some great continuities in the development of the British empire.

Several of these general observations about British imperial
historiography have recently found expression in the work of
P.J. Cain and A.G. Hopkins. They have come to the conclusion
that the fragmentary nature of the subject is such that 'no
acceptable interpretation of eighteenth-century imperialism'
exists.[23] This is indeed the case, but Cain and Hopkins also
make the equally important observation that many recent
advances within eighteenth-century domestic historiography
have not yet been incorporated into debate about the nature
of British imperialism. On the other side of the coin, developments located within areas of study related to British overseas
activity have not yet found a place in the history of the mainland.[24] In particular, imperial history has not been substantially revised in the light of new work that has served to question
long-held assumptions about, and contributed to a greater
understanding of, the complexities of Britain's society and
economy. In the economic sphere alone, many important

contributions have been made in recent years to our understanding of growth, industrialization, the development of the state, and the expansion of government finance and the service sector. However, the combined effects of these far-reaching changes have not served to inform general discussion of the eighteenth-century imperial process in any significant way.[25] In part, this perhaps reflects the fact that, in the light of postcolonial experience during the last two or three decades, the preoccupations of many eighteenth-century historians and teachers have moved away from examination of the development of Britain's foreign and imperial role to new and fashionable areas of study. More importantly, it also reflects a long-standing unwillingness among social and economic historians to give due weight to Britain's imperial experience through a consideration of imperialism as a two-way process in which expansion was shaped by metropolitan forces and overseas activity acted as a major agent of change within Britain itself. Consequently, few attempts have been made to integrate imperial issues into general interpretations of change and development in eighteenth-century Britain. For the most part, imperial issues seem to have been regarded as matters of rather marginal importance and many authors of general works or textbooks have contented themselves with a self-contained chapter or two of the 'trade and empire' type. Indeed, it is possible to read some accounts of eighteenth-century Britain in which the empire barely features at all. Such a narrow perspective can only lead to a seriously incomplete understanding of the forces behind the nation's development, both at home and abroad.

1688 AND ALL THAT: THE EMERGENCE OF THE MODERN STATE

The amount of historical attention devoted to 'new' imperial history in recent years has not been made at the expense of more traditional areas of study. On the contrary, the administrative structures, political institutions and commercial organizations which served to define the formal framework within which imperial expansion occurred have been subjected to intense levels of detailed examination. Not only has this helped to explore the subtleties of the commercial and political relationships between the core and the periphery of the empire, but also detailed work on the development of the state after 1688 has enabled historians to reassess the fiscal and administrative arrangements which allowed Britain to develop the capacity to wage war and deploy resources on a global scale. Indeed, Britain in the eighteenth century has recently been described as a 'fiscal-military state'.[26] The characteristics of this state that emerged after 1688 were such that the metropolitan authorities were more often than not able to offer significant levels of support and protection to those operating in overseas territories and possessions.

At the very heart of the processes which transformed England, and then Britain, into a relatively powerful state were the fiscal and government funding arrangements constituting the core of what is commonly referred to as the 'financial revolution'. By drawing on domestic and foreign resources, and by establishing mechanisms for the management of short-term debt and long-term borrowing, ministers were able to meet the sustained challenge posed by the Bourbon powers over more than a century of intermittent warfare and conflict.[27] Upon these foundations were built the administrative and military structures which heralded the emergence of a reasonably effective central government bureaucracy and this was to be of the greatest importance for the development of overseas colonies and territories. More and more ministerial and parliamentary time was spent dealing with various problems of empire, particularly after 1750, and, although the general quality and speed of decision-making often left much to be desired, recent historical work has stressed the considerable amount of attention and effort devoted to imperial affairs by officials and ministers in key positions of responsibility.[28]

Because of the way in which some parts of the empire developed within terms of reference defined by commercial enterprise rather than by the imperatives of the Crown or state, many imperial problems were dealt with beyond the formal bureaucratic machinery of government in organizations which held primary responsibility for key areas of overseas activity. These organizations, or groups of individuals, often acted in a quasi-official capacity and as such they represented informal extensions of central government. There were, for example, very close links between the East India Company and both the Treasury and the Southern Department, and most political decisions relating to East Indian affairs were based upon lengthy formal and informal consultations between the Company and ministers. Most decisions were arrived at long before matters were presented to Parliament for discussion.[29] This was much the same with other groups of merchants and colonial agents who often achieved considerable success through their lobbying activities, particularly before 1760.[30]

Of course, the East India Company was much more than a simple commercial organization. Over time, it became a sovereign power in its own right and, as a monopolistic body, it was the sole official vehicle of British activity and administration in India. The Company thus fell somewhere in the rather grey area between private profit-making body and representative of British national interests. It was successful in the former role before 1760 and detailed work on the Company has revealed that it became a sophisticated organization with a well-developed metropolitan management structure and decision-making machinery.[31] However, as the Company became a territorial power during the 1760s, it had to redefine its commercial strategy and it did this, initially at least, with conspicuously little success. There was also a growing sense of unease in Britain about the way in which the Company administered its Indian territories and, for these reasons, the Indian problem became a semi-permanent item on the domestic political agenda after 1767.[32] At the same time, of course, a quite different set of imperial problems relating to the developing crisis in North America was being addressed by ministers.[33] In other words, although the external threat posed to Britain's overseas possessions by France and Spain might have been overcome, at least in the short term, during the Seven Years' War, it remained to be seen how British politicians would respond to the internal threats to stability and security that emerged within various parts of the empire during the 1760s. Over the years, historians have examined and re-examined all aspects of the political responses to the imperial crises of the 1760s and 1770s, but only a few have considered the answers to problems arising in different geographical locations as being based upon a set of general ideas and assumptions about order and authority within the overseas empire.[34] There is still a need to identify common denominators and to consider how those in Britain were changing their attitudes towards the ways in which the activities of those in *all* Britain's overseas territories should be regulated and governed.

CORE AND PERIPHERY: GENTLEMANLY CAPITALISM AND THE EIGHTEENTH-CENTURY EMPIRE

Ever since Sir John Seeley started the historiographical ball rolling over a hundred years ago with his famous and oft-quoted remark that Britain in the eighteenth century seemed 'to have conquered and peopled half the world in a fit of absence of mind',[35] historians, theorists and polemicists representing all outlooks and persuasions have endeavoured to establish explanations for British overseas expansion. In doing this they have displayed far less indifference towards the empire than those predecessors and contemporaries Seeley criticized for showing little interest in imperial expansion while it was actually taking place. At the same time, a wide range of writers have also focused a great deal of scholarly attention on imperialist impulses generated within, and by, British domestic society and economy. While a wide variety of 'peripheral' factors have been identified as acting as important imperial dynamics in their own right, the search has gone on for explanations of expansion which link the core of the empire to its periphery. Each generation of historians has provided its own agenda for debate and this has meant that few attempts to create a general framework of interpretation for the development of British imperialism have survived intact for very long. In recent years, however, the question of the role of the metropole within the processes of overseas expansion has been brought very much to the fore once more. This has come about through the development of an interpretation which sees Britain's imperial fortunes inextricably entwined with the long-term evolution of a distinct form of capitalist enterprise culture which embraced several different elites in British society.

Over the last decade or so, P.J. Cain and A.G. Hopkins have produced an important body of work highlighting the mechanics and dynamics of British overseas expansion. Three articles in the *Economic History Review* have recently been followed by a two-volume book devoted to a major reassessment of British imperialism.[36] In creating a new framework of interpretation, they have attempted to sweep away many of the underlying assumptions about British imperial history. They have done this by linking important domestic economic and social historiographical developments to the enormous body of literature that has grown up in recent decades in the field of imperial studies. As a result, they have advanced a case for examining the influence of non-industrial forms of metropolitan capital on the process of overseas expansion. In particular, they have focused on areas of economic activity based upon, and underpinned by, gentlemanly notions of behaviour, conduct and endeavour. With regard to the period between 1688 and 1850, Cain and Hopkins hold the dominant element within what they call 'gentlemanly capitalism' to have been the landed interest. They have spent much time establishing a broad range of links between the City and the rentier class who derived its power, wealth and status from land and agriculture. They have then examined the ways in which gentlemanly capitalism 'imprinted' itself on the British overseas presence.

In some ways, as Cain and Hopkins themselves acknowledge,[37] the gentlemanly capitalist thesis can be seen as being set within a long-established framework of theory and explanation which has focused on the relationship between land and finance in the development of British capitalism and imperialism. As socioeconomic theories of imperialism developed during the course of the eighteenth and nineteenth centuries, two different elites, the landed aristocracy and the monied interest, were identified by a wide range of analysts as being deeply implicated in the expansionist process.[38] Often described as 'parasites' or, in Bentham's phrase, 'sinister interests', these representatives of a domestic alliance between land and money were held to have shaped and directed the imperial process in their relentless quest for place and profit. Influential commentators and analysts from Cobden and Bright, through Spencer, Hobson and Veblen to Marx, Kautsky and Lenin, often underpinned their economic theories of British imperialism with a sociological perspective. This concentrated on the expansionist impulses emanating from a society in which the traditional elements of a feudal/military landed interest were fused with the main features of an emerging capitalist class of financiers. Such analyses, which were often shot through with strong anti-Semitic prejudices, tended to be strong on assertion but weak on supporting evidence. Nevertheless they became widely accepted and were cast in stone by several generations of twentieth-century commentators, particularly those who had political or ideological axes to grind. By re-engaging this area of debate and discussion, Cain and Hopkins have brought the analytical tools of the modern historian to bear on a task which has long exercised the minds of those seeking to explain British imperialism, but which in different ways has produced few satisfactory answers.

In general terms, the work of Cain and Hopkins in its eighteenth-century context can be approached in a critical fashion in a number of different ways.[39] First, it can be argued that too much weight has been given to metropolitan factors in the imperial process and this has shifted emphasis away from expansionist impulses emanating from the periphery of the empire. In these terms, it can be maintained that factors such as indigenous politics or power struggles, the strategic ambitions of local military commanders, the expansive pressures exerted by expatriate or settler communities, to name but a few, are played down by Cain and Hopkins as they pursue their central belief that explanations of expansion ought to begin at home.[40] Moreover, in doing this, it could be said they have not only moved non-economic factors to a position of marginal importance, but they have also overemphasized the extent to which the 'Industrial Revolution' was ever perceived as being a major imperial dynamic by historians in the first place. In their book, Cain and Hopkins sought to disarm any critics who might attempt to develop arguments along these lines. They declared that they did not wish to play down the importance of politics and ideology in the imperial process and that they did not seek to deny that some of the causes of imperial expansion were to be found at the periphery. Rather, they were trying to emphasize that the 'generic causes' of imperialism were to be located in the metropolis, and they were endeavouring 'to understand why actors of a certain kind were where they were when they were, and why their views of the world inclined them to act in the way that they did.'[41] Such debate on the causes of imperialism has tended to be located primarily in a nineteenth-century context[42] and, as far as the eighteenth century is concerned, there is still a need to try and strike some sort of balance between the influence of metropolitan and peripheral factors within the expansionist process.

Second, given the amount of time that Cain and Hopkins have spent identifying expansionist impulses emanating from the metropole, it could be argued that their analysis of socio-economic developments in Britain needs to be subjected to close scrutiny. Their whole case rests on the belief that a distinct form of innovative capitalist culture was forged after 1688, thereafter helping to mould and shape the British imperial experience in different ways. In a direct sense, the financial resources of the British elite were channelled into the wider world through a number of different commercial and business mechanisms. Less directly, some of the central features of metropolitan elite culture were brought to bear on the imperial process through their export to the periphery where they helped to influence the nature of Britain's overseas presence.[43] However, although gentlemanly capitalism in its partially evolved eighteenth-century form is held to have been dominated by the traditional landed elite, it can be demonstrated that, in purely financial terms, in some areas and contexts it was the metropolitan non-landed elite who provided the bulk of the resources that underwrote the process of imperial expansion. Of course, the gentlemanly capitalist case rests on much more than simple analysis of patterns of investment or capital flows, and Cain and Hopkins are primarily concerned with the 'broader set of connections [between elites] arising from the financial revolution and the increased degree of social integration that it encouraged.'[44] Even so, any critic, with one eye on the various 'interest groups' that used to feature so prominently in Hanoverian political historiography, could ask whether or not the significant differences, tensions and divisions between different elites in British society were such that they would make it difficult to bring these groups together under one broad gentlemanly capitalist banner. Or, to put it another way, it could perhaps be argued that differences in outlook, lifestyle, behaviour and assumptions were such that, while various groups of individuals might be described by the historian as being gentlemanly capitalists, they might in reality have little in common with one another. If this was the case and, if in an eighteenth-century context, elite groups formed only a series of loose alliances with one another, then the phrase 'gentlemanly capitalist' could be regarded as a very imprecise term and a rather blunt analytical tool. It might then serve little purpose in explaining the development of British overseas expansion. Rather than being seen as a central dynamic within the imperialist process, gentlemanly capitalism could become little more than a very general background influence.[45] There is a need therefore to examine in some detail the nature of elite involvement in different aspects of the imperial process. At the same time, there is also a need to consider the ways in which various elites stood in relation to one another, in both the overseas empire and Britain itself, and to establish whether or not they were able to develop any sense of a common or 'national' interest transcending narrow sectional interests. Only then will it be possible to come to some sort of a conclusion about the extent to which, if at all, the influence of elite groups headed by the landed interest was imprinted on the imperial process during the course of the eighteenth century.

Third, throughout the work of Cain and Hopkins, the metropolitan focus of attention is very much on London and gentlemanly capitalism largely represents an alliance of mutual benefit forged between the City of London and a landowning elite based predominantly in the South of England. The effect of this is firmly to locate the development of the gentlemanly capitalist within a particular *English* cultural environment. Of course, many individuals with origins in Ireland, Scotland, Wales and provincial England found a place for themselves within that frame of reference and many of them became key figures in the world of metropolitan finance, politics and imperial decision-making. So much so was this the case that it could be argued that much more weight needs to be given to Celtic (and indeed non-British) influences in the eighteenth-century British imperial experience. Individuals drawn from across the Celtic nations increasingly made their mark as investors, merchants, officials, soldiers and settlers and their traditions and cultural behaviour had the effect of diluting the strength of English influence at both the core and the periphery of the empire. This is not to deny that these individuals were themselves anglicized or acquired the gentlemanly trappings of the

English elite but simply to point out that they came from very different cultural, religious, and social backgrounds from the archetypal gentlemanly capitalist described by Cain and Hopkins. Overseas activity was a truly *British* enterprise and as such it represented a manifestation of all the complexities, contradictions and cross-currents to be found within eighteenth-century metropolitan society.

These questions about the gentlemanly capitalist thesis have been raised and these broad lines of inquiry have been defined because, although Cain and Hopkins have attempted to point a way forward to a general explanation of the development of British imperialism from 1688 through to the present day, they were primarily concerned with the period after 1850. As a result, some central areas of their work have not been developed in any depth in an eighteenth-century context. Indeed, as has been pointed out in one review of *British Imperialism*, 'Cain and Hopkins do not linger long in the eighteenth century.'[46] Much of what they have said about the characteristics of Victorian imperialism has been supported with detailed case studies of overseas expansion, but this is not the case with regard to the eighteenth-century empire. For the early Hanoverian period, the analytical balance is heavily in favour of the evolution of a gentlemanly order at home rather than British activity in the wider world. This means that important issues, such as the nature of the processes which forged the links between the core and the periphery of the empire in the eighteenth century, still require detailed analysis. Attention still needs to be devoted to the emergence of gentlemanly elites in the overseas territories under British control. In short, the individuals who belonged to eighteenth-century elites need to be identified; their assumptions, attitudes and motives need to be assessed; and their commercial and financial activities need to be quantified and analysed. Above all, there is a need to assess the bold claim that the interpretative approach to British imperial history embodied in the work of Cain and Hopkins 'is in principle applicable to the whole history of British expansion'.[47] As things stand, the case offered by the gentlemanly capitalist interpretation is neither proven nor disproven in its eighteenth-century context. Indeed, the jury has not yet even begun to consider the evidence.

2 The Dynamics of Expansion

The expansion and development of British overseas activity in the eighteenth century was based upon foundations established well before 1700. At the end of the seventeenth century, English settlements in North America were scattered throughout the politically demarcated colonies running along the coast from the Carolinas to Maine, while the Hudson Bay Company engaged in commercial activity in an amorphous region between the Great Lakes and the Arctic littoral. In the Caribbean, Britain had settlements on Antigua, Barbados, Jamaica, Montserrat, Nevis and part of St Kitts. In the Orient, despite several serious setbacks suffered at the hands of the Dutch in the East Indies during the course of the seventeenth century, the East India Company had established itself at Bombay, Madras and Surat. Just before the turn of the century, the Company had acquired several small villages in Bengal and this settlement became Calcutta which grew to be the second city of the British empire by 1775. These footings of empire might not always have been firm and secure and, in some cases, the British presence might not have been represented by anything more than small forts and trading settlements, but their location served to determine much of the subsequent course and direction taken by British overseas activity during the eighteenth century.[1] Of course, trade and discovery continued to take Britons into new ventures and spheres of influence, but the main focus of overseas activity remained in North America, the West Indies and India. In all these three areas, a variety of factors combined to transform footholds into well-established colonies and possessions as threats from rival powers were eliminated, trade was developed and territory was expanded.

THE MILITARY CONTEXT

In a world of fierce and prolonged competition between European powers, the most important dynamic within the processes serving to expand the British empire from 1700 arose from warfare and armed conflict. Between 1688 and 1775, England or Britain fought four major wars: the Nine Years' War, 1689–97; the War of Spanish Succession (which was known as Queen Anne's War in the colonies), 1702–13; the Wars of Jenkins' Ear and Austrian Succession, 1739–48; and the Seven Years' War (or French and Indian War as it was referred to in North America), 1756–63. The effects of this long, intermittent and ultimately successful struggle against France and Spain were not simply to be judged in terms of the conquest of territory, the rewards gained from peace treaties, and the growth of the army and navy. Warfare also acted as an important catalyst of change within Britain itself, most notably in the realm of government organization and finance. But whatever the long-term importance of developments within the state and government, the most immediate and tangible gains made from warfare were, as contemporaries recognized, those represented in the form of newly won territory, possessions and untapped sources of wealth.

As Britain continued to rise through the ranks of the great powers, conflict against European powers increasingly took on an extra-European dimension which meant that major and minor theatres of war were to be found in the wider world.[2] This meant that the spoils of war invariably included overseas territory and possessions seized or returned from defeated rivals. In the Treaty of Utrecht of 1713 Britain secured Acadia (renamed Nova Scotia), Newfoundland, Hudson Bay and part of St Kitts from France; at Aix-la-Chapelle in 1748 she regained Madras from the French in exchange for Louisbourg; and at Paris in 1763 Spain conceded Florida, and French influence was all but eliminated from both India and the North American mainland. These gains made by the Crown at the expense of European rivals were buttressed in the east by the fruits of successful military campaigns waged by the East India Company during the late 1750s and 1760s. Military conflict against the combined forces of the Mughal Emperor, the Wazir of Awadh and the Nawab of Bengal culminated in the Company's victory over Indian forces at the battle of Buxar in 1764. This paved the way for the Treaty of Allahabad of September 1765 which saw the British assume near-sovereign authority over the Mughal provinces of Bengal, Bihar and Orissa.

Before 1763 and beyond times of formal conflict against European powers, British ministers did not see any great need for a strong and permanent armed presence to control and regulate the nation's overseas possessions. In North America, the small garrisons of regular troops that were established in New York, Newfoundland and Nova Scotia tended to be neglected by the metropolitan authorities to the point that contemporary observers were often moved to comment about the shocking condition of the soldiers and their equipment.[3] Such neglect, however, should not be taken to indicate that the peacetime use of military force did not have any part to play in the development and expansion of the British empire during the eighteenth century. On the contrary, in all spheres of British activity, peacetime advancement and consolidation were based ultimately upon force, or the threatened use of force, and the metropolitan authorities were usually responsive to specific requests for assistance from the periphery when valuable possessions were thought to be at risk. Trade, colonization and revenue collection were often dependent upon the deployment of British arms to support, defend and extend commercial enterprise, and by the the eighteenth century Britain already boasted a long tradition of state support for overseas economic activity.[4] Unlike their French counterparts, English governments had never taken an active role in coordinating or directing particular trading activities in the national interest, but they had always been prepared to intervene in order to smooth the way forward for merchants and trading companies. In general terms, government intervention often came in the form of legislation to establish monopolies, proprietary colonies or systems of trade such as those embodied in the Navigation Acts, for which in return the state often received payment, long-term loans and increased income from customs revenue.[5] More directly, though, state assistance for beleaguered Britons overseas often took the form of diplomatic or military action. In virtually all areas beyond Europe, British overseas trade was, in the last resort, an armed trade and the government often acknowledged this by exercising, or threatening to exercise, military power on behalf of merchant or planter communities. This was particularly so when strong representations were made in London on behalf of those whose lives or property were at risk.

Although the deployment of troops overseas during peacetime was limited before the 1760s and there was little that might be considered to have resembled a 'policy' on such matters, the metropolitan authorities were prepared to sanction the use of regular forces in the colonies when the need arose. In other words, colonists were not left to their own devices in matters related to defence and security and, provided they were willing to contribute to some of the costs, those in colonies that were perceived to be valuable could usually rely on support from London.[6] During the first Maroon war (1730–9), for example, military support in the form of two regiments and a squadron was sent to the planters of Jamaica as they endeavoured to counter the threat to stability posed by the former Spanish slaves inhabiting the interior of the island.[7] Of course, extended military operations in the wider world were risky ventures and Britain did not sweep all before her, despite her developing naval strength. This was very much the case, for example, during the War of Jenkins' Ear when, in the wake of Admiral Vernon's widely acclaimed defeat of the Spanish at Porto Bello in 1739, an expedition was sent to the West Indies in order to try and exert further pressure on Spain's South American empire and commercial activities. In spite of meticulous planning, the operation went badly wrong. An attack on Cartagena failed, and a large number of British and American troops were lost through disease and illness.[8] Such disastrous setbacks, which in this case prompted a public outcry and contributed to Walpole's removal from office in 1742, illustrated the hazards associated with mounting combined military operations a long way from home waters. In recognition of this, attempts had already been made to try and address logistical and support problems through the building of a number of naval bases in the Caribbean by the 1740s. This helped to give Britain a permanent naval presence in the region which could be used, in part, to help meet the strategic threats posed by the French and Spanish and which could also serve to provide rapid responses to local crises and difficulties. By 1740 bases had been built at Port Antonio and

Port Royal in Jamaica, and at English Harbour in Antigua. This commitment of resources to the periphery by the metropolitan authorities served to provide some security and reassurance to the local British population.[9] Even so, in terms of a permanent presence, the overall commitment of men to the periphery of the Atlantic empire remained very limited indeed, and as late as 1754 there were only some 4000 regular troops in the West Indies and North America.

In the east, to take a case from an entirely different sphere of commercial operations, the metropolitan authorities were again prepared to respond to crises in a positive fashion. The East India Company received help from Crown forces as it endeavoured to overcome pirates and corsairs in the Indian Ocean and Persian Gulf.[10] Naturally enough, this type of assistance was extended during times of war and in all spheres of British commercial activity the Admiralty responded to requests from maritime interest groups by organizing and coordinating convoys in order to offer protection to merchant fleets. Over time the protection of trade became increasingly well organized and efficient, and the successful extension of state support to the commercial community was reflected in the diminishing losses of merchant shipping during the wars that occurred after 1713.[11] All the evidence points to continued commercial growth and expansion often being dependent upon the exertion of influence based upon a military presence,[12] and this was an element in economic development that could not be ignored by ministers and officials. Only on very few occasions were British interests not defended when trade-related disputes of a serious nature occurred. This served to reassure the merchant community at home and overseas colonists, for they knew that in the last resort they had the apparatus of the state reasonably close at hand to help them realize their ambitions.

Throughout the period, the Bourbon powers posed a dangerous threat to Britain's overseas possessions and news of French and Spanish military activity always prompted a swift response from Britons at both the core and the periphery of the empire. In particular, the threat posed by the French played on the minds of policy makers, politicians and essayists alike. This helped to strengthen the case of those who advocated conquest and annexation as the best means of colonial defence, while it enabled those of less overtly aggressive tendencies to argue that territorial expansion was both justifiable and un-avoidable.[13] Steps were often taken to deny the French or Spanish strategic advantage and these measures could develop into an important dynamic within the expansionist process as they drew colonists forward into new areas of territorial activity and settlement. In North America, for example, some Virginians sought, with great vigour, to extend their western frontier during the 1740s. Their eyes were not closed to the commercial opportunities that would arise from such a territorial advance, but they were also seeking to improve their defences in order to protect the colony from the French threat. In this, the pressure and lobbying activity of the Ohio Company met with some local opposition but, following approval from the metropolitan authorities, a land grant of 200,000 acres was eventually made by Virginia's governor and council, providing that a fort be built and garrisoned by the Company.[14] The general strategic and military situation after mid-century dictated that there was a quickening of the pace of this sort of defensive annexation, despite fears continuing to be expressed in London about the spiralling costs of administering and defending an extended territorial empire.[15] After the conclusion of the Seven Years' War, when the French presence was removed from Louisiana and the Spanish withdrew from Florida, the scope for expansion of this sort was widened considerably. It forced the government into action through the establishment of the Proclamation Line of 1763, designed to define boundaries for old and new colonies alike and to prevent uncontrolled movement into the interior of the continent.[16] Even then, responses to the general question of how best to regulate the frontier were complicated by continuing anxieties over the possibility of a Bourbon resurgence in the region, and the London press indulged in lengthy speculation on how best Britain could defend her old colonies as well as her new ones such as Canada.[17]

The nature of the British reaction to French military activity in Asia was once seen by some scholars in similar terms to the response made by colonists in North America. The defensive annexation of territory for military and strategic purposes was held to have represented an important factor in the expansion of the East India Company's possessions in India.[18]

This argument no longer seems so compelling, not least because the strength and potency of the French threat to British India during the second half of the century has been reassessed by historians. Yet, although this danger undoubtedly diminished after the end of the Seven Years' War, the spectre of a Bourbon resurgence in India was often uppermost in the minds of ministers, politicians and East India Company directors as they assessed Britain's military and strategic position in Asia. On several occasions, rumours and reports of French activity in India prompted the metropolitan authorities into sanctioning the deployment of additional military and naval units in the region.[19]

The part played by Britain's armed forces within the imperial process went well beyond the deployment of military power to secure territory and win battles against the French, Spanish and local powers. The long-term presence of the army and navy in overseas colonies can be seen as playing an important part in helping to determine patterns of development within local economies and societies. Yet, attempts to define colonization as part of a process involving the creation of militarized British overseas societies in which 'garrison government' formed the cornerstone of the relationship between the dependencies and the imperial authorities have met with resistance from scholars whose interests lie with the North American colonies.[20] This, however, should not deflect attention away from the fact that in many areas of British activity the army, navy and local militias played an important part in supporting and sustaining local elites and the representatives of metropolitan authority. They pacified frontiers, deterred rival European powers and patrolled hostile sea lanes. In addition, military expenditure could play an important part in the growth of colonial economies, particularly those of recent settlement where frontiers were threatened by European or native armed forces.[21] Throughout the period, the deployment of arms, the use of force and the organization of society on military lines was a fundamental feature of everyday life in many spheres of British overseas activity. The militia ensured that in North America, for example, colonists 'were armed and more or less trained for war'.[22] Meanwhile, in the West Indies the militia might have been a notoriously ineffective fighting force, but it nevertheless played an important part in local society by acting as an agency for the maintenance of law, order and internal security.[23] The Jamaican militia, comprised of local free-men of all races, numbered 5,398 during the mid-1760s and this meant that, with only a small garrison of regular troops on the island, it represented the main defence force.[24] Indeed, at times, local forces could rise to the occasion as the Antiguan militia proved when it showed itself to be more than a match for a small company of regular troops early in the century.[25] Furthermore, the militia also had an important part to play in a social context. Service in the militia was a central aspect of the lives of the planter elite in the West Indies, as elsewhere, if only because the holding of rank helped to define and reinforce individual relationships and the social hierarchy in general.[26]

In an Asian context, contemporaries had long accepted that in the last resort the East India Company's trade was an armed trade.[27] This, together with the need to provide for the defence of British settlements, meant that the Company had slowly developed the capacity to deploy force whenever it considered it to be necessary. In India, every aspect of the Company's activities was defined and reinforced by military activity of one sort or another after 1750. From an early date in their respective developments, the Company's main coastal settlements at Bombay, Calcutta and Madras had been fortified and heavily defended.[28] Moreover, the Company developed a number of additional military functions beyond those necessary to support trade and meet the semi-permanent threat posed by the French and other rival powers. The Company's army was used to maintain internal peace and stability; it served as a police force; and when revenue-collection responsibilities were assumed in the mid-1760s military units played an important part in the process by ensuring that the native population paid their taxes and customs duties on time.[29] One consequence of this was that as the Company consolidated its presence and defended its position in India it offered employment and economic opportunities to countless numbers of Indians and their families. The rebuilding of Fort William in Calcutta during the 1760s needed a considerable labour force (30,000 coolies were at work on the new fort in 1761), and a wide range of other military and administrative construction projects employed large numbers of craftsmen and labourers.[30] Because of the long-term consequences of such developments, early nineteenth-century India has recently been described by one historian as a 'garrison state' in which the army acted as a dynamic force for change in a wide variety of economic, political and social contexts.[31] Yet, well before any fully fledged 'garrison state' might have come into being, the Company's army was already playing a significant part in helping to determine the shape of the society that had been brought under British control.

As the militarization of British India gathered pace, so the methods chosen by the East India Company to meet and support the needs of its fast-growing army came to represent a powerful dynamic of expansion in their own right.[32] Small garrisons of a few hundred men grew in size dramatically after 1740 so that by 1770 the Company's Bengal army had alone grown to around 30,000 men. From 1760 onwards, the need to pay the European and native troops employed by the Company represented a major problem for local administrators. Solutions were increasingly sought through the annexation of revenue districts, and subsidy payments were demanded from the local rulers on whose land the troops were stationed. This process gathered a momentum of its own and the eventual outcome in 1765 was the grant of the *diwani* to Robert Clive by the Mughal Emperor. This not only gave revenue collection rights in the provinces of Bengal, Bihar and Orissa to the British, but it bestowed upon the Company the status of *de facto*, if not *de jure*, sovereign power in the region.[33] The Company found that in the pursuit of revenue it was drawn further and further into Indian administrative, diplomatic, legal and political life and the transformation from commercial company to territorial ruler was well under way.

The *diwani* revenues were used by the Company to offset spiralling military expenditure, but only a small minority of observers recognized this at the time. Clive estimated that he had secured a potential income of £4 million a year for the Company, and, although events were to prove that this was an overgenerous, if not fanciful, assessment, many assumed that the *diwani* represented a large financial windfall for the British. They failed to see that, in reality, the revenues had to be applied first and foremost to the processes that were underpinning the continued transformation of British India into a highly militarized state. Consequently, the Company ran into serious difficulties when it proved impossible to transfer revenue surpluses to Britain on a scale that could satisfy the demands of stockholders and covetous politicians in Westminster. At the same time, the army in Bengal continued to swallow huge amounts of revenue income. Annual military expenditure in Bengal almost doubled from £550,000 in 1764/5 to £1,093,000 in 1770/1, when the *diwani* revenues had fallen to £1,267,000 from their peak of £1,817,649 in 1766/7. Further expenditure on extravagant civil and military capital projects was also heavy, with the rebuilding of Fort William costing £1,602,000 between 1762 and 1772. It took some time for this fundamental mismatch of resources and expenditure to become apparent to those running the Company's affairs, although local representatives undertook some rather half-hearted cost-cutting measures in response to pressure from London. Of far greater importance for the development of the British imperial presence in India was the drawing of the Company into a much closer supervision of long-standing native revenue-collection procedures. Thus a self-perpetuating process had come into being: for defensive purposes the Company required a large army which could only be paid for by territorial revenue income, but that income could only be collected from territories that were stable, well governed and well protected. This was not by any means a process that was easy to control and supervise in the turbulent world of North Indian politics and diplomacy. The former Governor of Bengal, John Holwell, warned of the danger of being drawn into new unwanted areas of expansion when he wrote in the 1760s that: 'New *temporary* victories stimulate and push us on to grasp new acquisitions of territory. These call for a large increase in military force to defend them, and thus we shall go on grasping and expanding until we cram our hands so full that they become cramped and numbed, and we shall be obliged to quit and relinquish even that part which we might have held fast.'[34] The army was pushing back the frontiers of British India, but at the same time it was also playing a critical role in defining the shape and structure of important parts of the society under Company control.

TRADE AND EMPIRE

For all the importance they attached to the military victories
that paved the way for the seizure of new overseas territories,
it was trade, not conquest, that captured the attention of most
of the contemporary observers who had an interest in Britain's
affairs in the wider world. As Namier put it, Englishmen [*sic*]
saw commerce as the 'dominant factor' in the existence of
their country.[35] Yet trade and empire were inextricably linked,
and no one could ignore the increase in the volume of British
commerce which had occurred at the same time that Britain
had extended her imperial presence in the wider world.[36]
Moreover, contemporaries were well aware that the possession
of colonies and territory was not simply to be regarded as a
means by which Britain could develop her trade. The empire
was seen to be located at the very heart of the various interactive processes that helped, in general, to sustain and develop
national power, prestige and prosperity.[37] Straightforward trade
with the overseas empire was in itself of the greatest importance, but contemporaries recognized that much more than
the simple exchange of goods was derived from the commercial relationship between Britain and her colonies. Trade routes
were, in the words of one historian, 'the most elementary
material structures of the empire'.[38] They provided the path-
ways along which travelled news, information, goods, troops
and migrants, and they represented the essential link between
the core and the periphery of the empire. The colonies were
important as markets and sources of raw materials, but the
nature of the colonial trade was such that it provided innu-
merable additional benefits. The colonies helped to promote
domestic industry and employment, while the shipping employed in the colonial trade was manned by a large number of
merchant seaman whose skills could be used by the state in
times of war.

The importance of trade with the empire had been reinforced by the legislation embodied in the Navigation Acts of
1650, 1661 and 1690 which had been used to establish England as the entrepôt through which colonial goods flowed to
the Continent.[39] Most colonial produce (the exception being
cod from the Newfoundland fisheries) could only be shipped
to Europe via England in ships that were 'English-built', that

is in ships that had been built in England or her colonies.[40] Similarly, most European goods could only be sent to English colonies from English ports. This legislation also helped to create what one historian has described as a 'huge "sterling" trade area', a trading world in which, in theory if not in practice, all balances between individuals and companies at the core and the periphery had to be settled in sterling.[41] Thus, although the foundations of the Atlantic trading system were laid by, and built upon, individual initiative and private enterprise, the Atlantic empire and British maritime strength in general were, to a considerable degree, developed with the needs of the state firmly in mind. Indeed, it has recently been argued that the primary purpose behind the establishment of the Atlantic empire was, from the state's point of view, to 'foster commerce and shipping' rather than to secure extended territorial acquisitions for their own sake.[42] Few could deny that Britain owed much of her wealth and naval strength to the possession of an overseas empire.

Official representatives of British interests repeatedly professed, like their European rivals, that they preferred trade to conquest and this became a generally held maxim among metropolitan decision-makers.[43] The directors and officials of the East India Company could, for example, plead that trade not conquest was their primary interest, even after the beginning of the process that saw them acquire an army of 50,000 men and control over the lives of millions of Bengalis.[44] Yet, despite this wide gap between theory and practice and the fact that the ultimate logic of the pursuit of armed trade was that trade and dominion would become inextricably linked, contemporaries consistently adhered to the belief that the assumption of territorial responsibilities was dangerous and to be avoided at all costs. If, however, local circumstances were such that conquest and control by Britain's commercial and administrative representatives could not be avoided, then territorial acquisitions were to be kept to an absolute minimum. Expansion beyond established spheres of activity was always frowned upon by those directing overseas affairs from the metropolis and, in the first instance, the British were always concerned with the cultivation of peaceful trade and commerce. A major worry throughout the period was that the administration and defence of overseas territory would be difficult and expensive and the burden of such responsibilities could ultimately render commercial activity unprofitable. As one historian of the Atlantic empire has recently remarked, the British preference before 1750 was for informal or limited empire and, in pursuing a 'minimalist' policy, the metropolitan authorities repeatedly shied away from committing resources to the colonies and sanctioning the acquisition of new territory.[45] Only after 1763, as the full potential of North America began to be realized and the focus of British imperial attention was switched from the Caribbean to the mainland colonies, did London begin to deploy significant amounts of men and materials to the colonies on a permanent basis.[46]

Even those contemporaries who were active in their attempts to discourage territorial ambition could not have denied that a direct connection had been established between the expansion of trade and the acquisition of an overseas empire. Shifting patterns of British trade reflected the extent to which commercial activity was increasingly located in areas where Britain had a formal imperial presence. The dynamic focus of British trade moved slowly but surely away from Europe towards her developing and increasingly populous possessions in Asia and the Atlantic empire.[47] Demand for British goods in these areas was an important determining factor in the general growth of the export trade. In particular, the ninefold increase in the white and slave population of the North American colonies between 1700 and 1775 helped to provide an outlet for woollen goods, but the lack of industry at the periphery of the Atlantic empire also meant that a wide range of other manufactures including linen, silks and metal products also found their way across the Atlantic.[48] The overall effect of the reorientation of English trade in the first three-quarters of the eighteenth century was such that while the value of manufactured exports from England to Europe rose from £3,201,000 in 1699–1701 to £3,617,000 in 1772–4 (a 13 per cent increase), the value of similar exports into territories bordering on the Atlantic Ocean rose from £475,000 to £3,981,000 between the same periods (a 738 per cent increase). By 1772–4, 40.4 per cent of English domestic exports went to Europe, while 42.4 per cent went to North America, the West Indies and Africa, 9.9 per cent to Ireland and the Channel Islands, and 7.3 per cent to Asia. In other words, while Europe remained the major destination for re-exported goods (63.2 per cent of the value of all English re-exports went to the Continent between 1772–4), just about half of English exports of domestic manufactures, foodstuffs and raw materials were finding their way into the wider world.[49]

The growing importance of British commercial operations in non-European spheres of activity was also reflected in similar important shifts in the composition of the import trade. Again, Europe was displaced from a position of dominance during the course of the first three-quarters of the century, so that by 1772–4 only 36.7 per cent of English imports came from the Continent. This fall (from 60.8 per cent in 1699–1701) was offset by a steady rise in the value of imports from the Atlantic and Asia, so that by 1772–4 they accounted for just over half of the total. Of particular note was significant growth in the importation of calicoes, silk, sugar, tobacco, tea, coffee and rice from the wider world, while producers closer to home provided England with increasing amounts of a broad range of raw materials and, from mid-century, with corn. By the 1770s, the import trade from Europe and Ireland was dominated, in very general terms, by raw materials and a smaller amount of manufactured goods. The emphasis within the import trade from Asia and the Atlantic was very much on foodstuffs for the domestic market and re-exportation. Nevertheless, the importation of naval stores such as timber, pitch, tar and hemp from the North American colonies also proved to be of great strategic significance because, even if the British economy was unable to become self-sufficient in such materials, it was able to break away from its dependency on northern Europe for such goods.[50] Contemporaries devoted a considerable amount of time and energy to analysis of these quite profound changes in the pattern of British overseas trade and, perhaps not surprisingly, some well-informed observers were moved to use a revolutionary analogy when they described what had taken place. While there was some debate about the relative merits of the Atlantic and Asian trades, no one could deny that Britain's emergence as a great power by the 1760s was closely allied to the processes which had allowed her to expand her commercial influence in all quarters of the globe after 1700.[51]

Of course, British commercial success in the eighteenth century was built upon foundations that had been laid during the century and a half before 1700. Thus, in general terms, the importance of trade as a dynamic of expansion in the eighteenth century lay primarily in its increasing volume helping to sustain and extend the British overseas presence. This is not to say that commercial factors, such as the search for unexploited sources of goods, raw materials and bullion, did not play a part in establishing contacts and opening up entirely new areas of activity between 1688 and 1775, or that exploration and discovery in themselves were no longer considered to be worthy enterprises.[52] But in a formal imperial context, the primary importance of trade was that it enabled the British first to consolidate their territorial presence and then move forward from existing, often very small and long-established, footholds in North America, the West Indies and Asia. Moreover, the organization of trade and commerce must also be seen as playing an important part in shaping the very nature of Britain's imperial relationships and helping to forge the links between core and periphery. Within the Atlantic empire, the Navigation Acts played their part in bringing settlers and colonists into a world of goods that was defined to a considerable degree by metropolitan patterns of consumption, standards and fashions.[53] Meanwhile, in an Asian context, the nature of the close relationship between the state and the monopolistic East India Company was such that it allowed British authority and administration in India to be vested in a trading company whose activities were supported by a large private army and were largely beyond effective control and supervision from the metropolis.

INDUSTRIALIZATION AND IMPERIALISM

For many years one of the truisms of modern British history was that an industrial revolution, the 'Industrial Revolution', had occurred between *c.*1750 and *c.*1830. Because a large territorial empire had also been established during that same period, many historians (particularly those with ideological axes to grind) spilled a great deal of ink trying to establish causal links between the process of domestic industrialization and the acquisition of overseas territory. Although it is possible to make a case for overseas trade helping indirectly to promote industrial expansion through its contribution to the general strengthening of the British economy before 1800,[54] historians of the eighteenth century have not been able to make many direct connections between industrialization and the growth of territorial empire. Indeed, they have failed on two different counts. First, specific territorial conquests or annexations cannot be shown to have been motivated by the need to establish markets for manufactured goods; and, second, on the other side of the coin, it is not possible to demonstrate that the profits of the slave trade, or plunder looted from the empire, primed the pump of an industrial revolution in mid-eighteenth-century Britain.[55]

Recent work has not helped the cause of anyone who might be tempted to resurrect such attempts to establish 'industrial' connections between the core and periphery of the empire. This is not least because the concept of an Industrial Revolution, as classically formulated, has come under fire from those who have used revised figures and statistics to suggest that economic development in Britain was much more gradual than was once thought. This interpretation has in itself become a matter for controversy and this has served only to underline the complexity of the issues involved when attempts are made to establish a pattern of overseas activity based upon a chronology formulated with reference to landmarks in domestic history. More important, though, has been the recent suggestion that, in seeking to establish direct links between industrialization and imperialism, historians have been addressing the wrong issue. It has been argued that a much more fruitful line of inquiry can be pursued if the focus of attention is shifted away from the factors promoting the initial acquisition of territory to the question of how subsequent expansion and the extension of influence was sustained. Thus, for example, it is clear that the process of industrialization played no direct part in the original seizure of Bengal in the 1760s, but it has been argued that the East India Company's links with an 'industrializing metropolis' were essential in allowing the Company to develop the capacity to wage sustained large-scale warfare on the subcontinent.[56] Much of what J.R. Ward has written about this issue falls beyond the period being examined here for he is primarily concerned with the period between 1790 to 1820. Nevertheless, his general point about the central importance within the expansionist process of the relationship between the Company's tea trade and the emerging industrial economy is also valid for the third quarter of the eighteenth century.

Important indirect links between industry and empire found expression in the China tea trade which by the 1760s had become the fulcrum of the East India Company's commercial operations. This trade represented a vital mechanism that allowed the Company to transfer to Britain any surplus accruing from its newly acquired territorial revenues in Bengal. As there was only limited home demand for Bengal goods, the Company chose to focus its commercial energies on a product that was being widely consumed in Britain. However, this was not a straightforward process because the trade between India and China had first to be expanded in order to give the Company's representatives at Canton the resources necessary to enable them to purchase large consignments of tea for shipment home. Thus, during the initial stages of this development of the China trade in the late 1760s, the Company invested as much of the revenue surplus as possible in Indian goods for sale in China and it also pursued the potentially hazardous policy of shipping bullion from Bengal to Canton.

As a result of this strategy, more and more tea was shipped from China to London, to the extent that the amount almost trebled to 12,787,113lb a year between 1768 and 1772.[57] But, of course, sales destined for the domestic market were dependent upon buoyant demand, and Ward makes the important point that the growth of the manufacturing sector within an expanding economy played a key role in helping to stimulate tea sales in Britain. Income growth in the industrial sector and the development of the tea drinking habit in an expanding urban population after 1750 played their parts in increasing per capita consumption of tea.[58] In spite of fierce competition from smugglers, this allowed the East India Company to generate a substantially greater volume of domestic tea sales after 1765, even though annual growth rates were erratic. Yet, encouraging though this trend was for the directors of the Company, home demand was not sufficient to consume all of the tea imported from China. Between 1765 and 1774 88,202,945 lb of tea was shipped into Britain by the East India Company but only 63 per cent of that amount, 55,782,300 lb, was sold for the home market.[59] A substantial, and growing, amount of unsold tea (17,755,000 lb which was worth £2,052,922 by 1772) lay in the Company's London warehouses. This represented 63 per cent of all the Company's unsold goods and concern about this deteriorating asset led to the ill-fated attempt to force the product onto the American colonists in 1773.[60] As those directing the Company's affairs fully recognized, there was little point in shipping huge quantities of goods half way around the world if they could not be sold. They also knew, however, that, although they were far from satisfied with the overall level of Company sales, the significant proportion of imported tea that they did manage to sell in the home market played a crucial part in oiling the financial wheels of the empire. While much of the revenue surplus was used to sustain the Company's military and administrative presence in India, the sale of China tea to ordinary consumers throughout Britain allowed for the partial realization of the profits derived from revenue collection in Bengal. In the short term, this satisfied Company stockholders who received increased dividend payments and it was well received by ministers who secured an annual share of the revenue for the government after 1767.

The capacity of the domestic population in an industrializing economy to absorb goods from overseas was thus of considerable importance in helping to forge one important link between developments at the core and the periphery of the empire. It is worth stressing that this indirect link between the process of industrialization and the consumption of goods from overseas was by no means limited to the East India Company and the tea trade. Recent work has acknowledged the extent to which coffee, sugar and tobacco also became products that belonged to the world of consumption in Britain during, and indeed before, the eighteenth century.[61] In general terms, the process of industrialization helped to increase consumption rates of these goods and this played an important part in sustaining Britain's position in the wider world.

LANDS AND SEAS OF OPPORTUNITY: ENTERPRISE AND EXPANSION

The empire offered endless opportunities to Britons drawn from all walks of life[62] and those who took up these opportunities often played an important part in helping to expand Britain's overseas interests. Individual enterprise and initiative in a wide range of economic activities often acted as a central dynamic within the expansionist process. At one level, speculators of all sorts moved beyond formal territorial frontiers and often acted as the vanguard for the development of large-scale British interest and investment. At another level, many individuals were content to focus their entrepreneurial energies on spheres representing a long-established British presence and their activities helped to improve and diversify old areas rather than to open up new ones. Expansion of different sorts was thus occurring simultaneously both within and beyond British overseas possessions, and it was not unusual to find an individual engaged in both types of economic activity.

Beyond an entrepreneurial context provided by long-distance overseas trade and commerce, the empire offered many different ways for an individual to seek out place and profit. In the military sphere, for example, serving officers in the army and navy were often swift to develop business interests and buy land in the areas they visited on tours of duty and, at times of conflict, they were able to secure rich pickings from prize money.[63] As a larger British military presence was established in North America after the mid-1750s, the financial and material needs of this force were serviced by prominent merchants and monied men who were contracted by government to supply provisions and hard currency to the garrisons at the periphery.[64] More generally, members of colonial and British elites channelled resources and investment finance into a wide range of business and commercial schemes designed to sustain, improve and develop the colonies.[65] Those from a more humble background were not excluded from this process, and settlers and migrants from different social classes in Britain sought the opportunity that would enable them to establish themselves and their families in colonial society. Some secured themselves in a profession before attempting to move into trade and land; others sought the small plot of land that would enable them to become a farmer or planter. Of course, personal advancement and the search for profit, rather than concerns about the development of the wider British imperium, were the primary motivating factors for most of these people and the empire offered them more and better openings than the situation in

Britain. Nevertheless, a combination of the labour, resources, wealth and skills of all these people played no small part in sustaining the processes of growth and expansion that were already well under way, and this contributed to the widening of spheres of British activity in every quarter of the globe.

For some, both in the colonies and Britain itself, the acquisition and purchase of land at the periphery offered the prospect of considerable financial gain and personal advancement. Although in reality few investors ever realized their expectations of securing large returns from their involvement in land speculation, they nevertheless often played a key part in extending the frontiers of settlement by recruiting settlers in Europe and then shipping them across the Atlantic. Having established a claim to territory, it was essential to people the land in order to clear it, cultivate it and so increase its value. This required a large labour force that could only be recruited from Europe and thus in North America a strong link was established between land speculation, westward expansion and patterns of settlement in the colonies.[66] The lure of the interior exercised a strong influence on settlers and speculators alike for, as George Washington advised a fellow Virginian in 1767, there was always 'an opening prospect in the back country for adventurers, where numbers resort to, and where an enterprising man with very little money may lay the foundation for a noble estate in the new settlements . . . for himself and posterity.'[67]

Even those without access to the resources and connections that were necessary for land purchase and speculative activity on a grand scale were offered the prospect of rapid economic and social progress. In particular, military service in both the British army and colonial forces offered numerous opportunities to officers and men alike. Such a large number of British officers became landowners in North America that the historian of the army in the colonies has commented that perhaps 'only unusual sloth or ineptness kept an officer from getting a sizeable grant somewhere in America during his service'.[68] Those drawn from the ranks were also able to benefit from the distribution of land. When units were disbanded, or individuals left regiments after their term of service, troops were often paid off with a land grant which encouraged them to settle in the colonies.[69]

Beyond the military, there were opportunities for those who migrated to the colonies either individually or as part of organized land-settlement schemes. In Philadelphia during the 1680s, for example, William Penn's revised scheme of arrangement for the First Purchasers allowed for 20 feet of frontage on the River Delaware and a 26-foot-wide high street site to be given to an individual when a 1000 acre site was purchased in the country. The entire package cost £20 and in some cases this allowed even artisans to become merchants and members of the local elite within a short space of time.[70] These individuals were assisted by the fact that in 1720 it was estimated that land in Philadelphia, bought for £10 in 1685, was now worth £300.[71] In total, Penn, who had been granted 45,000 square miles of territory by Charles II, managed to sell off some 715,000 acres of Pennsylvanian land to just under 600 purchasers between 1681 and 1685.[72] Not all of these First Purchasers could match the later success of William Branson, the son of an English shoemaker who arrived in Pennsylvania in 1708 and who was worth over £36,000 when he died in 1760.[73] Yet even early settlers, such as the Welsh and Cheshire Quakers who came from an impoverished region of Britain, were able, on average, to accumulate estates of over 700 acres.[74] The cheap land on offer from Penn in the early days might make Pennsylvania a special case, but more generally the experiences of those seeking opportunities in the colonies illustrate that North America often offered, or at least seemed to offer, far better prospects to the individual than did the mother country. The general situation was much the same in the West Indies and there are numerous examples of merchants and professionals who were able, from modest beginnings, to acquire land and develop large estates and plantations.[75]

Others chose to move beyond the formal boundaries of the empire in their search for profit and prosperity, and their individual actions often served to act as powerful dynamics within the expansionist process. In some cases, these individuals crossed back and forth over the thin line between legal and illegal activities and, by doing so, they helped to develop and sustain informal areas of British overseas activity. On the high seas, pirates in peacetime could become officially sanctioned privateers in wartime and, under both guises, they were able to conduct their activities on a global scale and establish their own extensive network of bases and supply lines after 1680.[76] Poachers often became gamekeepers and a pirate, such as the infamous Captain Kidd, was able to become a pirate hunter whose missions were funded by leading members of the British political elite. A more respectable figure such as Admiral Sir Peter Warren was able to use marriage and the investment of prize money and booty to establish a comfortable position for himself in colonial society.[77] The collective impact of such aggressive entrepreneurial activity could be considerable and the early development of Jamaica's plantation economy was based largely upon proceeds derived from privateering, freebooting and the contraband trade.[78]

On land, traders moved into the North American interior where their activities helped to extend territorial frontiers and turn informal spheres of activity into areas under formal British control. They often became embroiled in unofficial disputes with Indians or those representing French and Spanish interests.[79] In some cases this could lead to war, the deployment of troops in support of those engaged in conflict and, ultimately, to the acquisition of huge tracts of land.[80] Neither the colonial authorities nor those in London condoned, or welcomed, the actions which set these events in motion, but in practice they could do little to curb the aggressive commercial activity of those operating well beyond the frontier and the rule of law. Such was the level of concern about this sort of problem in the 1760s that some officials in North America and London were arriving at the conclusion that only the deployment of armed force would serve to regulate the activities of private traders involved in the Indian trade.[81]

In Asia, private traders played an even more important role in determining the course of British territorial expansion. The East India Company represented the official vehicle of British commercial, military and political activity on the subcontinent, but one of the most important dynamics of imperial expansion was provided by the small number of private traders who operated alongside the Company's employees in the world of commerce and industry. Thus, even though those directing the Company's fortunes from both London and Calcutta were often dedicated to the consolidation of British influence within strict territorial and political limits,[82] the vigour and enterprise of the small private sector was such that economic and commercial activities were often developed in areas, trades and industries well beyond those engaged in by the Company itself.[83] There were undoubtedly limits to the extent to which trade could influence politics, but there were several parts of India where the activities of private traders led to the British acquiring an economic stake well before they secured political control.[84] In other words, informal empire developed alongside, or ahead of, formal empire. As this happened, there were clashes between private British traders and local rulers over a wide range of commercial issues and this drew the Company into new spheres of involvement and activity. Although it was always concerned about overstretching its resources, the Company was usually willing to deploy force on behalf of beleaguered British entrepreneurs. This meant that after 1740, when the British had more and better troops at their disposal, the force used to defend trading activity or extract commercial concessions from local rulers was such that the Company became an important player in Indian politics. This was no better illustrated than during the 1760s when a whole series of private-trade disputes prompted the great war against the Nawab of Bengal and his allies which eventually led to the British securing control over Bengal and its neighbouring provinces.

This chapter has identified some of the dynamic processes that underpinned and sustained British overseas expansion between 1688 and 1775. But, of course, no process has a life of its own. All processes require resources to prime them and individuals, or groups of individuals, to make the decisions that spark them into life. Attention now turns, therefore, to those who deployed the resources and made the decisions that led to British overseas activity taking the forms and directions that it did. These are the individuals whose willingness to invest, innovate, and take risks was part and parcel of a domestic enterprise culture which took on new forms after 1688 and which increasingly extended itself into the overseas commercial arenas provided by the British empire.

Part Two
Metropolitan Elites
and the Overseas Empire

3 Gentlemen and Entrepreneurs: Landowners, Merchants and Bankers

At the forefront of the various dynamic processes that contributed to the expansion of the British empire during the eighteenth century were constituents of several different elites. These powerful groups, both at home and abroad, held the levers that served to regulate and determine the form and direction taken by British activity in the wider world. Within metropolitan society, a political elite dominated by the landowning classes defined the features of state development and plotted the general course taken by commercial activity, diplomacy, and military action; a mercantile elite supervised and directed the growth of overseas trade; and a financial elite provided much of the capital and resources to support both the state and private enterprise at home and abroad. There was, of course, considerable overlap between these leading sections of British society, and this only served further to concentrate power and influence at the core of the empire. This is not to overlook, or understate, the contribution made by countless thousands of ordinary men and women to the various processes that underpinned British imperial expansion and, equally, it is not to deny that the form an empire eventually takes is fundamentally conditioned by factors well beyond the control of the metropolitan elite. However, the focus in much of what follows in this chapter will be on those individuals of the first or second ranks of British society whose attitudes, decisions and, above all, resources played a key role in helping to define some of the main characteristics of British imperialism during the eighteenth century. Sixty years ago, Richard Pares observed that 'Colonial history is made at home: given a free hand, the mother country will make the kind of empire it needs.'[1] Even if this view is only partially accepted, then it must also be

47

accepted that colonial history is made at home by members of
the economic, political and social elites.

In a domestic context, the eighteenth-century empire was
established, extended and governed by a relatively small co-
hort of individuals. One recent estimate has put the size of the
elite, that is those wielding political power and influence, at
no more than 20,000 individuals out of a total population of
some six million in 1750.[2] This is a reasonable estimate and it
will serve as a convenient overall figure for the various kinds
of individuals discussed in this chapter. Leading members of
this elite were drawn from across Britain into a tight-knit political and business community whose main point of contact
was to be found in London.[3] They all benefited, directly or
indirectly, from metropolitan involvement in a wide variety of
overseas activities and enterprises. Bankers, politicians, military officers, landowners and merchants contributed capital
and skills to the development of the empire and, in return,
drew benefit in the form of employment, opportunity, prestige
and profit.

In a formal sense, the interests of these people were represented at a national level in institutions like Parliament and
the offices of state, but they also wielded great influence
through investment and active involvement in powerful organizations such as the East India Company. Their position was
further reinforced by membership of the many houses, partnerships and companies which operated in the City of London.
This business community was based upon a series of City-wide
and nationwide networks and connections which provided
points of contact for those who operated at the different
frontiers of British overseas activity. Thus, North American
merchants often worked closely with West Indian planters who
in turn rubbed shoulders with East India Company directors
or investors. Indeed, at times there was considerable overlap
between groups of businessmen with overseas interests. A North
American merchant, or West Indian planter, might well dab-
ble in East India Company stocks or bonds, and this was reflected in the way that such individuals increasingly sought to
diversify their activities into different sectors of the empire.
They shared the same problems, faced the same difficulties and
fought the same wars, and, not surprisingly, they borrowed
extensively from one another's experience and expertise.

Decisions about future courses of action were not taken in isolation, but with reference to a worldwide British system of obligations and commitments, all of which had to be carefully weighed and balanced against one another. Because of this, it was not enough for the business elite simply to have access to the resources necessary for overseas trade and investment. In order for those resources to be deployed effectively, and for investments to be protected, they needed the support of the state and those who directed the nation's foreign and overseas affairs. Before committing themselves to long-distance trade and business ventures, individuals needed to know that in time of emergency they could rely on government to deploy ships and troops to uphold their interests. In return, they had to convince the political, landowning, elite that their commercial operations would bring wealth, benefit and prestige to the nation at large without imposing an unacceptably heavy burden on the taxpayers who funded the state's activities in the wider world. An alliance of mutual benefit needed to be forged between two very different metropolitan elites – the business community and the landowning classes – and, in the event, the processes that served to extend British overseas influence helped to bring this powerful sociopolitical concordat into being. Imperialism played an important part in redefining economic, political and social relationships within the metropolis by drawing different elite groups together under a banner of common interest.

THE LANDED ELITE

All forms of power and authority in eighteenth-century Britain were based upon, and determined by, property and proprietary rights. Although the development of a commercial society had multiplied and diversified the forms of property that could be held by an individual, land ownership still formed the cornerstone of the social and political system. Land provided security, stability and status. Hence, there was widespread concern when these certainties were disturbed by increases in the rate of sale and turnover of land, not least when these transfers were accompanied by the arrival of those whose purchasing power was based on new wealth. Moreover, there was also concern that while landed wealth was unmovable and therefore dependable, other forms of property such as goods, money and paper assets could take flight at moments of crisis. Whereas long-established owners of land or real estate held a permanent stake in society and observed well-defined social obligations, those with transportable wealth had no such ties, and, not surprisingly, they were considered to be unreliable. Such attitudes underpinned the general hostility towards the monied interest expressed by the landed interest and their apologists as they attempted to define, redefine and defend their place in the order of things.[4]

Debate has raged among modern historians about whether or not the social elite constituted an 'open' elite during the eighteenth century,[5] but analyses made by contemporary social observers suggested that the proportion of families in England and Wales occupying the highest rung in society remained fairly constant. A small elite of between 1.2 per cent and 1.4 per cent of all families were variously assigned to the category of 'High titles and gentlemen' by Gregory King in 1688, Joseph Massie in 1759 and Patrick Colquhoun in 1801/2.[6] This group accounted for some 18,000 to 27,000 families and their combined income represented between 13.9 per cent and 17.9 per cent of the total amount earned in England and Wales. This does not take into account all income derived from land, because 'freeholders' and 'farmers' constitute a separate category in the social tables, but it does nevertheless give a good indication of the extent to which a small landed elite exercised economic influence out of all proportion to their actual numbers on the ground. Modern historians have stressed that the work of King, Massie and Colquhoun has to be treated with some degree of caution, but their estimates do allow reasonably accurate guesses to be made about wealth-holding and distribution. With this in mind, G.E. Mingay calculated that in 1790 there were 400 'Great Landlords' who earned an average income of £10,000 a year and owned between 20 and 25 per cent of the cultivated land in England and Wales. Beneath them in the social tables were between 14,000 and 25,000 members of the gentry. They enjoyed between £300 and £5000 a year and held between 50 and 60 per cent of the land.[7] This pyramidical structure of wealth- and land-holding illustrated the fact that economic resources and power remained concentrated in a small number of hands. This general state of affairs was reflected in the way in which formal badges of status and prestige, such as peerages and other titular ranks, were distributed to an exclusive group of individuals whose numbers fell significantly between 1700 and 1770. While the number of English and Irish peers increased slightly, this was more than offset by a marked decline in the number of baronets, knights and Scottish peers. As a result, a landed social elite that had stood at 1546 in 1700 had fallen away to 1138 seventy years later.[8] In other words, any 'openness' or upward social mobility within British society in general was not yet managing to disturb or recast the upper ranks of the social tables. On the contrary, and despite what many contemporaries believed, the lines around the landed social elite were in fact becoming evermore tightly drawn.

In Parliament and the central offices of state, the landed elite exercised political influence out of all proportion to their actual numbers. The cabinet was dominated by aristocrats and, in addition to activity in the House of Lords, peers were also capable of exerting significant influence over local parliamentary constituencies, so much so that it has been calculated that in 1715 around a fifth of the seats in the House of Commons were under their control.[9] More generally, the central importance of landed property in eighteenth-century society was reflected by membership of the House of Commons being based upon a landed wealth qualification (£600 for county members and £300 for burgesses) rather than on a more general personal wealth or property assessment. This restricted the number of those eligible to stand for election to somewhere between ten and twelve thousand landowners in the 1780s, and it meant that those men of trade or finance who did not move into land were debarred from entering the legislature. Of course, the need for such a qualification proved no barrier to the commercial or professional man of substance with real political ambitions, and estate purchase allowed increasing numbers of businessmen of various sorts to enter the Commons during the course of the eighteenth century. By 1790 around a sixth of all MPs were from the business community.[10] But, although these were men able to exercise an ever-increasing degree of influence on policy-making, this should not obscure

the fact that parliamentary politics and matters of state continued to be dominated by those who formed the backbone of
landed society.

In spite of its small size, the landed elite was far from being
a homogeneous group. In the political realm, for example,
landowners divided into factions and parties in both the Lords
and the Commons and there was no united landed 'interest'
in Parliament or anywhere else. More generally, there were
often great social and economic differences between and
among the peerage and other landed gentry groups. Indeed,
some members of the aristocracy were far less wealthy than
prosperous untitled landowners.[11] Ultimately, however, there
was much more to unite the landed elite than there was to
divide it, and lifestyles, social responsibilities and general outlook were all fundamentally shaped by a set of shared core
experiences which overrode regional, political and economic
differences. In the realm of religion and education, for example, there was an increasingly uniform pattern of belief and
instruction. Unlike the situation during the seventeenth century, most members of the aristocracy adhered to the Anglican
faith and were hostile towards Catholicism and the dissenting
traditions and, as the eighteenth century progressed, more
families turned their back on private tuition in order to send
young nobles to public school and university.[12] Underpinning
these developments were powerful cultural and social influences emanating from London. This served to bring regional
landed elite groups together into a world of fashion, style and
goods which not only helped to forge a sense of common
identity but also served to reinforce their position at the top
of the social hierarchy in the localities. Landowners in the
provinces imitated the ways of metropolitan life, and in some
distant parts of Scotland and Wales this acted as a powerful
agent of anglicization within the elite.[13]

Running parallel to trends promoting conformity of belief
and experience within the landed elite were a number of influences which served quite fundamentally to reshape attitudes
towards the role and activities of the landowner. Improvement
and innovation characterized developments in traditional
areas of agricultural interest, but many members of the landed
elite also tried to extend their economic horizons well beyond
their estates as they sought new methods of wealth creation.

Diversification, either through choice or necessity, was the order of the day and this helped to broaden perspectives on the world of business and finance. Recently, a number of historians have emphasized the extent to which interaction occurred between the practitioners of different forms of economic activity during the eighteenth century. Thus, just as merchants moved into the worlds of finance and industry, so too they were followed, albeit to a lesser degree, by members of the landed elite. The economic and social effects of this trend were quite profound and, as Mingay has remarked, 'one of the basic facts' of eighteenth-century life was that 'the process of economic expansion since the fifteenth century had resulted in land, trade, industry, and the professions becoming inextricably mingled'.[14]

Seeking improvement and expansion, landowners endeavoured to extend the range of economic activities undertaken on their estates, but they also sought better rates of return on investments placed elsewhere.[15] Merchant wealth in Britain had long been based upon a willingness among individuals to undertake risk through investment in a wide range of different types of property and enterprise, but historians have also argued that the reasonably secure nature of government funds after 1688 meant that an increasing number of landowners were prepared to distribute their financial resources more evenly between land and financial assets.[16] The extent to which this occurred across the country has long been a matter for debate, but a clearer picture is now beginning to emerge as more case studies of individual investment portfolios appear in print. These suggest that a significant number of landowners drawn from across provincial England, Scotland and Wales were not only looking to the City to boost their fortunes but were also becoming involved, with varying degrees of success, in a wide range of industrial, banking and overseas investment schemes.[17] Not all landowners looked to exploit financial opportunities beyond their estates,[18] but many extended their range of economic activities significantly during the course of the eighteenth century.

The development of a broad range of economic interests among the landed elite is well illustrated by the case of the Fuller family of Rose Park (now Brightling Park), Sussex. By the 1750s, John Fuller (1705–55), who had strong West Indian connections and interests, not only earned £2270 from plantations managed by his brother, Rose, in Jamaica, but also earned £1200 from investments, £2200 from an ironworks at Heathfield which supplied cannons to the Board of Ordnance, and £1780 from the family estate.[19] The Montagus of Beaulieu, notably John the 2nd Duke who was nicknamed 'The Planter', were a naval family who diversified their activities in similar fashion. Ambitious (and unsuccessful) attempts to establish plantations in the West Indies and a sugar port in Hampshire found a place alongside considerable investment in estate forestry schemes and, when the royal dockyards were unable to meet demand for new vessels during the 1740s, naval shipbuilding began at the commercial yards on the Beaulieu estate.[20] Families such as these who had a tradition of overseas activity were by no means alone in seeking to place capital resources into very different types of enterprise,[21] although they were considerably more fortunate than the 1st Duke of Chandos whose enthusiasm for economic diversification was not matched by similar success. Indeed, Chandos's experiences might well have served as a salutary reminder to his fellow landowners that, rather than speculate in new forms of enterprise, it was perhaps better to remain in the relatively safe and familiar world of agriculture. Virtually every form of investment that Chandos undertook turned to dust, but his failures at least bear testimony to his willingness to innovate. He invested in building, mining and manufacturing; he purchased land at home and abroad; and he speculated in South Sea stock. The last activity was his undoing, as it was for so many others, and his financial empire collapsed around his ears in the 1730s.[22] Such misfortune did not deter others in the long run, however, and even members of a minor provincial gentry family like the Wilkins of Llanblethian in South Wales were able to develop diverse economic activities embracing the law, banking and colonial trade with such success that they eventually became powerful agents for industrial change in their region.[23]

All of these cases point out that a growing number of landowners had the necessary resources and information at their disposal to enable them to engage in a wide range of investment activities. As part of this process, some capital was channelled towards the City of London, but it is difficult to determine in aggregate terms just how much investment finance found its way from the landed elite to the stock market. Where historians have risked making an informed guess on the issue, they have tended to err on the side of caution and argue that the landed interest did not contribute much to the City and its activities.[24] Yet, in spite of great practical difficulties surrounding the transportation of capital to London, it is clear that English provincial finance, including a significant amount derived from the landed gentry and the genteel leisured classes, had been finding its way to London bankers throughout the seventeenth century.[25] This trend had accelerated during the 1670s, by which time families such as the Verneys of Claydon and the Fitzwilliams of Northamptonshire were channelling over a third of their rent income towards London. Bankers such as Sir Richard Vyner and Edward Backwell were servicing their needs as well as those of clients drawn from within the capital itself.[26] Even if a national capital market did not exist in the eighteenth century, most regions were served by reliable channels through which funds could be transferred to London.[27]

Of course, it is one thing to assert that some surplus capital was flowing from the provinces to the City, but it is quite another to determine what those managing funds on behalf of clients then did with the finance committed to their safekeeping. In the seventeenth century, there had been a relatively straightforward choice between private lending or mortgage, but the overall picture is more complicated for the eighteenth century when a broader range of investment options had become available through the development of public and joint-stock finance. Diversification can be seen, for example, in the case of the group of West End London bankers whose business was based to a considerable extent upon servicing the needs of the aristocracy and gentry. Not only did large private banks, such as Hoares, Childs and Goslings, invest their own considerable assets in a wide range of stocks and government securities, but in a quasi-broking capacity they also handled similar investments on behalf of some of their clients.[28] In this sense, high finance often represented only one element in a broad portfolio of investments held by the landed elite, and stock market activities could prove to be a useful supplement to more traditional forms of income.[29] Although landowners might not have contributed large amounts of capital to the City, they were nevertheless prepared to make use of the stock market when conditions were right and when it suited them. Meanwhile, braver souls within the landed elite were looking to deploy financial resources in the wider world well beyond London and their investment horizons were broadening in a literal as well as a metaphorical sense.[30]

THE MERCHANT ELITE

Few contemporaries would have endorsed Wyndham Beawes's remark that 'the antiquity of the free profession of a merchant may justly entitle it to claim precedency to nobility of birth, and all hereditary, or new created dignities conferred on men by emperors and kings'.[31] Nevertheless merchants, or entrepreneurs engaged in large-scale overseas trade, occupied an important place in eighteenth-century society. This was not simply because of the wealth they generated through their commercial activities, but because they formed close-knit elites who wielded important political and economic influence in many of Britain's major ports and cities.[32] Indeed, by the middle of the eighteenth century a popular view was that the 'virtue' of British merchants was such that they had become key agents in the further development of the nation's power and prestige.[33] The individuals belonging to this elite are not to be confused with domestic retailers, middlemen or traders because, while some overseas merchants branched out into a variety of domestic industrial and banking activities,[34] the scale of the main branch of their commercial operations was such that they became figures of considerable substance and standing in their particular communities. Equally, it has to be stressed that not all of those who exported goods to overseas markets can be classified as merchants. The overseas trading community had a broad base and, as detailed work on Bristol has revealed, many exporters were small tradesmen who simply contributed to cargoes and played little or no part in the import trade.[35]

Recent research has emphasized that a sizeable, continuing commitment to overseas trade demanded access to significant levels of initial and working capital. Long-distance trade was always a hazardous business and the normal risks associated with storm and accident loss were made much worse by the threat posed to ships and cargoes by enemy action during times of war.[36] Even in times of peace, profits or returns were often two or three years in the making. A great deal of trade had to be funded through the extension of credit (for up to two years in some cases) to producers and consumers both at home and overseas and, thus, merchants had to borrow on a regular basis to sustain their operations.[37] The need for initial capital outlay and security meant that only men with resources in the region of £1000–5000 at their disposal could contemplate entering overseas trade with any confidence, and in some branches of trade up to £10,000 was required.[38]

Because individuals had to commit a high level of finance to overseas trade, and in view of the fact that more bankruptcies were recorded for merchants than for any other occupation during the course of the century,[39] it is not surprising to find that many traders sought to place their capital in enterprises that were based upon on the partnership principle. Large firms or partnerships could better withstand the risks and uncertainties associated with long-distance trade in an age of almost continuous warfare. Thus, resources tended to be concentrated in the hands of a small number of firms or individuals, and particular branches of trade came to be dominated by powerful groups of firms, as was the case, for example, with the London–Chesapeake tobacco trade or the Glasgow–West Indies trade.[40] In London during the early part of the century, overseas trade was dominated by 10 to 20 merchants who left fortunes of over £20,000, and their success was reflected by the fact that, as the century wore on, the ratio of their income against that of the peerage improved quite significantly.[41] Leading provincial merchants were also able to generate wealth on a similar scale and in 1785, for example, it was calculated that half a dozen of those engaged in Bristol's West Indian trade had left estates of over £30,000 when they died.[42] The average merchant operated on an altogether more modest scale, but in London such an individual still had resources in the region of between £5000 and £15,000 to his name at the time of his death.[43]

Estimating the size of the nation's merchant class during the eighteenth century is not an easy task, partly because of the problem of deciding if an individual should be classified as a full-time merchant rather than as someone for whom overseas trade formed only part of his business activities.[44] Even so, on the basis of informed contemporary guesses, the figures for England and Wales suggest that the total number of individuals involved in overseas trade was relatively small. In 1688 Gregory King estimated that the number of 'merchants and traders by sea' with an income of over £400 was 2000, while seventy years later Joseph Massie put the figure at 3000.[45] These contemporary estimates of the size of the merchant community are broadly acceptable to the modern historian. They are consistent with recent estimates that have been produced for London alone,[46] bearing in mind that the capital still dominated Britain's overseas trade during the eighteenth century despite the advance of several of the western outports such as Liverpool, Whitehaven, Bristol and Glasgow.[47]

These figures might seem to suggest the existence of an open, expanding and increasingly cosmopolitan merchant elite,[48] but there is a need for caution because detailed research points to a trend in which the main branches of the Atlantic trade, in both London and the outports, were becoming specialized and dominated by an ever-diminishing number of firms and individuals.[49] In the tobacco and sugar trades, in particular, fewer firms were importing a greatly increased volume of goods, while smaller operators fell by the wayside. Thus, as trade expanded during the course of the century, there was a marked growth in the average size of firms. Whereas the largest firm of Glasgow merchants in 1713 had a capital of £7000, there were several firms with capital of over £50,000 by the 1770s and this placed them in the first rank of Scottish private companies.[50] The evidence from Bristol, Glasgow and London suggests that small merchants or newcomers might well be able to find an opening into overseas trade (there were no formal restrictions on entry), but they were often unable to compete with the large well-resourced firms which concentrated their attention on particular branches of trade.[51] It was therefore not easy to become a successful merchant. It was an expensive business which required specialist skills and knowledge, but, once established, the rewards could be significant even though the spectre of potential bankruptcy loomed large in the business life of every overseas trader.

Most firms and individuals developed specialist activities and concentrated their resources and assets in one particular branch of overseas trade, but from the middle of the seventeenth century there had been a growing number of exceptions to this general rule. Individual merchants had been prepared to diversify their business activities both in terms of the areas with which they traded and the products in which they dealt.[52] For a few, overseas trade had become an endeavour to be conducted on a global scale and their investments were channelled into Asia and Africa as well as into the North Atlantic Empire. Maurice Thompson, for example, was an interloper in the East Indies who by the 1640s had also nurtured extensive business interests in Canada, New England and Virginia.[53] By the beginning of the eighteenth century, the Heathcote family had established a vast trading network that embraced the Baltic, Spain, the Mediterranean, the West Indies, North America and the East Indies. Sir Gilbert Heathcote (1652–1733), who has been described as 'perhaps the most successful merchant of his day', carved out a position of great influence for himself in the world of metropolitan politics, serving as Lord Mayor of London, director of the East India Company, and as director and governor of the Bank of England. This enabled him to serve at the very heart of several of the decision-making processes that determined the nation's financial and commercial strategies.[54] Thomas Hall (1692–1748), initially the purser of a ship engaged in the China trade, subsequently established business connections in Europe, South America and the Far East, engaging all the time in an ever-widening range of commercial activities.[55] Further down the scale, a small-scale overseas trader such as the druggist Joseph Cruttenden, who concentrated most of his activities on Barbados and Massachusetts, dealt also with customers as widely spread as Antigua, Jamaica, Madras and New York.[56] This type of geographical diversification was also occurring beyond London in some of the outports. In Bristol, for example, the major merchants involved in the slave, sugar and tobacco trades remained in discrete specialist groups, but a small overseas operator like Stephen Bagg, who was a tradesman dealing in leatherware, was able to maintain business links with the Carolinas, Jamaica, Newfoundland, Quebec and Virginia in 1773.[57] Bagg was not alone, and his commercial activity represented part of a general trend which saw individual entrepreneurs broadening the scope of their economic activity. From an imperial point of view, this meant that more and more individuals were taking advantage of the unity and integration of the British empire and were tying their personal fortunes to the different areas being brought under metropolitan control.

THE FINANCIAL ELITE

During the early stages of its development, English-style banking, unlike its continental counterpart, was located firmly in the world of domestic trade rather than foreign trade. Overseas merchants, however, became increasingly enmeshed within the complex web of financial connections and arrangements centred upon London.[58] By the beginning of the eighteenth century, many members of the City's mercantile community were branching out into a wide range of financial activities and as the century progressed merchants in provincial cities followed them and became quasi-bankers.[59] This process was accelerated at times of war when slumps in trade led to merchants seeking to divert their unused financial resources into new areas of investment. Evidence from the 1690s points to mercantile investment in a wide range of areas, with there being a marked preference for the joint-stock of the City's monied companies.[60] Necessity forced merchants into an evermore flexible approach towards the commitment of their resources, and the establishment of a system of public finance based upon transferable stocks and shares facilitated moves towards the establishment of broad portfolios of investment which outlived the wartime conditions in which they had been created.

These trends troubled contemporary observers who feared that investment capital was being diverted away from trade and commerce,[61] but it is not surprising in view of the growth of the capital's financial institutions and the general expansion of credit. Indeed, the growth of personal fortunes within Britain's merchant community was often based upon a willingness among individuals to seek out new investment opportunities. Land title-deeds, shares in industrial schemes, government contracts, state securities and the stock of the great monied companies were often represented alongside commercial investments in merchant portfolios.[62] Individuals such as William Braund moved easily and naturally between the closely related worlds of trade and finance and, as they did so, they developed broad-based commercial and financial interests.[63] As Sir John Clapham remarked about the 'projectors' of the 1690s, these were not 'single-project men but regular promoters' of a wide range of speculative business activities.[64] A similar situation occurred in Scotland where the Glasgow business elite developed an interest in private banking, as was demonstrated when the Ship, Arms and Thistle Banks were established by prominent members of the tobacco-merchant community during the mid-eighteenth century.[65]

The investment opportunities presented by the 'financial revolution' also helped to facilitate the development of a specialist financier class which operated beyond the long-established areas of scrivening, goldsmith banking and money lending.[66] This was the group known rather indiscriminately to contemporaries as the 'monied interest'. Their primary concerns were banking, broking and all aspects of public finance and, collectively, they formed a powerful part of the nascent financial service sector. The resources and skills of these individuals played a key role in the development of the state, trade and empire, and the wealth that they created allowed them to establish an influential position within the wider British metropolitan elite. In terms of numbers, the financial elite might have been much smaller than the merchant elite, but their position was comparable in terms of political influence, wealth and status.[67]

Some of the most prominent members of the monied interest belonged to the banking community. Central to this community – indeed central to the financial revolution in general – was the Bank of England which serviced the financial needs of government. Founded on the joint-stock principle in 1694, the Bank received deposits, made loans (mainly to government), handled much of the national debt, discounted bills and issued notes.[68] The 24 annually elected directors of the Bank had close personal links with government and the other monied companies, and the stockholders included many individuals who were prominent in the world of national commerce, finance and politics. But beyond this powerful institution were an increasing number of private banks both in London and, after mid-century, in the provinces. They were of great importance in the processes which led to the emergence of something approaching a nationwide financial system.[69] Indeed, in the words of one modern authority, London bankers 'become indispensable linchpins in the system, connecting the country banks not only with the London money market but also with one another.'[70] One might add that they also helped to forge an investment link between British provinces and the wider world.

Some of the banking firms in London emerged from the long tradition associated with goldsmith-banking, and some were established by newcomers who were men of substance from the world of trade and industry able to provide the capital necessary for the successful establishment of a partnership.[71] This was reflected in the way that, as London's private banking community expanded, a broad division appeared between the West End banks and the banks in the City. The former tended increasingly to base their business upon handling the accounts of the landed interest, while the latter, based in and around Lombard Street, worked closely with the mercantile community. The total number of firms involved in private banking in London was not large, but it did rise quite steadily, despite short-term fluctuations, from around two dozen in the 1720s to fifty or so on the eve of the American War for Independence. Partners came and went, and firms divided to form new partnerships, but one common feature of the private banks was that they operated on a relatively narrow capital base in the region of £20,000 to £50,000. They therefore depended upon the need to attract deposits, both interest-bearing and non-interest-bearing. This meant that because the banking community, like the merchant community, had members drawn from a wide range of cultural and ethnic backgrounds, factors such as kinship, connection and religion had a significant influence on the development of particular business interests. Although no general pattern emerges, there are some notable specific instances such as the case of the Freame-Barclay bank whose North American and Quaker associations brought in a great deal of business from merchants in the Chesapeake trade as well as from Quakers. Similarly, the bank of Prescotts, Grote, Culverden and Hollingworth exploited the commercial connections of one of the principal partners, the tobacco exporter Andrew Grote, by attracting business from, among others, a number of Jewish merchants involved in the tobacco trade. These bankers, whatever their origins, were on the whole well regarded figures in metropolitan society. This was partly because they provided essential services for other members of the elite, and partly because they seemed to act with moderation and caution. As a result, the profession acquired all the trappings of gentility. Few contemporaries would have dissented from the view expressed at the time that 'bankers are generally Gentlemen of large estates and monied property, and though some have unhappily failed, it is an uncommon catastrophe, the business being certainly as lucrative as it is genteel.'[72]

Although banking represented an acceptable financial activity in eighteenth-century society, observers were far from convinced about the moral worth of the functions performed by those who focused their profit-making activities exclusively on the stock market. From as early as the 1690s the number of brokers allowed to operate in the City of London was, in theory, limited to 100 and several codes of conduct were drawn up in order to regulate the behaviour of those who traded in stocks and shares.[73] In effect, however, the stock market remained unpoliced throughout the eighteenth century. Anyone could deal in stocks and set themselves up as a broker, and it was recognized by those in government that sharp practice and price manipulation could not be restricted or controlled. During the 1770s, moves towards the self-regulation of the markets were made when the Stock Exchange was established but by then the damage had been done. Stockjobbing was held to be the cause of a wide range of economic ills, and brokers and jobbers were singled out for sustained and ruthless criticism from a wide range of commentators. Thus, not only professional brokers, but many of the private individuals who invested in stocks and securities ran the risk of being indiscriminately denounced as a 'jobber', and it was not uncommon for those prominent in government and public life to conceal the extent of their speculative activities behind a screen of nominee holdings. In effect, the broking profession remained outside the bounds of polite society, despite the ironic fact that brokers acted as the essential point of contact with the market for many of those who wished to take advantage of the opportunities presented by the 'financial revolution'.

IDEALS AND ALLIANCES

It has recently been argued that the establishment of a close alliance between land and finance helped to dictate the general pattern of British economic development and overseas expansion during the eighteenth and nineteenth centuries. As this occurred, the representatives of the financial and commercial interest were drawn towards traditional elite culture, thereby becoming gradually infused with the ethics, ideals and prejudices of the gentleman: the 'gentlemanly capitalist' came into being.[74] In addressing this issue, there can be little doubt that the extension and diversification of individual economic activity that occurred during the late seventeenth and early eighteenth century served to reshape many of the social, cultural and political relationships between different metropolitan elites. In very general terms, this manifested itself in the creation of a sociopolitical alliance between land and business that was based upon the removal of barriers between practitioners of very different types of economic activity. British elites were drawn together by the ownership of property, be it land, capital or paper investments. As this happened, members of elite groups were brought into close working contact with one another and this inevitably served to redefine their ideas about what was, and what was not, in their own interest and the national interest.

Any recognition of reasonably harmonious interaction between elite groups in British society has, however, to be reconciled with historians having long drawn attention to economic and social differences, as well as to general 'antagonisms' and conflicts, between members of the landed 'interest' and an emerging monied class.[75] Indeed, it can not be denied that tensions between sections of different elites remained evident throughout the period. As the emergence of a 'country' opposition indicated, hostility towards the monied interest helped to fuel the belief held by many of the landed elite that their position, as well as the nation's moral well-being, was being undermined by developments in the world of high finance and stockbroking.[76] Thus, although the capitalist spirit in general escaped sustained censure during the eighteenth century,[77] all forms of City-based financial activity were the target of many different types of criticism.

The modern historian might regard the 'financial revolution' as one of the most important economic advances of the period, but contemporary observers were not so sure. By the mid-eighteenth century it could not be denied that the City had been instrumental in helping the nation come to terms with the many problems associated with almost continuous warfare,[78] but a wide range of critics nevertheless condemned City institutions and the emergent financier class in no uncertain terms. Throughout the century, the Bank of England attracted great suspicion and hostility, and its long-term position remained a matter for debate.[79] More generally, the all-pervasive influence of the manners, methods and ethics of the City was seen to be helping to undermine the economic, moral and political stability of the nation. Radicals attacked the close and mutually beneficial links between governments and chartered institutions. Those drawn from the narrow circle that subscribed to government loans in times of war were seen to be profiting in a tax-free environment from the nation's misfortune. At the same time, the landed interest laboured under a tax burden which was deemed to be excessively heavy in times of war precisely because of the need to pay attractive rates of interest to those who provided loan capital to the state. All forms of new wealth generated in the City (or overseas) were perceived to be corrupting forces which could upset the aristocratic settlement and recast the social tables.[80] Above all, perhaps, speculative activity was seen as promoting sloth, greed, 'luxury' and avarice, which in turn led to the gradual abandonment of traditional forms of endeavour such as trade in which notions of moderation and responsibility played a central part in the creation of wealth.[81] Speculative entrepreneurial activity of the financial type often sat very uneasily alongside codes of conduct based upon a gentlemanly ideal in which, among other things, honour played an important part.

Tension between elites was not simply fuelled by criticism from those seeking to protect a gentlemanly ideal against the corrupting influences that were thought to be at large within the business and financial community. There is evidence to suggest that, on the other side of the coin, the City of London in its broadest sense was often quite resistant to aristocratic modes of behaviour. One authority has declared that there was a 'residual contempt for aristocratic degeneracy',[82] and this prevented the ready acceptance of all forms of gentlemanly conduct by the practitioners of trade, finance and business. In general, 'aristocratic' ideals were often subjected to hostile criticism, and they could be decried as being effeminate, foppish and 'foreign', particularly when a more vigorous and aggressive response to British setbacks in the wider world was demanded from those directing the nation's political and strategic fortunes.[83] Not everyone chose to play the game by gentlemanly rules.

It cannot be denied that members of elites demonstrated deep hostility and suspicion towards one another from to time during the eighteenth century. Nevertheless, it seems clear that tensions diminished after 1720 as different socioeconomic groups realized that they could all draw benefit from the financial and political arrangements that had served to reshape the British state and extend the overseas empire after 1688.[84] The representatives of land and finance were prepared, with some degree of unease, to make use of one another's skills and resources in an arrangement of mutual benefit and convenience. This is a point made recently in a similar context by Linda Colley with reference to attitudes towards traders and the commercial interest. Just as the relationship between land and trade was a mutually beneficial one,[85] so too was that struck between land and high finance. John Cannon has touched briefly on this theme as he has endeavoured to explain why the aristocratic settlement remained unchallenged, and was even strengthened, during this period. No other form of regime held any attraction for the business, commercial and industrial communities, he has argued. Instead, the existing system, which in its political form was managed by the aristocratic elite, offered them encouragement, stability, the prospect if not the reality of upward social mobility, and plenty of opportunity for investment free from heavy taxation and government interference.[86] The conduct of overseas affairs could create deep divisions between different elites, but concerted pressure from the merchant community could also force a government dominated by landowners into action against its instinct and better judgement. This was perhaps most notably the case during the events leading up to Walpole's declaration of war against Spain in 1739, when a widespread and well-organized public campaign helped to convince ministers that the nation in general would benefit from decisive action in the West Indies.[87] This is a good example of the way in which a 'national' interest which transcended different sectional interest groups was slowly beginning to emerge.

By the mid-eighteenth century, some contemporary observers were beginning to draw attention to this state of affairs by questioning the notion that in the economic sphere the landed classes enjoyed any separate form of identity or special status. It was argued that landowners were in fact 'deeply implicated in commercial society',[88] and this was reflected in Parliament, which devoted a great deal of its time to matters of trade, commerce and empire. Contemporary observers also drew attention to neither landowners nor businessmen alone being in possession of all the qualities necessary to govern a changing modern society and an expanding empire. As Sir Josiah Child wrote in the late seventeenth century, businessmen and the gentry complemented one another, so that in a political context 'a mixt assembly of noblemen, gentlemen, and merchants, are the best constitution that can be established'.[89] The acquisition and expansion of the empire played a key role in sustaining this 'mixt assembly' of different elite groups and it helped, at least in part, to focus attention on the evolving national interest rather than on narrow long-standing sectional concerns.[90]

In spite of the underlying tensions sometimes evident in the relationship between different elites, individuals were often able to bury hostility and mistrust beneath a shared sense of common identity and belief. As Paul Langford has recently stated, '. . . most contemporaries understood well, that it was no longer rational to assume hard lines of distinction between the diverse enterprises of Hanoverian England.'[91] Reflecting this state of affairs at local level, a growing body of evidence based on studies of Cumbria, Cheshire, Norfolk, Lancashire and Yorkshire points to a situation in which provincial elites embraced families drawn from the land, the professions and commerce.[92] On the whole, landed society managed to absorb newcomers with relative ease, part of the reason being that few businessmen seem to have wished to transform themselves into fully fledged landed gentry of the traditional type. Rather, there was a tendency for such men to purchase relatively small parcels of land of a few hundred acres or so. These were often located close to their urban homes which helps to explain why newcomers do not feature to a great extent in analyses of the great landed estates.[93] Many of the wealthy individuals who sought a home in the country were often not inclined to opt for all the accompanying trappings of a rural lifestyle. One foot was placed in the world of the landed gentleman, but the other foot was kept firmly in the world of business and, by selectively embracing the gentlemanly ideal, these men were adopting what the author of a detailed study has aptly called 'country life in miniature'.[94] The general picture was much the same in parts of Scotland. Glasgow tobacco merchants had little difficulty in procuring land and their purchases could be on quite a considerable scale. Like their English counterparts, however, they did not move entirely into the world of the country gentleman. Their estates were concentrated around Glasgow, not breaking their links with business. Although land-owning in Scotland, as in England, brought social prestige and political power, the tobacco merchants remained very close to their commercial operations and continued to exercise direct supervision over their trading interests.[95]

The local elites produced by the intermingling of land and business were defined by a wide range of characteristics. Individuals displayed a commitment to 'improvement', engaged in diverse economic activities, shared political and administrative duties within the community, and interacted at a social level. Moreover, relationships between families were often reinforced by kinship and marriage. Giving an overall sense of shape and coherence to groups drawn from a wide range of socioeconomic backgrounds was adherence to a gentlemanly ideal or code of politeness, and this allowed individuals to meet on common ground. The title 'gentlemen' was sufficiently flexible in its application to include all members of all elites, so that many others, and merchants in particular, found that they were increasingly identified by commentators as embodying all the qualities of a worthy English gentleman.[96] Indeed, such merchants often found that the conduct of business was informed by gentlemanly values. The whole system of credit was founded on honour and unwritten rules, and an individual's creditworthiness was often based upon his word as a gentleman. Social status in general was defined by the way in which lifestyles were conducted, and gentlemen were deemed to be polite, genteel and leisured because for the most part they had little routine day-to-day involvement with the world of work and the processes of wealth creation. All this was reinforced by the balance of exchanges of ideas, taste and general outlook between the representatives of elite city and country life often being such that many salient features of metropolitan style and behaviour were extended into landed society, thus helping to establish and sustain a sense of common identity between elites in different parts of the country.[97] Regular contact with London, either through part-time residence or correspondence and the reading of newspapers and periodicals, meant that ideas about metropolitan behaviour, standards and fashions were transmitted to the provinces by the elite, and this meant that the polite lifestyles of the well-to-do who lived in the capital were often imitated by many of those who belonged to the upper echelons of provincial society.[98] In a very loose and general sense, those embodying the characteristics of the gentlemanly capitalist were often to be found across many parts of Britain, and not simply in London and the south of England.

ELITES AND EMPIRE: AN IMPERIAL NATION?

By the mid-eighteenth century, the development of careers, business interests and investments had led to members of the elite becoming dependent upon Britain sustaining, if not extending, her position in the wider world. In view of this, it might be thought that Britons would have taken a close interest in imperial affairs. Modern historians, however, are far from agreed on the extent to which the British were concerned about their empire and colonies. At one end of the spectrum is a view which suggests that few people cared at all about the colonies. Jacob Price has recently argued that only a handful of the metropolitan elite had any experience of, or interest in, the American colonies. Few MPs or officeholders demonstrated much knowledge about, or understanding of, events and developments in North America, particularly before mid-century. Moreover, because the Atlantic trade was increasingly concentrated in a small number of major ports, many parts of the country lost direct contact with the world of North Atlantic commerce. Moving beyond a narrow definition of interest in the colonies based upon involvement in political and commercial activity, Price is unable to find much evidence of the population at large deriving any great direct benefit from the North American empire. His conclusion is that while a large number of people did care about the colonies, they were 'very unevenly distributed geographically and socially and quite diverse in their approach to American questions.'[99] In other words, while not indifferent towards America, many Britons did not yet find that the colonies captured their attention and interest on a regular basis.

At the other end of the spectrum is an argument which suggests that the empire had in fact become, or was becoming, deeply embedded in popular consciousness to the point that imperial issues had almost become part and parcel of everyday life. Kathleen Wilson has not only demonstrated the extent to which imperial themes were represented in the press, theatre and extra-parliamentary politics, but she has also drawn attention to the ways in which those outside the elite played a key role in formulating popular attitudes towards the empire, conquest and territorial acquisition.[100] All sections of society contributed to, and benefited from, the imperial process and moreover helped, in different ways, to bring the empire into a position of central importance as far as political discourse and the development of ideology was concerned. Where should the balance be struck? Had Britain become an imperial nation or can Price's analysis of the British-American connection be extended to sustain the general argument that Britons gained little from, and cared little about, their overseas possessions, colonies and territories?

One thing that observers of imperial affairs were increasingly certain about was that Britain drew great material strength and benefit from her overseas possessions. The empire represented an important, perhaps the most important, manifestation of Britain having become one of the great European powers. Possession of overseas territory was increasingly held to be synonymous with national wealth, strength and prestige, and observers and writers sought repeatedly to try and calculate the benefits brought to Britain by her colonies. In particular, they were keen to establish the various ways in which the empire had become a source of great strength to the mother country in a military and strategic context. The expansion of the empire and the related growth of trade and shipping had undoubtedly helped to provide manpower resources that could be deployed during times of military crisis and conflict. This was particularly the case, as contemporaries never tired of observing, with regard to the number of seamen that Britain now had at her disposal. The merchant fleet acted as a permanent naval reserve, through providing a pool of labour on which the state could draw when it needed. Indeed, the demands of the navy were such that at times the merchant fleet could be reduced to only a fraction of its peacetime complement. It has been calculated, for example, that during the 1750s the navy absorbed some 60,000 men from a merchant and fishing fleet that had numbered some 70–80,000 personnel before the hostilities.[101] In general, the existence of this reserve played a key part in helping to meet the threat posed by the Bourbon powers. More specifically, troops supplied by Britain's colonies and overseas possessions could at times defy metropolitan expectations of their abilities and help to inflict significant setbacks on the French. In a North American context this was demonstrated in 1745 when forces deployed by the New England colonies successfully assaulted Louisbourg, Cape Breton Island, while in India the great expansion of the East India Company's armed forces was based upon recruitment of thousands of native sepoys during the 1750s and 1760s.

The expansion of the British overseas empire had a considerable effect upon the domestic economy where it acted as a powerful agent of change and development. As we have seen, there is little detailed evidence to suggest that the profits of imperialism, be it Bengal plunder or the ill-gotten gains of the Atlantic slave trade, primed the pump of any British industrial 'revolution'. Nevertheless, in some regions overseas merchants began to channel resources into industry, and trade therefore did have a part to play in the all-important process of capital formation. More generally, there can be no doubt that the possession of an overseas empire assisted in stimulating growth, improvement and innovation, and this helped to strengthen the metropolitan economy. On one hand, the expansion of imperial trade and commerce brought an ever-increasing range and volume of raw materials into Britain, while on the other hand, as contemporaries increasingly acknowledged, the expansion of colonial populations played an important part in creating employment in the mother country by increasing demand for manufactured goods and finished articles. The purchasing power of the colonies was considerable and made itself felt across a wide range of British industries and services, particularly those located in and around London.[102] In some ways, too, even the limited strength of colonial industries was brought to bear on the general process of British economic development. On occasions, colonial producers were able to help overcome shortfalls in important areas of metropolitan output, notably in the shipbuilding industry. Those closely involved with British shipping were swift to condemn this development, but many contemporaries welcomed it as tangible evidence of the way in which possession of overseas colonies helped to augment and reinforce British commercial and naval strength.[103]

It was also clear to those contemporaries who held more than a passing interest in the world around them that possession of an overseas empire was beginning to have a considerable effect upon everyday life in Britain. Not only were many private fortunes dependent upon investment in empire, but goods imported into Britain from her overseas possessions were at the very heart of some of the most important changes occurring in patterns of domestic consumption. Diet, fashion and social habits changed as products such as tea, coffee, sugar, china and textiles found their way to Britain in ever-increasing quantities. Merchants stimulated demand for different products by directing them towards specific types of consumer. Heavy, durable cloth was marketed with workmen in mind, while chintz and fine cloth were aimed towards fashion-conscious ladies and gentlewomen. Such strategies met with notable success, and members of polite society proved themselves to be keen to avail themselves of new and different types of textiles, particularly Indian cotton. This had quite an effect on styles of dress and clothing within the upper echelons of society, so much so that at the end of the seventeenth century the political economist John Cary observed that, although

Indian cottons had rarely been seen twenty years before, 'now few think themselves well dresst till they are made up in Calicoes, both men and women, Calico shirts, Neckcloths, Cuffs, Pocket-handkerchiefs for the former, Head-Dresses, Nightroyls, Hoods, Sleeves, Aprons, Gowns, Petticoats, and what not for the latter, besides India-Stockings for both Sexes.'[104] Decorative style within the home also changed and the elite availed themselves of opportunities to purchase carpets and curtains from the empire and beyond.[105] If textile imports helped to change styles of clothing and dress, then so too did the importation of non-European grocery products alter dietary patterns, first among the well-to-do and then among the population at large.[106] Items such as tea, chocolate, coffee and tobacco were initially regarded as luxury goods but they developed into products of mass consumption as merchants stimulated widespread demand by mounting advertising and distribution campaigns on a nationwide scale.[107] These changes in patterns of consumption were, of course, then in turn reflected in the overseas empire as goods were re-exported by metropolitan merchants to the colonies.

Beyond the world of goods, it was also evident that the consequences stemming from successful activity in the wider world could be brought to bear upon the nation's financial fortunes. Improved returns from the East India investment at the end of the seventeenth century played a key part in allowing the metropolitan economy to take the strain imposed by war when hostilities against France were resumed in 1701.[108] More directly, and in a way that was much more obvious to contemporaries, the financial rewards and spoils associated with military victory and conquest could be considerable. This was most notably the case during the 1760s when the East India Company secured territorial revenues at the conclusion of its campaigns in northern India. Some were moved to the erroneous conclusion that the Company's success would provide a large part of the answer to the problems associated with the nation's spiralling National Debt. Success in the east was widely regarded as something akin to a gift from heaven. However, those with a keen eye on the interlinked technical and legal problems associated with the state securing access to the Company's newly won private riches were swift to recognize that the benefits stemming from short-term financial returns could be more than offset by long-term administrative, constitutional and political difficulties.[109] Nevertheless, those charged with management of the nation's finances could draw some immediate comfort when the East India Company agreed to make an annual payment of £400,000 to the Treasury after 1767 which would just about offset the loss of government revenue caused by the reduction of the Land Tax from four shillings a pound to three shillings a pound.

In other spheres of activity, conquest also brought financial rewards which could, in theory at least, help to alleviate the nation's burden of debt. Rather than follow the usual path of granting land to petitioners in return for the payment of quit rent, the authorities arranged sales of small lots in newly acquired Crown islands in the West Indies following the acquisition of territory from France in both 1713 and 1763. Although returns did not always match the expectations of those in government, considerable efforts were made by the authorities to ensure that a significant revenue was raised from new British colonies. The way was pointed forward through the sale of 10,000 acres in St Kitts. This eventually raised £110,997 for the Treasury in the years after the Treaty of Utrecht, but this early promise was not sustained during the course of later similar transactions. Only £138,851 found its way into the Treasury's coffers from the sale of 167,000 acres and a number of town lots in Dominica, Tobago and St Vincent during the decade or so after the Peace of Paris when a combination of unforeseen factors prevented officials from securing the return of the £700,000 or so that should have been forthcoming.[110]

Contemporaries did not need to be financial experts or close observers of domestic politics to appreciate that the empire was steadily growing in importance. By mid-century, there was little escape from exposure to imperial affairs and issues, and images of empire were to be found in a number of different spheres of public life. The different types of image that were brought before the public helped to contribute to the evolution of a broad set of imperial attitudes, and they served to shape perceptions of empire among significant numbers of the population at large. Wilson has helped to establish the extent to which members of the reading public were granted access to information about the empire through the medium of the newspaper and periodical press, and she has also indicated the ways in which imperial themes loomed large in the theatrical entertainment of the time.[111] As far as the latter context is concerned, it seems clear that the elite, together with members of other social classes, were drawn in large numbers to theatres in London and the provinces where productions were often based upon, or reflected, issues located in an imperial context. Building on a publishing tradition which reflected a broad interest in travel literature and alien cultures,[112] newspapers and periodicals increasingly began to fill many of their columns with items and articles about life and events in Britain's overseas territories. Interest in colonial affairs was not confined to the London press, as the provincial newspapers proved to be just as keen to bring the wider world to their readers. This did not simply arise from the provincial press following publishing trends dictated by those in the metropolis, but also indicated the extent to which regional newspapers were in touch with the broader interests and concerns of many of their readers. By mid-century, war, trade and 'foreign affairs' had become matters of primary importance to all provincial newspaper editors, and the inclusion of lengthy accounts of imperial affairs, often under the heading 'Plantation news', only helped further to extend the horizons of the reader.[113] Local news, by comparison, took up little space in many of the newspapers.

As Britain made significant territorial gains during the late 1750s and early 1760s, an ever-increasing amount of press attention was devoted to imperial affairs. Alongside detailed accounts of battles, expeditions and political developments at the periphery were to be found an extraordinary range of items related to the history, geography and topography of British overseas possessions. After the capture of Quebec in 1759, for example, readers of monthly magazines were treated to a large number of articles dedicated to descriptions of the Canadian economy and society.[114] A similar publishing trend was evident after the success of British arms in India between 1763 and 1765. In its role as *diwan* of Bengal, Bihar and Orissa, the East India Company was drawn into the administration of extensive territories, and a great deal of information was published in Britain about the societies that had fallen under British control.[115] In part, this went some way towards supplying the basic information that was necessary to enable Britons fully to comprehend the material gains derived from conquest and territorial acquisition, but such coverage also reflected a deep general fascination with the exotic or the unusual, and readers were brought lengthy accounts of the curiosities and customs that were revealed by British encounters with indigenous societies in the wider world.

At a less elevated level, the press also devoted a considerable amount of attention to coverage of imperial politics. This was assisted by the easing of restrictions on the reporting of parliamentary debates during the early 1770s and, as the affairs of America and India began to loom large in the Houses of Commons and Lords, the newspaper reader was able to follow in detail the development of imperial policy. In addition, the domestic affairs of the East India Company and the activities of miscreant Company servants, the widely despised 'nabobs', were laid before readers in the decade after 1765.[116] Indeed, such was the interest in these issues that reports of debates at the Company's General Court of Proprietors were, at times, given pride of place in the London press above the proceedings of Parliament and matters of state. The bitter and acrimonious nature of East India politics was also reflected in the publication of numerous pamphlets and polemical essays, many of which provided the reader with background information on the development of controversies and disputes in their Indian context. Moreover, as in earlier years, the provincial press also fed their readers on a diet based to a large extent on imperial affairs and colonial matters. In some cases this served a practical purpose beyond that of simply enlightening the general reader. In Scotland, for example, editors recognized their readers' interest and deep involvement in transatlantic trade, shipping and migration and, from 1760 onwards, they filled their publications with information about the American colonies.[117] In short, by the third quarter of the eighteenth century, few members of the British elite or general reading public stood much chance of avoiding contact with imperial affairs.

British success in the wider world always prompted enthusiastic bouts of public rejoicing and the elite were well to the fore on such occasions. They organized lavish entertainments funded by subscriptions, and these celebrations of overseas triumphs always attracted active participation from large numbers of people who had no personal stake in the empire.[118]

And, of course, the reverse was also true: the failure of British arms was widely regarded as a national disgrace and angry mobs could be brought onto the streets by news of military setbacks or the loss of territory to France or Spain. This illustrates the extent to which imperial issues had established themselves in popular consciousness, but beyond these short-term public expressions of celebration or anger were to be found a number of different media through which a rather more long-lasting interest in the empire could express itself.

The development of, and perception of, Britain as an imperial nation manifested itself in the cultural sphere through the medium of landscape architecture.[119] Throughout the period, monuments and gardens were dedicated to the celebration of British victories and the commemoration of British heroes, and the whole process gathered pace during the 1750s and 1760s in response to the military success enjoyed by the nation during the Seven Years' War. In total, well over a hundred surviving 'follies' have been identified as having been inspired by imperial activity between 1739 and 1815. Examples such as the Grenville Tower, built at Stowe in 1747, not only acted as memorials to fallen individuals such as Thomas Grenville, killed at the Battle of Finisterre, but also served as symbols bearing testimony to British supremacy and virtue. An entire estate such as that at Shugborough, the seat of the Ansons, could be devoted to an ostentatious celebration of family endeavour in the wider world, in this case the exploits of George Anson during his circumnavigation of the world between 1740 and 1744.

These types of declaration of faith in Britain's imperial ascendancy multiplied in both number and form during the Seven Years' War, and monuments of various sorts were built on many landed estates. Landscape architecture of this genre was influenced in particular by the neoclassical style that became increasingly popular in mid-century. An important figure in this process was James Stuart who acted as consultant for the series of victory medals produced for the Society for the Promotion of Arts, Manufactures and Commerce. He translated these designs into many of the architectural medallions set in the building at Stowe which was modified to become the Temple of Concord and Victory during the early 1760s, and he also used them on the Triumphal Arch that was constructed at Shugborough. Visitors to estates such as Stowe, which contained the most visited garden of its time, were left in no doubt about the close nature of the association between some landowning dynasties and overseas endeavour. Even the least discerning eye could not fail to note the symbolism that had been incorporated in the temples, arches and monuments dotted over the landscape. Empire, commerce and the fruits of victory were all depicted through design features and representations which played upon the central theme of Britain triumphant in the wider world. The metropolitan elite basked in the reflected glory of the expanding empire, and well they might, for many of them were deeply involved in every aspect of British overseas activity.

4 Investment in Empire

The establishment and gradual extension of British interests into the wider world opened up numerous business and commercial opportunities, and a large number of the British elite were drawn to economic activity based in the nation's overseas territorial possessions. While this acted as a dynamic for further imperial expansion, it also helped to strengthen imperial ties by entangling Britons in a global network of commitments and obligations which needed support from, and defence by, the state. As such, this had significant implications for the way in which Britain organized herself as an imperial power, and it played its part in shaping the contours of the modern state created after 1688.

THE SCOPE AND STRUCTURE OF EIGHTEENTH-CENTURY IMPERIAL FINANCE

The military and commercial wheels of the British empire were oiled by finance, but it is worth stressing at the outset that no aggregate figures are available which allow us to quantify the extent to which domestic financial resources were channelled into the wider world during the eighteenth century. This is partly because the surviving statistical data are fragmentary, but it is also difficult to disentangle the general costs of warfare from those incurred solely in an extra-European or imperial context. The whole issue is further complicated by the way in which the British imperial presence was structured in different ways in different parts of the world. Various organizations, institutions and agencies represented Britain abroad and they all operated within their own financial and administrative frameworks. Some were small private firms or partnerships, while at the other end of the scale was the East India Company, a semi-official representative of the Crown which held territory and possessed its own considerable armed forces and administrative personnel. As a result of all these difficulties confronting the economic historian, no detailed work on imperial finance has been attempted to complement that undertaken by Davis and Huttenback on expenditure, returns, losses and reinvestments in the nineteenth-century empire.[1] However, in spite of this large gap in our understanding of British imperial development, one important point seems quite clear. Beyond the part it played, via general military expenditure, in contributing to the National Debt, eighteenth-century empire building did not impose a particularly heavy burden upon the domestic economy, and it certainly did not cause a damaging drain of investment finance from Britain. This was because the capital requirements involved with the building of the eighteenth-century empire were not substantial.

Once colonies had been acquired and established, they did not often require subsequent regular injections of large amounts of investment finance from the mother country to sustain economic growth, expansion and settlement. Indeed, in some places, such as Jamaica, the resources used for the development of a plantation economy were almost exclusively derived from local sources.[2] More generally, the West Indies and North America both provide cases which illustrate that there was no need for any regular large metropolitan subsidy for colonial economies. Even though military expenditure by the metropolitan authorities was undoubtedly of vital importance to many colonial economies, peacetime defence and administrative costs were quite limited, reflecting the perennial concerns expressed in London about the need to keep the costs of empire to a minimum. Average annual British government expenditure of £148,000 on the North American colonies between 1740 and 1748 rose only to £417,000 during the decade before the War for Independence.[3] Even so, it cannot be denied that colonists everywhere were tied economically to Britain in many different ways. They needed metropolitan credits to meet short-term working capital requirements, and they needed Britain to provide services and manufactured goods, but their general level of prosperity was such that they were not dependent on Britain for investment finance to fund expansion and development.[4] Indeed, it has been argued that in North America the benefits gained by the colonies 'largely offset' the costs of belonging to the British empire when all aspects of the imperial economic relationship are taken into consideration.[5] On the whole, once colonies had been established, colonists accumulated capital through saving and they ploughed back profits into various enterprises, thereby prompting growth and expansion. Thus, Richard Pares was able to come to the conclusion that 'the wealth of the West Indies was created out of the profits of the West Indies themselves.'[6] In general terms, neither the defence nor commercial development of Britain's overseas possessions imposed a heavy direct burden on the British state or the domestic taxpayer. This only occurred during times of war against European powers when conflict increasingly manifested itself in struggles for colonial territory and overseas possessions.

Although the development and expansion of the established parts of the empire was not dependent on state subsidy or the export of large amounts of domestic capital, private metropolitan investment nevertheless played a crucial role within the various processes that sustained and supported British imperialism. There were, broadly speaking, four forms of investment in empire available to domestic investors during the eighteenth century, and each helped to shape the development of the British overseas empire in a different way. First, in a very general sense, investors could underwrite the activities of the state by subscribing to loans and buying into stock issues. In doing this, they reinforced the 'fiscal-military state' which in its turn supported and defended the empire. This type of investment, which lay at the very heart of the 'financial revolution', played a key part through establishing the general context and conditions in which overseas expansion could take place. Second, investment in a powerful imperial agency or corporation such as the East India Company represented a positive contribution to the extension of British influence overseas. After all, the line between trade and conquest, already blurred by 1750, had become non-existent a few years later as the Company evolved into a formidable territorial and military power in its own right. Third, there is what might be called direct investment in empire which took the form of private investment by individuals or consortia in overseas projects such as plantations, commercial and trading ventures, or land settlement schemes. Not only did such investment often help to establish and develop the very nature and form of the British presence overseas, but the metropolitan investors involved in such schemes acquired an interest in protecting and extending their activities. Finally, the availability of investment finance (whether derived from the metropolis or from the colonies themselves) was not by itself enough to secure economic growth and development, as considerable resources were needed to ensure the day-to-day operation of colonial business and commercial enterprises. In this context, the domestic mercantile and financial services sector played a vital role in sustaining imperial economic growth through the provision of loans, mortgages and commercial facilities to those at the periphery who sought credit for their activities. This was particularly the case in some West Indian and North American contexts where local financial markets, especially for credit, were often slow to develop.

FUNDING THE STATE

The conjunction of interests between the landed elite and the commercial, business and financial communities outlined in the previous chapter was based upon the economic and political arrangements which found expression in government finance and the creation and expansion of the National Debt.[7] These arrangements, and hence the alliance of elite interest groups, were forged during a century of almost continuous warfare. This placed a major financial burden on the state and during war years between 1689 and 1763 the army and navy never accounted for less than 64 per cent of annual government expenditure.[8] Where once historians believed that Britons were lightly taxed when compared with their continental European contemporaries, recent detailed work has shown that the burden of direct and indirect taxation was, on a per capita basis, heavier in Britain than it was in France. Indeed, aggregate annual returns based upon the excise, customs and the Land Tax more than trebled to over £12 million a year between 1689 and 1775.[9] In the first instance, this provided ministers with a sizeable regular income which could be directed in large part towards military spending. Just as important, however, was the fact that because government interest payments were secured on taxation, the state's creditworthiness was substantially reinforced. This facilitated more and more long-term borrowing to meet the increased levels of annual expenditure.[10] As one modern authority has argued, this was the most important factor underpinning British military success during the course of the long eighteenth century.[11] The National Debt rose from £16.7 million in 1697 to £242.9 million by 1784, and loans came to fund a greater and greater proportion of spending, so that by the time of the American War 40 per cent of expenditure was paid for by borrowing.[12]

The creation and expansion of the National Debt and the accompanying growth of a bureaucratic state brought benefits to all sections of the metropolitan elite. While there was much criticism of the mechanisms and techniques used to fund state activity, notably because they were thought to promote profiteering, speculative activity and stockjobbing, the landed elite as well as monied interest groups were able to take advantage of the new financial opportunities presented to them after 1688. Against a general background in which the landed classes enjoyed a reduction in the fiscal burden imposed upon them in terms of *direct* taxation, the aristocracy and gentry were able to invest in the funds if they chose. At the same time, more and more of their sons were able to enter public service as the number of offices of state multiplied during the course of the century.[13] Some country gentlemen rapidly took advantage of the opportunities presented by the 'financial revolution' but, as Dickson's detailed study of public finance reveals, the landed classes did not, in aggregate terms, subscribe a great deal to the stocks and government long-term borrowing schemes.[14] Indeed, as the eighteenth century progressed, the amount of investment capital finding its way from the provinces into government long-term loans decreased so that, in Dickson's words, by 1750 'the circle of home investors was based more solidly on London than it had been six decades earlier.'[15]

Changes in the profile of domestic investors during the first half of the eighteenth century served only to heighten contemporary interest in the activities of London's financial elite. Because of their large stake in the National Debt, the monied interest made gains from the new financial environment that were far more visible than those made by the landed elite and, as a result, they were liable at times of crisis to receive hostile criticism from all quarters. At the most basic of levels, it was believed that the monied men thrived during periods of national misfortune, since by making loan finance available to government they were thought to profit on a considerable scale when the nation's debts were spiralling upwards.[16] More insidiously, it was held that close links with ministers who needed their expertise, contacts and access to investment capital led to the financial elite exercising undue influence upon, and within, the decision-making process.[17] Although many of the tales about the influence of the monied interest were wildly exaggerated, there can be no doubt that a relatively close-knit body of London-based financiers, commercial men and merchants made large sums from underwriting state loans and by acting as government contractors.[18] Moreover, when this economic relationship was transferred to a political environment in the House of Commons it was unlikely that the money men would, in the words of John Brewer, 'bite the hand that fed them'.[19] This helped to form the essential connection in the relationship between the landed and monied elites and, despite periodic outbursts of antagonism between the two groups, the relationship grew stronger as the century progressed.

Beyond the landed and monied interest groups, there was a large and growing number of small-scale domestic investors in government securities who were based in London and its environs. These individuals, members of the 'middling orders', were often women, tradesmen and artisans who owned less than than £500 stock each, but in total comprised around 50 per cent of investors in government stock. This pattern of ownership was reinforced as the stockholding community became more concentrated in London. This should not be allowed to obscure the fact that big financiers, who represented a small percentage of domestic investors, controlled up to a third of most stocks.[20] It does, however, serve as a reminder that important sections of society well beyond the elite were deriving some income from long-term investment in the state and its activities. Moreover, foreign investors, particularly the Dutch, were important public creditors and their commitment to long-term government securities meant that they had more than just a passing interest in the part played by the Britain on the international stage.[21]

While the scale and scope of government finance was extended significantly as a result of activity and conflict around the world, it is of course difficult to argue that those investors in the National Debt knowingly sought to promote overseas expansion. Their investment was not perceived as being destined for any specific type of state activity and it is not possible to link particular sections of the investing community with even the most general areas of government action. Nevertheless, in addition to attractive rates of interest, investors benefited from secure national defence, political stability and a tariff policy which offset the need for an excessive land tax.[22] Overseas activity and commerce could develop in these conditions, despite the disruption caused by long periods of warfare, but the creation of the fiscal-military state did not by itself provide a financial dynamic for expansion. What it did do, however, was help to forge the mutually beneficial relationship between the landed interest and the financial and commercial community. In this way the City became the linchpin of the eighteenth-century state by providing a series of services which united the main branches of state activity, including overseas activity, and made them dependent upon one another. In this broadest of senses, the investing community in general, including members of the landed classes, undoubtedly had a stake in the empire for it was their financial resources which allowed the British state to deploy its military and naval power on a global scale. This military disposition allowed Britain to meet the challenge posed by the Bourbon powers, and, as this happened, overseas territories and possessions were acquired, secured and extended. In this general way, the state provided the essential framework in which overseas business and enterprise could flourish.

JOINT-STOCK INVESTMENT

If public creditors were a long way removed from direct involvement in the process of overseas expansion, then, similarly, domestic investors in overseas trading companies should not be characterized as back-seat empire builders. As K.G. Davies observed about the Royal African Company, 'The men and women who invested in the African Company did not do so in pursuit of an ideal of imperialism; their aim was to make money. They were interested in exports and imports, shipping and slaves, forts and factories, only in so far as they contributed to the making of profits.'[23] The joint-stock principle effectively separated investors from direct capital management, and supervision was undertaken by elected representatives or company directors. This meant that investors played little part in the day-to-day running of company affairs. The problems of empire were seldom discussed at meetings of stockholders, and even the directors of trading companies often proved incapable of exerting any significant influence over the pace and direction of overseas expansion.[24] Moreover, in an Asian context, the vehicle of British expansion, the East India Company, had by the middle of the eighteenth century reached a point in its development where capital input from Britain had a negligible effect on its operations.[25] Its domestic capital base was a very small one of £3.2 million, and working capital for its metropolitan operations was supplied by a short-term bond debt which fluctuated between £3 million and £6 million. India bonds, on which the yield moved between 3 and 6 per cent, proved to be a popular form of short-term investment,[26] but the scope for investment within the Company was quite limited when set against the broader context provided by government securities and the funded debt. Those who chose to place their financial resources with the Company were drawn almost exclusively from the well-to-do commercial and financial classes of London and the United Provinces, and there are few detectable signs of direct interest from the landed classes.

A further point worth stressing about expansion in Asia is that from the late 1750s onwards, British activity in India became almost self-sustaining as the Company began to adopt the role of territorial revenue collector. Important developments, such the recruitment and maintenance of an enormous army, did not require, or at least were thought not to require, any financial input from domestic sources.[27] When the Company did later receive additional capital injections from metropolitan investors in 1786, 1789 and 1793, this failed to alter the general *modus operandi*, and certainly did not act as a direct stimulus to overseas activity. Rather, this had much more to do with the urgent need to relieve the Company from a crippling burden of domestic debt. In short, domestic investors helped to provide little more than a broad institutional framework within which those overseas could operate.

If investment in East India Company stock did not influence the pace and direction of British expansion in India, individuals could nevertheless secure significant profits from the activities of trading companies in the wider world. These profits played an important part in the transfer and redeployment of financial resources in and around the nascent London money market. As early as the 1670s, bankers such as Clayton and Morris were able to finance money-lending activities from the profits made from investment in the East India Company, the Hudson's Bay Company and the Royal African Company,[28] and financiers continued to regard joint-stock investment as an attractive proposition despite many of them burning their fingers in the flames fanned by the South Sea Bubble crisis of 1720. The East India Company, which offered annual dividend payments of 6 per cent during the first half of the century, was particularly attractive to investors when the market rate of interest was restricted by the law of usury to 5 per cent. East India stock was generally regarded as a gilt-edged investment through this period, but an even closer interest in the Company's overseas fortunes was taken during the 1760s when military and political success in Bengal led to a sustained bout of speculative fever in the London financial market. After the Mughal Emperor granted the *diwani* to the Company in 1765, it was widely assumed that sums between £2 million and £4 million a year would soon find their way to stockholders in the form of increased dividend payments. In the event, the Company proved unable to realize any significant revenue surplus that could be transferred to Britain. Few recognized this at the time, however, and the annual dividend paid to investors rose from 6 to 12½ per cent which in turn prompted a marked rise in the price of Company stock as it attracted attention from a wide range of speculators. Many individuals, including Robert Clive and his immediate circle who made good use of their inside knowledge of Company affairs, were able to make substantial gains through their purchase of stock on a rising market in 1766, although their self-serving actions undoubtedly inflicted great long-term damage on the Company's finances.[29] Although this episode reflected no credit on many of the individuals involved, it nevertheless illustrates the extent to which the fruits of British overseas activity could be realized by those working in the metropolitan economy. Investment in empire could, in the right conditions, offer the prospect of easy financial pickings to those in the City without requiring any direct commitment of resources to the actual processes through which expansion occurred.

DIRECT INVESTMENT: TRADE AND LAND

It is possible to find a few examples of metropolitan business-men investing in overseas industrial enterprises such as the Virginia Bristol ironworks established in 1730 or the American Iron Company which developed operations in New Jersey and New York during the 1760s.[30] Direct investment in empire, however, was most common in the realm of trade and land. As far as the former was concerned, this was particularly the case with the 'store' system of operation which was used, most notably by Scottish firms, in the North American tobacco trade. This system, in which chains of wholesale stores and retail outlets were established to supply local planters with European goods and credit, allowed the direct purchase of tobacco to be made by Glasgow firms in the colonies through their local representatives.[31] Many firms owned and maintained stores, although a variation on the store-system scheme of operation was provided by some companies who dealt with independent and affiliated local merchant houses on a wholesale basis.[32] These closely related commercial practices stand in contrast to the 'consignment' system which was generally favoured by London and Bristol merchants before the 1770s.[33] Under this system, goods were transferred to the metropolis via an agent or factor who made all the transportation arrangements and charged a commission for the sale of goods in Britain and the purchase of products for the colonists. The critical difference between the two schemes of arrangement was that those plant-ers who consigned produce to others for distribution retained legal ownership of the goods in transit until the time of sale and they therefore bore all the risks involved with long-distance transportation.[34] As a consequence of this, few of the merchants involved in the consignment-system branch of the tobacco trade needed to acquire property in, and commit direct investment to, the Chesapeake. This was very much the case, for example, with the Bristol tobacco merchants.[35] Their gen-eral methods and type of investments, however, stand in marked contrast to those of a large number of their contemporaries in the sugar trade, who also used the consignment system but who were very active in taking up ownership of plantations in the West Indies.[36] This comparison underlines the extent to which the organization of trade varied and developed along different lines from region to region and from commodity to commodity.

From the point of view of metropolitan merchants, the primary advantage of the store system was that it allowed advance purchases of tobacco to be made so that the turnaround times of ships in American ports could be reduced. This helped significantly to cut freight charges and costs.[37] However, this system required considerable levels of capital investment to build and stock stores, purchase goods in the colonies, and then bear the costs of storage, transportation and insurance. An indication of the scale of such investment is that eleven stores in Virginia belonging to the Cunninghame group of Glasgow were valued at £11,450 sterling in 1775. This did not include the value of the slaves, horses, vessels and wagons used to service the stores, and, in addition, the Cunninghames owned and maintained at least six transport vessels for use on transatlantic trade routes.[38] Whitehaven tobacco merchants followed their Glasgow counterparts and also developed the store system of operation. They tied up investments in the Chesapeake in a similar way and some, such as John Gale, went one step further and moved into ownership of plantations in the colonies.[39]

The general context provided by Scottish commercial law meant that the largest British firms using the store system in the tobacco trade developed in and around Glasgow, and English firms could not compete effectively beyond the 1750s. Unlike English tobacco firms which did not expand beyond two or three partners, Scottish firms were based upon shares distributed between up to nine partners. These syndicates began life with initial capital of between £5000 and £20,000, but they could later expand in some cases to £100,000. An average individual share in such a firm during the period just before the American War fell somewhere in the range between £1000 and £2000. Of course, most of the individuals involved in these enterprises were sleeping partners, with the general strategy being determined by a managing partner who delegated responsibility to representatives (who themselves were often shareholders and/or relatives) in Maryland and Virginia.[40] Although most of the long-term finance required by these firms was based upon the reinvestment of profits, or was borrowed from within Glasgow itself, London's resources could play an important supporting role at times when the drawing of bills on agents in the City helped to provide the tobacco merchants with essential short-term credit.[41]

Beyond the world of trade and commerce, members of British elites were well to the fore in land speculation at the periphery, and they were particularly swift to take advantage of the opportunities presented by the addition of significant amounts of territory to British possessions at the end of the Seven Years' War. Land speculation, of course, had been a feature of the development of the North American colonies since the earliest days of settlement and while, in Bernard Bailyn's words, 'it was never a preserve of absentee capitalists',[42] British investors played a prominent role in the speculative process during the eighteenth century. They acquired vast tracts of land which they intended to settle, improve and later sell at a profit. There are few detailed studies offering a overview of this speculative process from the British point of view, but evidence provided by examinations of the American context for such investment suggests that many members of the metropolitan landed interest and business community were tempted to try and take advantage of the new opportunities presented to them. They did this either as individuals or as partners in syndicates.

During the first half of the eighteenth century, several of the British landed elite activated claims based on inheritance to huge tracts of territory in North America. After 1744, for example, John Carteret, Earl of Granville, acquired 20 million acres in North Carolina and by the 1760s a team of agents was collecting rents from settlers on his behalf. In similar fashion, Lord Fairfax established a claim to 5 million acres in Virginia in 1745.[43] Although the beginning of the war with France in 1755 interrupted this process of expansion and settlement, the likes of Granville and Fairfax, as well as the individuals behind enterprises such as the Ohio Company, established a pattern of development which involved the peopling of the land under their control as an essential part of the profit-making process.

Metropolitan landowners continued to be prominent as a wave of land speculation spread across British North America after 1763. Most notable, perhaps, was the Earl of Egmont who, in unsuccessfully pursuing the idea of setting up quasi-feudal communities with himself as 'lord paramount', established a claim to 65,000 acres in East Florida. He also set about developing 22,000 acres in Nova Scotia where, in total, five million acres was given away by the authorities before 1773. Operating on an even grander scale than Egmont was the lord advocate of Scotland, Sir James Montgomery, who incurred a significant loss on schemes designed to effect the settlement of the 100,000 acres he had been granted on the island of St John. In the south, visionaries such as Denys Rolle of Devon and Sir Archibald Grant of Aberdeen laid elaborate and fantastic plans for the development of settlements in Florida. Among others, Lord Dartmouth (who also had ambitions in Nova Scotia) and the Earl of Tyrone were granted 100,000 acres and 60,000 acres respectively in Florida. Although considerable energy was devoted to planning and promoting new ventures in all of these areas, by no means all those who established legal title to land then advanced much further with the territory under their nominal control. In East Florida, in particular, the amount of settlement actually effected by absentee owners was very limited indeed.[44]

In general terms, applications made for land grants during the 1760s reflected the extent to which all sections of the British elite were interested in the periphery of the empire as an attractive area for possible investment, speculation and development. Those applying to the Privy Council for grants of land in East Florida and the island of St John were drawn from across the highest ranks of society and the same was the case with the groups of speculators involved with abortive settlement projects such as the establishment of the colony of Vandalia in the Ohio Valley.[45] Whereas some land-purchase and settlement projects, such as the Scottish American Company established in 1773, involved many individual subscribers drawn from well beyond the elite;[46] aristocrats, merchants, financiers, officials, military officers and politicians (including cabinet members) were foremost among those seeking to jump onto the speculative bandwagon. In this sense, nowhere was the close nature of the alliance between land and business more clearly seen in an imperial context than during the race to acquire estates in North America between 1763 and 1775.

AN EMPIRE OF CREDIT

During the eighteenth century many colonists were less dependent on the mother country for investment capital than they had been during the earlier stages of development, but the provision of credit from metropolitan sources was still of paramount importance in the Atlantic empire. In general, credit facilities offered to colonists by British merchants and financiers not only enabled entrepreneurs to extend the scale and range of their commercial activities but they also helped, indirectly, to enhance the standard of living by promoting urbanization and frontier development.[47] An important role in the development of the empire was thus played by merchants and financiers in Britain who offered accommodation to those engaged in commercial and business activity at the periphery of the empire. Loans and credit extended to colonial entrepreneurs carried very obvious risks, but there were important potential advantages to be gained by borrower and lender alike. The colonist used credit to make purchases and improve his enterprise, while the metropolitan merchant could often use extended credit as part of a deliberate strategy to boost sales of goods.

One form of metropolitan credit comprised the colonial debts that were allowed to accumulate in the books of British merchants, while another found expression in the money-lending activities of the type favoured by the likes of Admiral Sir Peter Warren who engaged in extensive transactions in New England and New York.[48] As far as the latter context is concerned, the extent to which colonial economies were dependent upon non-commercial metropolitan credit facilities was determined by a number of important local factors, ranging from the type of staple crop grown to the size and diversity of the population, and the level of long-term commitment of settlers to their region.[49] As a result, some small colonies, like the West Indian island of Montserrat with its weak economy based upon sugar production, were closely tied to the London financial market for the provision of bonds, mortgages and promissory notes. The diverse South Carolina economy, on the other hand, generated enough individual wealth to enable a considerable part of its own borrowing needs to be met from within the colony. Even so, although some important indigenous credit mechanisms and networks had developed by the mid-century, they were often ultimately drawn into the financial webs that extended into the empire from London and other metropolitan financial centres.[50]

In general terms, the overall burden of colonial debt to the mother country had grown steadily since the middle of the seventeenth century, but by the third quarter of the eighteenth century the level of commercial credit extended by Britain to her overseas colonies had begun to increase quite dramatically. Of course, not all areas of British overseas activity were affected to the same degree at the same time. In North America, the rapid growth in the amount of credit offered to the colonies by British sources between 1745 and 1760 was not sustained thereafter as the metropolitan economy entered a long-term slump which was punctuated by a couple of short-term commercial booms and severe credit crises in 1763 and 1772.[51] Nevertheless, the way in which credit relations had developed was such that overall levels of colonial indebtedness had greatly increased by the 1760s and 1770s. By the beginning of the American War in 1775, colonists owed domestic creditors about £3 million, with nearly half that sum being held in the tobacco colony of Virginia alone.[52] Thomas Jefferson was not too far wide of the mark when he declared that planters had become a 'species of property annexed to certain mercantile houses in London'.[53] This view was supported by the calculation that in the mid-1760s eight London merchant houses were alone owed £956,579 by their customers and suppliers in North America.[54] Of course, not all firms were affected to such a degree but even a medium-size commercial operation such as the London Virginia merchant firm of John Norton & Son was owed £18,523 on 200 separate accounts in 1770.[55] Although contemporaries may have exaggerated the total amount of the American debt when they placed it at £4,450,000 in 1766, they quite correctly drew attention to the fact that creditors were drawn from across a range of commercial communities in London, Bristol, Glasgow, Liverpool, Manchester, Birmingham, Leeds, Sheffield, Whitehaven and Lancaster.[56]

Debts were often tied to particular branches of the North American trade. In particular, Glasgow tobacco merchants had committed considerable sums to the colonies in the form of credit to planters, but some merchants in Bristol, such as William Reeve and Henry Cruger Jr, also suffered badly from having been overgenerous in the credit terms offered to American merchants.[57] Many individual debts were often very small and fell below £10 sterling,[58] but the aggregate total was considerable. In 1791, after the upheavals caused by the American War for Independence, it was calculated that 200 British firms were still owed £4,984,655 5s. 8d. (including 14 years' interest of some £2 million), with London alone being owed almost £2,325,000.[59] Glasgow's merchants suffered in similar fashion. It was estimated in 1778 that America's debts to Glasgow amounted to over £1.3 million, and the burden fell heavily on the tobacco firms. One of the largest group of companies, the Cunninghame group, was owed over £100,000, and even smaller-scale enterprises, such as Logan Gilmour & Co. and Baird, Hay, & Co., were owed £20,000 and £16,000 respectively.[60] Given the extent of this indebtedness and the practical problems surrounding the liquidation of such assets, it is not surprising that Glasgow merchants were to the fore among those demanding a conciliatory approach to the colonists from the British government during the early stages of the war. In late 1775, Glasgow was the only Scottish burgh not to send a Loyal Address to the King.[61]

An even greater level of colonial indebtedness was to be found in the West Indies. Jamaica owed £2–3 million in the 1770s, while Grenada owed more than £2 million, and St Kitts £720,000 in 1773. A contemporary estimate put the aggregate planter debt to Britain at £6 million in 1766,[62] and the ever-rising level of indebtedness was indicated by another guess made 25 years later which placed the total West Indian debt at no less than £20 million.[63] This increased the sense of dependency on the mother country by linking the fortunes of the colonial economy to the prevailing state of the domestic financial markets, and the all-embracing nature of this close relationship was no better illustrated than during the great credit crisis of 1772.[64] At the metropolitan end of this imperial connection, British creditors obtained a stake in the empire which might become a very real one, rather than a paper one, when mortgage foreclosures took place and ownership of plantations changed hands.[65] As a contributor to the *Edinburgh Review* was to remark in 1804, 'For to speak the truth, the West

Indies have now chiefly become the property of the commercial body of the city of London.'[66]

The capital assets of the metropolitan merchants and financiers who offered credit to the colonies were often themselves quite limited, and finance to effect the provision of working capital to the periphery often had to be raised on a regular basis from domestic sources. Many trading companies and firms made routine use of a wide range of banking facilities, but for a variety of reasons banks were unable to meet the demand for credit from the merchant community.[67] Accordingly, borrowing on bond at four or five per cent interest from individuals was commonplace within the commercial community, and thus a large number of investors drawn from across the middling and upper ranks were to be found standing behind the merchant community. The savings of these small investors produced a better return when consigned to merchants than when invested in low-yield government stocks and securities.[68] Many of those who made such loans on bond to merchants were from provincial British towns and cities and they were not in any sense fully paid up members of a gentlemanly capitalist elite. Devine and Price have underlined this important point in their detailed studies of the British-Chesapeake trade. They have identified those who provided the credit necessary for the operation of the trade as being drawn from a wide range of local individuals and groups, although family connections often served to provide a link between lender and borrower.[69] These investors included widows, retailers and craftsmen, as well as merchants and landowners. They often held a very limited portfolio of investments in comparison with similar types of London-based investors, and, in general, they did not contribute to the public funds.[70] This meant, however, that their fortunes were closely and directly tied to the rise and fall of Britain's imperial fortunes.

The keen interest in overseas trade displayed by provincial investors is not surprising because, as has been pointed out in a study of the regional aspects of the 'financial revolution', such people could exercise little control over any investment they placed in the hands of London agents or attorneys. It was much more convenient and productive for them to take advantage of regional investment opportunities, and this often meant an involvement in particular branches of overseas activity.[71] This small-scale investment was vital because it released the long-term credit that was so necessary for the development of long-distance trade and private enterprise, and it was precisely the sort of commitment of resources that was often unpopular to those in the City who were seeking a swift, low-risk return on their own or their clients' money.

Of course, metropolitan provinces could not provide an inexhaustible amount of direct or indirect financial support for colonies, and their limitations were exposed after mid-century when the West Indies began to run into heavy debt.[72] With the savings of local inhabitants increasingly being diverted into new alternative channels of investment in the metropolitan economy, outport slave merchants, for example, were no longer able to provide all the long-term credit that was required to sustain the development and expansion of planter operations in the Caribbean. Consequently, as part of a general reshaping of the organization of the slave trade during the late eighteenth century, recourse was made to London commission agents who were better placed to tap the resources of the City's financial markets. The agents extended long-term credit arrangements to planters and they provided Liverpool merchants with the cash remittances that were necessary to fund the purchase of cargoes for Africa. Thus, although outport merchants continued to supply the West Indies with slaves, it was increasingly the London agency houses who underwrote and determined the course of West Indian trade, finance and production.[73]

The structure of British commercial operations was very different in Asia. The extension of metropolitan credit to the periphery played only a limited role in a region which had its own long-established commercial and financial infrastructure, markets and practices. The British community in India was heavily dependent on locally raised working capital to fund its trading activity both in a corporate and a private context. Few men in Bengal, Company servants and licensed free merchants alike, took much capital with them from Britain and rarely did they take more than was necessary to set themselves up in trade: £1000 was a typical sum.[74] Thereafter, they drew on Indian financial resources to a considerable degree. The need to do this was acute because the system of procuring goods required that a significant part of the purchase price, often over 50 per cent, had to be paid out before production began. It was a risky business to tie up capital in the region for a long time in this way, and it was also a costly undertaking despite eventual rates of return on such investments being high. Interest charges were much higher than in Britain, and European borrowers seem to have been charged about 12 per cent by local lenders. Most Europeans in Bengal were indebted to Indians at one time or another and the sums involved could be quite considerable. Senior figures in the British community like Francis Hare and Samuel Middleton owed around £70,000 and £170,000 respectively at the times of their deaths, and the East India Company itself was dependent on advances from a variety of sources amounting to £1.2 million in 1772.

The credit extended to the British in India came from sources within a fairly tight-knit business and financial community which had established a close working relationship with European traders. The great banking institutions, such as the House of the Jagat Seths at Murshidabad or the Banaras banks, supplied much of the capital needed by the British, but at a more humble level were the local money lenders who offered a wide range of services to those in need of credit. As far as individuals were concerned, many Company servants retained a *banian* as a form of local agent to conduct financial or commercial transactions on their behalf and they were also able to draw on them for loan finance.[75] Of course, as profits were realized over the years so British capital began to accumulate in Bengal. Entrepreneurs became less dependent on their *banians* and this allowed the merchant community to shape commercial conditions to their own particular needs. Many personal fortunes were remitted home, but not everyone chose this course of action. Some capital was reinvested in trade; some was placed at low risk with the Company; some was made available to private borrowers; and the whole process was institutionalized through the establishment of European banks and agency houses.

The pattern of development was much the same on the west coast of India at Bombay, although as early as the 1740s some merchants had accumulated enough surplus capital to allow them to lend to Indians as well as to their fellow countrymen. Yet, as the activities of Francis Pym in the 1750s illustrate, the British were at times heavily dependent on Indians to advance them long-term credit, and it took until the 1780s before agency houses with considerable resources could emerge and exert influence on the region's trade, not to mention the development of the China trade as well.[76] In general, the examples offered by detailed studies of Bombay and Calcutta suggest that, although by the end of the eighteenth century the British were far less dependent on Asian capital than they had been fifty years previously, local financial resources played a crucial role in supporting the expansion of trading activity and British influence in general.

EMPIRES OF INVESTMENT

Chapter 3 drew attention to some individuals within the metropolitan merchant community who developed trading and investment empires which reflected the geographical diversity of the nation's own imperial interests.[77] Peter Marshall highlighted this largely unexplored trend when he examined the validity of Harlow's assertion that the focus of British interest and policy had shifted eastwards after 1763. His disagreement with Harlow was based in part upon a review of British overseas commercial ventures during the third quarter of the century which suggested that expansion 'was general rather than distinctively Eastern or Western in nature'. He observed, quite correctly, that 'Contemporaries were not aware of the need to choose, and invested without geographical restraint wherever a profit seemed likely. East Indian interests proved no bar to speculation in the West Indies, in Nova Scotia, or the Ohio.'[78]

In some cases, the development of individual and family economic fortunes was determined by the general course followed by the nation's imperial fortunes. The business attitudes and outlooks of many metropolitan investors were flexible enough to enable them to adapt with relative ease to changing conditions within the empire, and this meant that they sought to redeploy their skills and resources as new frontiers were opened up. Some families used British overseas expansion as a vehicle for the creation of their own empires in miniature, and they were able to establish links and connections on a worldwide scale. The Franks family, for example, not only dominated the London diamond market, but by the 1690s they had developed an extended kinship network with closely connected branches and offshoots in Jamaica, New York, Philadelphia, Bombay and Surat.[79] A similar pattern of geographical diversification is also seen in the case provided by the relatives and descendants of James Russell (1708–88). As was the case with many Scottish families, the Act of Union of 1707 broadened the scope of the Russells' activities. A world that had once extended no further than Edinburgh soon embraced the trading world of London and the Chesapeake. Then, in the wake of the American Revolution and the disruption of long-established transatlantic trading networks and relationships, attention was switched to Madras and service in the East India Company.[80] The remarkable resilience and adaptability of the Russell–Lee–Clerk family connection might be untypical, but it does serve as one example of the extent to which the empire allowed individuals to survive and develop traditions of movement, migration and economic activity on a global scale.

There were plenty of individuals who were prepared to try their luck in more than one sphere of British overseas endeavour, and in more than one type of financial or commercial enterprise. Admiral Sir Peter Warren used his naval career as a means of developing a wide range of business activities in North America, Ireland and Britain, and he moved with ease and success in the worlds of trade, money-lending and land speculation during the 1740s and 1750s.[81] A little later, Sir George Colebrooke, MP for Arundel, combined extensive banking and investment activity with the chairmanship of the East India Company, and he developed a close interest in a wide range of commercial and speculative ventures in the West Indies, North America and Europe.[82] The Codrington brothers established a similarly wide range of interests during the 1760s. Sir William Codrington, MP for Tewkesbury, was a Barbadian sugar planter who accumulated a large East India stockholding in the 1760s, while his brother Edward, a merchant, made good use his of filial connection with the world of high politics and was granted the military provisioning contract for West Florida in 1766.[83] The family's status and standing was based almost entirely upon economic activity at the periphery of the empire. Men such as these, and London-based Scottish businessmen like Richard Oswald, Alexander Grant and John Sargent,[84] involved themselves in a wide variety of economic activities on a global scale. The channelling of metropolitan investment finance into different areas of British overseas activity gave these investors a large personal financial stake in the empire and it ensured that they would take a close and sustained interest in the conduct and development of Britain's imperial affairs.

Evidence drawn from a wide range of sources suggests that the metropolitan elite were deeply implicated in the imperial process. Landowners and businessmen alike helped to channel resources into the empire and they took a keen interest in the periphery as a potential source of wealth, opportunity and profit. It is nevertheless important that the strength of this connection is not overstated, for that would do scant justice to the complex nature of the problem being addressed. In particular, two general points need to be stressed.

First, by focusing exclusively on the commercial and financial elite it is possible to marginalize the role played by a wide range of small investors drawn from across Britain, and this can serve to overstate the influence of the large-scale operators in the City. As we have seen, savings were often invested locally rather than in London, and the availability of such resources gave provincial merchants and businessmen access to the funds and working capital that allowed them to strengthen and broaden the scope of their overseas activities. In other words, sight should not be lost of the broad nature of the enterprise and investment base that supported British trade and commerce.[85] The empire in its financial context should not be seen as being shaped solely by the needs of the City and investors located in the south of England.

Second, whatever the scale and structure of domestic investment in empire, very few metropolitan investors were able to, or even wanted to, exercise direct influence on the pace and direction of overseas expansion. In most cases, domestic resources were entrusted to, or placed at the disposal of, others operating at the periphery, and it was they who made the specific decisions and determined the particular courses of action that resulted in the expansion of territory or the extension of British influence. It is for that reason that consideration must now turn to those who lived and worked in the overseas empire.

Part Three
Overseas Elites in the
British Empire

5 Imperial Ties and the Anglicization of the Overseas Empire

The tangled web of credit and investment outlined in the previous chapter represented one important connection between Britain's overseas settlements and the metropolis, but a wide range of other links also helped to give the empire a sense of form and structure. These ties were not, for the most part, unwelcome to those at the periphery because they provided more in benefits than costs and ensured colonists their defence, liberty, opportunities and material goods. Less tangibly, perhaps, the empire also provided colonists, and especially colonial elites, with a sense of belonging, identity and order. In the absence of a strong and regular element of coercion within British imperial relationships, the ties that bound most British overseas subjects to the mother country were based upon free association which maintained the empire's integrity until a series of crises disrupted long-standing patterns of communality and dependency during the 1760s. The realities of time, space and geography were such that administrative control from the centre was often very weak indeed, and in areas of overseas settlement the British empire developed along lines defined by consent and cooperation rather than coercion and control. This was so much the case that the authority of London was only ever legitimized by being accepted by those in the colonies.[1] As William Pitt argued in 1766, when he warned the House of Commons about the dangers of redefining relationships with the North American colonies, the colonists needed to be bound with 'the golden cord of equity and [moderation]'. They could not be held within the empire by 'cords of iron'.[2]

Reflecting this situation, peacetime overseas deployments of British troops were very limited before the 1750s. A shared desire for peace, security and stability placed most colonists on the side of the local authorities, so much so that for most of the seventeenth century the number of regular troops stationed on the North American mainland only ranged between 300 and 1000, with perhaps twice as many serving in the West Indies.[3] These levels had not altered much by the mid-eighteenth century. In November 1754, for example, Parliament voted funds to maintain 3755 troops in Gibraltar, Minorca, Bermuda and the American colonies, and an additional force of 2290 men was recruited for service with General Braddock in North America. In the same year, 900 Crown troops were dispatched to India to reinforce the East India Company's small private army.[4] This meant that when very real fears were mounting about French military activity in the wider world, no more than 10,000 men of various nationalities were enlisted under British colours in overseas stations.[5] These numbers represented little more than token forces, dedicated to defence not coercion, and before the 1760s troops were not required to play an active role in keeping Britain's overseas possessions within the imperial fold. Although force, or the threat of force, always remained an important and powerful instrument within the processes of imperial consolidation and expansion, and regular troops were used on occasions to maintain law and order in the colonies,[6] the metropolitan authorities did not need to make systematic use of violence to keep local white populations under control.

THE EMERGENCE OF A TRANSOCEANIC ELITE

Unlike the mother country, white colonial societies did not, in a formal sense, possess aristocratic or gentry classes. Nevertheless, by the eighteenth century the passage of time had seen the emergence of colonial elites containing individuals and families who possessed all the defining characteristics of an aristocracy or gentry, even though they did not hold, or for the most part have access to, the same privileges, rights and titles as the metropolitan elite.[7] Indeed, many contemporary observers, not to mention modern-day historians, have made use of the terms 'aristocracy' and 'gentry' to describe members of different colonial elites. By doing so, they have, in the absence of the traditional benchmarks associated with title and rank, often used replicated patterns of behaviour and lifestyle, as well as the holding of wealth, influence and political power, to define the criteria through which individuals might be placed in an elite group in colonial society. Moreover, the use of the terms 'aristocracy' and especially 'gentry' has been extended beyond a narrow range of wealthy landowners or great planters. These terms have often been used to describe the 'better sort' to be found within the colonial urban sphere as well as those located in a rural environment. This was remarked upon by the Anglican clergyman, Arthur Browne, when he considered the ways that elites had emerged in North America in spite of the lack of a nobility or 'orders of gentry'.[8] He observed that the 'richer merchants' in some towns 'together with the clergy, lawyers, physicians and officers of the English navy who had occasionally settled there were considered as gentry.' This 'superior order' of gentleman was, in Browne's opinion, based upon 'better property and more information', and this social group was able, in magnanimous fashion, to accept jealous criticism from other sections of society because it was 'a specie of inconvenience which a liberal mind pardoned as compensated by the comfort and independence which produced it.'

In part, Arthur Browne's observations pointed to several different types of elites having emerged in overseas colonies. From the very beginning, elites in the mainland American colonies developed along lines determined by immigration and settlement, but over the longer term the composition of elites was also conditioned by patterns of mortality and succession. The interaction of various demographic trends meant that the founding elites in some colonies, such as Maryland, Pennsylvania and Virginia, could prove to be, in the words of one historian, 'fragile and short-lived', as many of the first generation failed to produce successors and new arrivals continued to find their way to the top of colonial society.[9] Over decades, as North American colonies developed and the social structure became more ordered, native-born individuals or creoles eventually began to outnumber those of British birth within the elites of different regions.[10]

The emergence of elites followed rather different patterns in other areas of British overseas activity. Native-born white elites failed to develop at all in India where permanent settlement was never attempted. The nature of the British presence was defined by the commercial and military operations of the

East India Company, and the traditional structures of Indian society remained intact outside the small enclaves granted to the Company by local authorities. Britons thus found themselves representing a tiny minority in a highly developed society which offered few opportunities for land purchase. Moreover, the climate was deemed unsuitable for long-term settlement. As a result, most of those who went out to India from Britain perceived overseas service as a means by which a fortune could be generated and then remitted home to provide for later comfort. Those who did not die at the periphery invariably returned to Britain after their term of duty. The white elites in the regions of India where the British established footholds had few long-term continuities in terms of personnel, and circumstances dictated that they often coexisted alongside powerful indigenous rulers, family dynasties and business groups. Although they were eventually able to exert considerable political and economic influence in some areas, the British elite were only ever free to build the sort of society with which they were familiar in the forts and settlements where they had full control over their own affairs.

In the British West Indies, members of the white elite often fell somewhere between the type of permanent settler seen in North America and the transient resident common to the British settlements in India. Accordingly, creole elites emerged more slowly than they did in mainland America,[11] but historians have nevertheless identified increasing signs of elite commitment to their islands and identification with local society after mid-century.[12] Although this interpretation serves as an important corrective to the old and stereotypical view of the Barbadian and Jamaican elite as absentee landowners, many planters still sought an eventual return to Britain where they could enjoy retirement living off investments consisting of enterprises run on their behalf in the Caribbean.[13]

The eventual repatriation of some very long-term settlers reflected the fact that in all areas of British overseas activity, there were always numbers of people within local elites who sought sooner or later to return to Britain.[14] Remigration played an important part in ensuring that many of Britain's overseas communities always contained individuals whose status was transitory and who, as a consequence, were only partially embedded in local society. Within the elite, merchants, factors, military and naval personnel, administrators, functionaries and professionals were always to be found alongside planter and settler families of several generations. These temporary residents often remained firmly tied to the mother country during periods of service which, although initially perceived as being short-term, could in fact last up to twenty years or more.[15] Such individuals exerted considerable influence, especially in ports and garrison towns. Their presence was not only to be found in the administrative, political and economic spheres of colonial life, but it also played a considerable part in helping to determine the development of social and cultural trends.[16] In particular, the army helped to forge a wide range of links between the metropolis and the colonies and, although the extent to which parts of the American elite were anglicized through regular contact with British armed forces has been a matter for some debate, the overseas officer corps represented an important social institution shaped by metropolitan aristocratic and gentlemanly ideals.[17]

It is clear, then, that various parts of the overseas empire created elites that were in some ways quite fundamentally different from one another. The British in India, for example, found themselves operating within a social, economic and political framework quite alien to those who lived and worked in North America. There were few individuals who developed a broad range of imperial experience by moving between the Atlantic empire and the empire in the east.[18] Even within the Atlantic empire there were important distinctions between the free colonies and the slave colonies.[19] Yet, the diversity of elite experience within the British overseas empire does not mean that no common denominators existed between those pursuing a variety of activities in different quarters of the globe. Many of those at the periphery who shaped the development and expansion of the empire before 1775 were to all intents and purposes members of one English-speaking imperial elite. Even those who can be defined as members of native-born or creole elites often considered themselves to be Britons abroad,[20] and all overseas elites used Britain as their major point of reference when defining their political, economic, social and cultural relationships. Some white colonial societies did develop their own distinct cultural characteristics, but all European overseas colonies looked to the Old World for guidance.[21]

Thus, throughout this period many of those in the British overseas empire who focused their attention on new frontiers or spheres of activity also regularly looked backwards over their shoulder to the country they or their forefathers had left behind. This general tendency for many colonists to seek the reassurance of an existence and lifestyle based upon patterns of social and cultural behaviour developed in metropolitan society was reinforced by a wide range of individual links maintained between overseas elites and their counterparts in Britain. Such was the nature of connections based upon marriage, kinship and business activity that one can point to the emergence of a transoceanic elite, that is an elite whose associations, characteristics and interests transcended national and regional boundaries.

The business conducted within the Atlantic commercial world was to a large degree based upon extensive cooperation and the pooling of resources between elites at the core and the periphery of the empire. Arthur Schlesinger's opinion of this relationship is as appropriate today as it was nearly eighty years ago: it was a 'business entente' which represented a 'centripetal force of great importance'.[22] Not only was the general conduct and organization of business much the same in the colonies as it was in Britain, but enterprises such as shipowning and land-speculation often brought together investors from the colonies and Britain into transatlantic partnerships and powerful interest groups.[23] In trade and commerce, British merchants made use of their colonial counterparts as agents and correspondents where they did not have their own representatives on the spot, and in spheres of operations such as the supply of the armed forces they became heavily dependent on their connections in colonial towns and ports. Naturally enough, they made use of people and firms that were known to them, and relationships based upon family, kinship, personal ties and religion played an important part in determining the way in which business and commercial enterprise developed within the Atlantic trading world.[24] Thus, for example, when a contract for provisioning troops in North America was granted to Moses Franks and three associates in 1760, the American end of the operation was handled by Franks's father, Jacob, who was a New York merchant, and his brother, David, a prominent Philadelphia merchant.[25] Numerous similar cases existed in a wide variety of different contexts and they all served to act as a strong tie between the core and the periphery of the empire. At the same time, ties were being established between different commercial elites at the periphery, and important inter-colonial relationships were based upon cooperation between businessmen in different parts of North America and the West Indies.[26]

In all of these contexts, marriage was used to cement commercial relationships where no family connection existed, and there are plenty of examples of the sons and daughters of British and colonial merchants marrying into families with whom transoceanic business links had been established. On the other side of the coin, of course, colonial merchants not only made used of correspondents and representatives in British ports but many of them, as outlined in Chapter 4, were dependent on credit from metropolitan sources. A few even allowed metropolitan firms to manage financial investments on their behalf.[27] In general, family connections were again of considerable importance in establishing and maintaining these links.[28] The creation of such multilateral transoceanic connections was reflected in the way in which junior members of families were often sent across the Atlantic, either from Britain to the colonies or vice versa, to serve a business apprenticeship under the supervision of a relative. Indeed, such a journey might represent only one of several occasions when an individual might cross the ocean on commercial or family business.[29] All of these connections illustrate the extent to which members of merchant communities belonged to, and perceived themselves as belonging to, an interdependent elite in an increasingly interdependent Atlantic trading world. As the merchants of Philadelphia put it in 1769, when they wrote to the Committee of Merchants of London explaining why they wanted the unpopular Townshend Duties to be repealed, 'We consider the merchants here and in England as the links of the chain that binds both countries together.'[30]

Important connections between metropolitan and colonial elites also existed beyond the world of trade. Again, the institution of marriage played an important part in helping to forge these connections. As early as the mid-seventeenth century, intermarriage had consolidated the position of elites in the West Indies by creating unions of interest between planter and merchant families. It had also helped to establish strong familial bonds between the Caribbean elite and their counterparts in Britain and North America, and this led to the eventual development of what has been described as a 'sort of Atlantic society'.[31] Large numbers of British military officers in America married women from leading colonial families, as was the case with Admiral Sir Peter Warren who married into the De Lancey family of New York in 1731. This allowed officers to establish themselves in the upper echelons of colonial society and, as in Warren's case, it could give them access to the financial resources necessary for them to move successfully into the world of land speculation and business development.[32]

Metropolitan society, and London in particular, offered many attractions to the colonial elite and, despite the cost and difficulties involved, there was a considerable and increasing eastward traffic across the Atlantic before 1775 as colonists travelled in search of the business, political and educational opportunities not available at home.[33] Inevitably, those who returned to the colonies, often after lengthy sojourns in Britain, carried with them many of the latest ideas and fashions. At times, this was a quite deliberate process which had specific aims and objectives in mind. Some colonial travellers gathered information from around Britain on a wide range of business and industrial matters so that recent developments or improvements could be imitated at the periphery, and young colonial merchants were sent across the Atlantic to acquire commercial skills and expertise. In such cases the very outlook and assumptions of the colonial visitor could be reshaped, or perhaps reinforced, by exposure to metropolitan society and this, in itself, was considered to be an important part of the visiting experience. This was particularly the case with those who were sent to Britain to take advantage of the educational opportunities available in the fields of law and medicine, and this learning process was not restricted to the classroom but was extended to include imitation of the types of behaviour, ideals and manners expressed in the upper echelons of British society. Many of the several hundred or so young colonists educated in Britain in the style of a gentleman moved in polite circles during their stay, and they endeavoured to make good use of any connections that they might have with the aristocracy or gentry. This was all part of a learning experience designed to give the young colonist a firm grasp of the ways of the world.

Although the wisdom of sending children to Britain for education was increasingly questioned by wealthy colonial parents after mid-century,[34] it was still hoped that close-quarter observation might lead to the imitation and replication of some of the better general characteristics of genteel metropolitan society. As Benjamin Rush, who studied as a physician in Edinburgh and London during the 1760s, later advised his son, London 'is an epitome of the whole world. Nine months spent in it will teach you more by your eyes and ears than a life spent in your native country.'[35] Of course, travel to Britain was only ever experienced by a small number of colonists, and many Americans did not like what they found in Britain, but those who undertook the transatlantic crossing nevertheless played an important part in forging behavioural and cultural links between the colonial elite and their metropolitan counterparts. The company of those who had recently been to Britain was much sought after by those members of the elite who never ventured abroad and, as one colonial newspaper correspondent commented in 1754, no traveller was more popular in polite circles than the one who:

> can move a minuet after the newest fashion in England; can quiver like a butterfly; is a perfect connoisseur in dress; and has been author to all the new cock't hats and scratches in town; has learnt the art of address from the gentility of Covent Garden, which, by Jove, he swears, had ruined his constitution. Amongst the accomplished beaux, he had learned those elegant expressions, *Split me, Madam; By Gad; Dam me*; and fails not to use them on all occasions. So entirely is he taken up with England, that he always mentions guineas when he speaks of money.[36]

HOME AND IDENTITY IN THE WIDER WORLD

The fact that many members of overseas elites retained a close connection with their counterparts in metropolitan society profoundly affected their perceptions of themselves and the colonial world in which they lived. At one level they found themselves at the top of a social hierarchy located within a distinct colonial society and cultural environment, and, naturally enough, much of their time and energy was taken with matters of local interest and concern.[37] At another level, however, they were part of a much wider elite whose cultural, political and social horizons extended well beyond their colony or region. Their position and fortunes were in many ways dependent upon factors which transcended regional or local boundaries, and this played an important part in defining the scope of the world in which they moved. With their feet located firmly in two quite different environments, it was often difficult for elites to reconcile their local concerns with wider British interests. In America, it also raised the important question of whether such people regarded themselves first as Britons, as Virginians or New Yorkers, or even perhaps as the representatives of some sort of dual Anglo-colonial society. Whatever the case, few colonists considered themselves to be Americans, and most of them identified with Britain and all things British.[38]

From the time that an overseas presence was first established, many of those who left Britain to pursue careers in the wider world continued to regard metropolitan society as home. This occurred even in areas where settlement rather than short-term service characterized the British presence, and members of some colonial societies proved reluctant to redefine notions of what should be regarded as home. Indeed, this tendency, which was common among all European colonists, frequently outlived the original settler and survived for several generations within a family.[39] Not only did this mean that settlers focused as much emotional and cultural attention on the Old World as they did on their new surroundings, but when they had accumulated sufficient resources they sometimes sought to return whence they came.[40] Some West Indian planters, such as Charles Price of Jamaica, never set eyes on Britain, yet they always regarded it as home. They went to elaborate lengths to ensure that their dependants were able to use the mother country as a safe haven to which they could retreat in order to escape from a debilitating and often insecure existence in the Caribbean.[41]

Contemporaries with a close interest in the West Indies believed that the position of Caribbean planters in relation to the mother country was quite different from that of the North American colonists, with the economic and cultural ties being held to be much closer in the former case.[42] Yet even in America colonists in long-established areas of settlement with strong regional identities saw themselves as belonging to something that was much more than a distant British imperial outpost which had little in common with the metropolis. They too could believe that they were members of a transoceanic community which had close ties to the mother country. Francis Hopkinson articulated this belief in the 1760s when he observed that 'We in America are in all respects Englishmen, notwithstanding that the Atlantic rolls her waves between us and the throne to which we all owe our allegiance.'[43] For Thomas Pownall, a former Governor of Massachusetts Bay and an Englishman who knew the colonies better than most, the nature of the relationship between Britain and America went far beyond simple allegiance or dependency. He argued that until the 1760s the American colonists regarded Britain as their true home and 'native country', and such had been the strength of this sentiment that 'it had been wrought up in them to a vigilant and active zeal for service.'[44] In short, many in North America held the firm belief that they were Britons as well Americans. As William Pitt declared, after arguing that Americans were entitled to enjoy all the 'peculiar privileges of Englishmen', 'The Americans are the sons, not the bastards of England.'[45]

LANGUAGE, GOODS AND INFORMATION IN THE ATLANTIC EMPIRE

While the task of delineating important regional differences in colonial society and culture has recently occupied many scholars, this should not be allowed to obscure the fact that historians have increasingly focused attention on some of the forces that established common ground between different groups of North American colonists.[46] As with some historians of British India and the British West Indies, they have devoted considerable energy to efforts to try and identify the various ways in which Britain's overseas possessions became 'anglicized'.[47] This has happened to such an extent that the phrase 'anglicization'

has now found its way into textbooks and general surveys of
the colonial period.[48] Indeed, by adopting a broad comparative approach it has been possible to advance the argument
that 'social and cultural convergence' created a 'common Anglo-
phone cultural order in the western Atlantic' during the century after 1660.[49] Although all Britain's colonies in the northern
hemisphere retained their own distinct regional features, characteristics and identities, they all increasingly came under the
influence of powerful economic, social and cultural forces
emanating from the metropolis.[50] While, of course, some colonies were more successful, and more willing, than others in
their attempts to develop their societies along British lines, the
historical view on this matter is no longer as clear-cut as was
once the case. In particular, it used to be widely assumed that
the New England colonies much more closely resembled England than did those of the Chesapeake. However, the reshaping of the English historical landscape in recent years has
prompted a re-evaluation of the comparisons between the core
and periphery. This in turn has led to a reinterpretation of the
relationship between the colonies and metropolitan society.
While acknowledging the existence of tremendous regional
diversities in colonial America, it is now possible to argue not
only that the seventeenth-century Chesapeake was more like
England than were the New England colonies, but also that
later settlements developed many of the socioeconomic characteristics evident in Chesapeake society.[51] In sum, as Britain
consolidated and then extended her influence across North
America during the second half of the seventeenth century,
colonial society increasingly took on some of the main characteristics of the society that the settlers had left behind.

One consequence of these developmental trends was that
ethnic groups with European origin found themselves assailed
by various processes of anglicization. This was particularly the
case with the Dutch in North America.[52] The final English
capture of New York was confirmed by the Treaty of Westminster in 1674 which followed the third Anglo-Dutch War, and
thereafter the colony's first assembly established a naturaliza-
tion act and a charter of liberties based upon English precedent. This transformation of public life in the colony met
with little opposition from the well-to-do merchant and cleri-
cal elite, but resistance from those lower down the social scale

manifested itself in the abortive rebellion led by Joseph Leisler in 1689 and the subsequent migration of poorer farmers from New York to New Jersey.[53] In later years a hybrid form of Dutch vernacular culture survived in the rural areas populated by these farmers and their descendants, but this also began to lose its strength and vitality as the process of anglicization began to take a firmer hold. In New York itself the linguistic balance had changed to such a degree by the 1740s that one commentator was moved to observe that: 'The Dutch tongue declines fast amongst us, especially with the young people. And all affairs are transact'd in English and that language prevails generally amongst us.'[54]

The large number of German speakers in British North America represented about ten per cent of the total population in 1775. They retained a much sharper sense of cultural identity than settlers of Dutch origin, and at first sight this would seem to suggest that they managed to resist the process of anglicization to some degree. Many German immigrants belonged to transcolonial and transatlantic religious networks which reduced their sense of isolation at the periphery, and they were able quite successfully to maintain several distinct forms of cultural behaviour. Philadelphia and, to a lesser degree, Charles Town served as centres of religious, political and legal activity, and, unlike the Dutch, Germans made use of their own press to publish newspapers, pamphlets and tracts. A hybrid form of Anglo-German was often used for the conduct of public business, but pure German was used in the home and in German taverns and coffee houses. This prompted mutterings of discontent from some English-speakers, and in 1751 Benjamin Franklin asked why Germans should be permitted 'to swarm into our [Pennsylvanian] settlements, and by herding together establish their language and manners to the exclusion of ours.'[55] Nevertheless, there were few signs of the sort of open hostility and violence that had characterized Anglo-Dutch relations in the late seventeenth century. Although few Germans were willing or able to play a part in the public and political life of the colonies, most were content to make good use of the opportunities presented to them by an imperial system headed, after 1714, by a Hanoverian king. They were free to pursue their own course of religious and cultural development, and they tacitly acknowledged that they belonged to a society whose main social and economic contours were shaped by British ideas, assumptions and values.

In a few areas, the English-speaking elite were able to exert little cultural and linguistic influence over the ethnic groups under their control. This did not pose any great problem for the authorities when such groups were represented by no more than small isolated religious sects and groups, but the situation was quite different when large numbers of people were involved. In Nova Scotia (which was ceded to Britain in 1713) the process of anglicization met with such determined resistance from members of the local French-speaking population that British metropolitan influences played little part in shaping the development of colonial society. The problem could only be solved by the infamous deportation of the recalcitrant Acadians during the 1750s, and this served to underline just how hazardous and difficult the process of anglicization could be where Britons were thin on the ground. Indeed, as has recently been pointed out, the general situation in Canada after the British conquest was such that the coming together of Britons with French-Canadians, members of mixed-blood society and settlers from New England produced an imperial region of 'extraordinary cultural complexity'.[56] Yet, in spite of the emergence of such hybrid communities, the advances that were occurring in English linguistic culture acted as a strong cement within the empire and helped to bring colonists from diverse ethnic and cultural backgrounds into the wider British imperium.[57] Membership of the English-speaking world was reinforced after 1740 when a parliamentary statute naturalized all foreigners who migrated to the American colonies. This helped to give new colonists a much closer and more formal sense of identification with Britain and all things British.

The sharpening definition of the north American colonies as a well integrated part of the British empire was, of course, based upon much more than the establishment of the English language as the colonial *lingua franca*. In the realm of material goods, colonists were increasingly drawn into a system of trade and commerce in which the metropolis determined the course of individual consumption and expenditure at the periphery. As has recently been argued, not only did the commercialization of the North American economy and the establishment of transatlantic credit networks serve to bind colonists to the mother country much more tightly than political or constitutional ties, but individuals were also brought into the world of metropolitan fashion and style.[58] Inevitably, the elite were at the forefront of those purchasing imported goods, but all sections of colonial society were eventually able to avail themselves of the opportunity to buy an extremely wide range of provisions and manufactured goods shipped in from Britain. This has made it difficult for historians to find much evidence for either the survival of a heroic breed of independent-minded, self-sufficient American yeomen farmers or the development of a unique American culture.[59] Indeed, even the remotest parts of the colonies have been shown to have been integrated to some degree into the international world of goods.[60]

The colonies were supplied by the metropolis with a wide range of products for use in the home, in business and on the farm. Detailed analysis suggests that colonial households were heavily dependent upon imported goods, so that by the 1770s up to 30 per cent of the per capita income of any one of the American colonies was spent on goods imported into that colony, with around 75 per cent of those goods being consumer commodities. The effects of the Navigation Acts were such that most of these imports (62 per cent between 1768 and 1772) came from England and the colonists were particularly dependent upon the mother country for the provision of textiles and clothing.[61] The effect of this development on aggregate British overseas trade figures was quite striking, as was seen in Chapter 2, and economic historians have, over many years, spoken of the 'Americanization' or 'Westernization' of English foreign trade as the Atlantic replaced Europe as the main destination for exported manufactured goods between 1700 and 1775.[62] Yet this trend must not be seen simply in a narrow overseas colonial context. Consumers of all sorts played their part in a process which embraced the whole of the British North Atlantic empire, metropole and periphery alike, and developments of this sort allowed one observer to comment early in the eighteenth century that 'I have no notion of any more differences between Old-England and New than between Lincolnshire and Somerset.'[63] Similarly, by focusing on the international dimension rather than on the regional or local context of economic development, historians have been able to write about the 'Atlantic community of nations as one economy' in the eighteenth as well as the nineteenth century.[64] The empire provided colonists with access to the same world of goods that was enjoyed by those in the metropolis.

The various processes of cultural and material integration taking place within the British Atlantic empire were facilitated by significant improvements in the speed, regularity and reliability of transoceanic communications during the first half of the eighteenth century. These improvements were such that regular and swiftly transmitted news and information enabled merchants in Britain to broaden their entrepreneurial horizons and exert much greater control over their overseas activities. They also allowed those in Barbados and Massachusetts to receive news from London just as fast as some of the furthest outposts on mainland Britain.[65] More and more ships (1500 by 1740 compared with 500 in 1675) were making Atlantic crossings each year and, although conditions in the North Atlantic dictated that journey times from west to east were always considerably shorter than those from east to west, this meant that news, as well as goods, could be brought to the American colonies much quicker and more regularly than had previously been the case. A simple measure of this improvement in transatlantic communication was seen in the way it had taken Philadelphia only 49 days to receive news of war from London in 1739, while it had taken 170 days for similar news to be conveyed in 1689.[66] Of course, some North American ports enjoyed seasonal and geographical advantages over others but even the longest haul, the Hudson Bay to England crossing, averaged a respectable six weeks by the 1730s. Journey times to and from the West Indies were, on average, longer than those to mainland America. Even so, although the Jamaica to England passage averaged 14 weeks, the run between Barbados or the Leewards and England was only eight weeks in both directions.

The lengths of journeys, if not their comfort, encouraged some individuals to cross the ocean several times during their lifetimes. Although many contemporaries regarded a transatlantic crossing with such fear and trepidation that they were dissuaded from even attempting the journey,[67] the Atlantic was to some travellers, and an increasing number of modern historians, almost as easy to traverse as the Severn or the Tay. As Bernard Bailyn has recently remarked, analysis of movements of people suggests that 'The Atlantic . . . was a highway rather easier to cross, despite all the dangers of ocean voyages, than the land passages across the British Isles.'[68] And in similar vein, another modern historian has commented that 'one of the great achievements of the early modern age was the transformation of the North Atlantic Ocean into an English inland sea.'[69] This was very much reflected in the movement of goods, information, ideas and people from Britain to her overseas provinces.

As a consequence of the improvement of transatlantic communications, a reduction in colonial isolation and provincialism was fostered by the growth of a newspaper press which dedicated itself to the dissemination of news about Britain and Europe. Five papers served Boston's population of 15,000 by 1735, and only one of them focused on New England news to any great degree. Not only did the newspapers provide several alternative sources of news for the reading public, but competition between publishers played its part in helping to increase the speed at which news arrived from London. The 'age' of London-datelined news in the papers was halved to 83 days between 1702 and 1739, and this helped to bring the colonies much more closely in touch with political events and social developments on the other side of the ocean. Not all papers devoted as much attention to news from Britain as did the Boston press, but even those that granted considerable space to local items or literary pieces nearly always allowed these contributions to be overshadowed by information relating to the wider Atlantic community. By 1740 there were 13 newspapers in North America and, although they and their successors eventually played an important part in developing local identities and loyalties, they initially helped to bring isolated colonies into the news and information network that formed such an important part of the British Atlantic.[70]

BELIEF AND LIBERTY: RELIGION AND POLITICS

Britons in all overseas communities, but most notably those in the colonies of the Atlantic empire, were bound together by their adherence to a set of common religious beliefs and constitutional ideals that had been exported from the mother country. English liberty and the Protestant faith provided the cornerstones of everyday life in all parts of the overseas empire, and colonists everywhere drew from the same general fund of religious and political traditions. Protestantism might have fragmented into a number of different denominations, and colonial commitment to the preservation of English liberties might have owed more to misplaced idealism than to constitutional reality, but religious and political attachments brought form and structure to the empire, gave identity to colonists, and helped to reinforce transoceanic connections and associations.[71] Whatever the view of the empire was from the centre, colonists did not doubt that they were entitled to the full benefit of English law and constitutional rights, even if there was often some confusion over precisely which form of legislation and the law should hold sway in the colonies.[72] Rightly or wrongly, colonists believed that Magna Carta, the Bill of Rights and the Toleration Act were as applicable to them as to any other Englishman.

Although colonists were located firmly within the world of English ideology and constitutional thought, they did not, of course, formally participate in the British political process through the election of individuals to represent their views and interests in Parliament. This is not to say, however, that the colonies were without influence at the heart of the empire. Some thirty men born in the West Indies and four or five men born in North America secured seats in the House of Commons between 1754 and 1790, and there were a significant number of MPs who had connections with the colonies through trade, business or military service. These men often contributed to debate and discussion on colonial affairs, but they were by no means united and, despite contemporary opinions to the contrary, they did not form well-defined and powerful interest groups in the House. Individuals did speak out on behalf of the colonists from time to time, and those with Caribbean links were capable of acting as a group when West Indian matters came before the House, but in most cases primary allegiance was owed to domestic political associates rather than to colonial connections.[73]

Much the same general argument applies to the rather different context provided by British activity in India. There were plenty of MPs who had connections with the East India

Company, of whom a number had served in India, but there was no united East Indian interest in Parliament. Although contemporaries feared the collective corrupting effect of 'nabob' influence on the body politic, the position of 'East Indians' in the House of Commons was in most cases determined by domestic political considerations rather than by membership of any imperial interest group. The East India Company itself was capable of exerting considerable political pressure from time to time, but it chose to do this through the lobbying of officials and ministers, not through the marshalling of parliamentary votes. The number of bitter private battles fought out by East Indian factions in the parliamentary arena and beyond well illustrated that any attempt to establish a united East India interest in the House would have been doomed to failure.[74]

Denied an effective voice in the British legislature, colonists instead devoted considerable attention to influencing imperial decision-making in other ways. From the 1620s, North American and West Indian colonies had appointed official agents to promote their interests in London, and colonial merchants and religious groups also cultivated metropolitan contacts in a systematic and well-organized fashion.[75] As members of extended transatlantic communities, merchants and religious groups were often able to work closely and effectively with like-minded interest groups in Britain, and the system took on a formal appearance as committees were established to coordinate activities and campaigns. In view of the small size of the colonial lobby within the Commons, agents and interest groups found it difficult to influence the decisions of Parliament. They nevertheless ensured that colonial voices were often heard in the corridors of power, notably those at the Board of Trade and the Treasury. Americans did not always get what they wanted when powerful interest groups were ranged against them, but concessions were made, legislation was altered, and favourable measures were introduced as a result of lobbying activity. This was especially the case between 1721 and 1754 when the development of lobbying helped to establish a relationship of mutual benefit between London and the colonies. Colonial interest groups pressed their claims on ministers and officials who, in return, made use of colonists' specialist knowledge and expertise as they endeavoured to come to terms with the problems of imperial administration and government. This relationship was later to be recast when the Board of Trade found its influence diminished as Parliament took a much closer interest in imperial affairs, but for most of the first half of the eighteenth century 'colonists cooperated with the British government because they were getting what they wanted out of it.'[76] At a practical level, this ensured that colonial political activity retained an important transatlantic dimension and, throughout the period, colonists focused considerable attention on events in London.

In addition to its transatlantic political and constitutional framework, the British Atlantic empire was also given definition, if not uniformity, by being a Protestant empire; that is to say that most of the non-indigenous members of the overseas societies under British control adhered to Protestantism of one form or another. Although Protestantism was at this time characterized by the existence of deep tensions between Dissenting denominations and the Anglican community in the English-speaking world, it nevertheless played an important dual role in the establishment and development of imperial identity. At one level, it served to highlight one of the fundamental differences between Britain and her Catholic European rivals, and colonists did not need to look far around them to be reminded of how the liberty and tolerance of the British empire stood in marked contrast to the Popery of the Bourbon powers. At a second level, many members of Protestant communities within the empire belonged to transoceanic faiths which had roots well and truly planted in Britain. To many of their co-religionists in the mother country, the colonists were 'brethren beyond the seas'.[77]

The churches, chapels and meeting-houses scattered across British overseas possessions were often, in theory if not in practice, part of extended religious communities and organizations which were regulated and controlled by metropolitan authorities. Nothing better symbolized these religious ties between core and periphery than the Anglican Church refusing to devolve any of its authority to the colonies. Despite pressure for the establishment of an American episcopate, the colonies remained under the ecclesiastical jurisdiction of the Bishop of London throughout the period.[78] The situation was the same in the West Indies where the the Anglican church in

Jamaica has been described by one historian as 'no more than a collection of qualified individuals, representative of a British institution'.[79] Consequently, any colonist seeking to enter Anglican holy orders was obliged to travel across the Atlantic for ordination. In a North American context this did not happen often before 1720 when the Church relied upon an English-born priesthood to fill its posts, but thereafter an increasing number of native-born Americans sailed to London to be received into holy office. The majority of the 150 or so Americans to undertake this type of pilgrimage in the years before 1776 came from the Chesapeake and Lower South where the Anglican Church had become progressively more entrenched during the first half of the eighteenth century.[80] Yet, for all this display of metropolitan authority and the fact the Anglican cause had been reinforced by the establishment of the Society for the Propagation of the Gospel in Foreign Parts in 1701, the Church in America was handicapped by the fact that it lacked unity and organization in the colonies.[81] This stood in marked contrast with the Dissenting faiths, several of which had assiduously developed connections with the metropolis and also organized themselves in the colonies through the establishment of associations and conventions.[82]

All the constitutional, political and religious sinews that bound the overseas empire together were strengthened during the course of the eighteenth century. The improvements that were taking place in communications meant that the channels through which political and religious ideas, information and instructions flowed between Britain and the colonies became much more effective. Again, this helped to reduce colonial feelings of isolation and it helped to integrate the colonies much more effectively into the wider English-speaking world. Although the East India Company's servants in India remained well beyond the control and supervision of the metropolitan authorities, the situation was different in the Atlantic empire where the improvement in communications helped imperial integration and centralized authority. By 1700, the regularity and speed of Atlantic crossings were such that royal governors of colonies were no longer permitted to take important action, such as declaring war, without approval from London, and colonial legislation was submitted to the metropolitan authorities for review as a matter of administrative routine. 'Government by instruction' provided the formal basis of core–periphery relations, and the 3124 letters exchanged between the governors of royal colonies and the Lords of Trade, Council of Trade or their secretaries between 1675 and 1737 bear ample testimony to the fact that the government and administration of the Atlantic Empire had developed within a context provided by ever-improving communications.[83] Of course, the same processes that centralized imperial authority also served to establish better connections between opposition political groups and religious dissenters on both sides of the Atlantic, and this helped to bring a transoceanic dimension to the development of ideological and theological discourse in the English-speaking colonial and imperial world.[84]

A variety of different ties bound the overseas empire to Britain and, to varying degrees, these ensured that the colonies developed along lines determined by the mother country. Taking advantage of these increasingly close connections between the core and the periphery of the empire were local elites, and it was they who exercised the greatest influence on the shape and structure of the societies under their control. They ensured that many of the defining characteristics of the colonies resembled those evident in contemporary British society, and they brought their own adapted forms of metropolitan enterprise culture to bear on the process of economic expansion and improvement. It is to these individuals that attention must now turn.

6 Merchants, Planters and the Gentlemanly Ideal

As part of the important historiographical trend which has recently focused on the various processes contributing to the anglicization of the British empire, much attention has been devoted to examinations of the ways in which Britain's overseas presence was shaped by dominant metropolitan gentry values, assumptions, tastes and fashions. Many of the social and cultural forces within metropolitan society that were identified in Chapter 3 as emanating from London and the South East of England also made their mark in the overseas empire. In the same way that regional differences in Britain were diminished as the well-to-do sections of provincial society adopted a common code of polite and genteel behaviour, so too the British overseas elite were brought together by their pursuit of a form of gentlemanly ideal. If the view that the 'spread of gentility created in America a conscious class of gentlemen united by common standards across colony lines' is broadly acceptable,[1] then the extension of such an argument suggests that all elites within the British overseas empire were drawn together, united and given a sense of identity by the same standards and codes of behaviour.

From the very beginning of overseas settlement, members of the British elites in different parts of the empire had been given a sense of identity and belonging by their adherence to sets of values, ideals and assumptions forged at home. While this allowed settlers to distinguish themselves from other European and native ethnic groups at the periphery, it also helped them to create a sense of dual identity. While settlers were committing themselves to a new world, they were also seeking to retain associate membership of metropolitan society. Britons from all classes and backgrounds took their cultural, material, religious and ideological baggage with them when they went overseas. This meant that, although some of their actions were undoubtedly shaped by the conditions in which they found themselves, they also attempted to recreate many of the social and economic characteristics of the society they had left behind. They often did this even when basic local factors such the heat and climate dictated that this was not a sensible or practical course of action to follow. Indeed, in the West Indies dogged replication of metropolitan styles of clothing, diet and housing was taken to an extreme and even absurd degree at times. In these matters of everyday life, adaptation to local conditions was thus often a slow, painful and long-term process.[2] As this process of creolization took place, adherence to the gentlemanly ideal continued to play a significant part in shaping the British imperial experience, so that even second or third generation members of the overseas elite, who had no direct experience of Britain, enthusiastically embraced forms of behaviour that had first been created in a metropolitan economic, social and cultural environment. Whether or not they were eventually to return home, overseas elites often in many ways represented an extension of the elites that dominated metropolitan society.

THE GENTLEMANLY IDEAL IN ITS OVERSEAS CONTEXT

With the exception of the important part played by the ownership of slaves in helping to define gentlemanly status in the Chesapeake, the southern American colonies and the Caribbean,[3] the criteria that contemporaries applied to the definition of a gentleman in the overseas colonies were similar to those used in Britain. The possession of land, wealth, leisure time, manners and a sense of honour were all considered to be of central importance when establishing an individual's position within the hierarchical order of colonial society. These characteristics enabled the elite to distance themselves from others around them. With a gentlemanly position established, the individual would engage in the same sorts of convivial, social, philanthropic and political activities as members of the metropolitan elite. Yet, as in Britain, self-perception and the perception of other people also helped to confuse the issue by ensuring that the term 'gentleman' was often used in a loose way to describe individuals who possessed little in terms of real wealth or possessions. In these cases, as in metropolitan society, the word 'gentleman' instead embraced other qualities such as birth, education and politeness.[4] Even so, the gentlemanly ideal played an important role in helping to shape and differentiate overseas society as it became more comfortable and affluent. Adherence to this ideal also helped to forge a strong bond between colonial elites and their metropolitan counterparts by allowing them to share many of the same general outlooks, attitudes and assumptions. Notions of 'improvement' in the cultural and intellectual sphere, as well as in terms of material advancement, often played an important part in the development of the colonies during the eighteenth century. This involved the implicit assumption that the new societies being created would carry all the genteel, ordered and hierarchical hallmarks of life in Britain.[5] In addition, different colonial elites displayed the same willingness as their British counterparts to diversify their economic endeavours beyond a single all-consuming activity. In the Atlantic empire, not only did wealthier merchants trade a wide variety of different products on a global scale,[6] but also powerful regional merchant-planter elites emerged. These elites contained individuals who, like those in metropolitan society, based their wealth, status and influence on the simultaneous development of several different forms of economic enterprise which encompassed land, industry, trade and finance.

Because the gentlemanly ideal provided a model for lifestyles in the overseas empire, elites in some quarters failed to develop, or developed only very slowly, their own distinct forms of cultural and social activity. Instead, they applied metropolitan patterns of behaviour to local circumstances and, hence, despite some very obvious climatic, economic and topographical differences, there was a great deal of similarity between elite lifestyles in different quarters of the world. A member of the New England elite would undoubtedly have found much familiar had he ever travelled to the West Indies or to one of the major British settlements in India. For, wherever British control was established, the representatives of authority recreated aspects of metropolitan life in miniature, be it in terms of clubs, societies, lodges of freemasons or general forms of social activity. Local administrative and legal institutions were developed along metropolitan lines in order to help regulate colonial societies, notably urban societies, in the same way that

British towns and provinces were controlled and ordered. Political institutions were based upon English models, and assemblies often bore a striking resemblance to Parliament.[7] Familiar names were applied to all these institutions as well as to the many homes and buildings that were built in the prevailing architectural styles of the mother country. Finally, in order to keep a close eye on developments, trends and fashions in Britain, overseas communities received news and information whenever possible through newspapers, periodicals and books sent out from family and friends at home. With this establishment of forms of metropolitan behaviour taking place on such a wide scale and in so many different contexts, it is not surprising that many contemporary observers were able to draw attention to similarities between elite lifestyles at the core and the periphery of the empire.

Of course, members of colonial elites were not all cast in a perfect mould of the English gentlemen. Indeed, as far as some contemporary observers were concerned, they could never become true gentlemen because more often than not they did not possess the necessary genealogical credentials. In the Caribbean, as elsewhere, attempts made by the elite to embrace the metropolitan gentlemanly ideal were sometimes deemed to be vulgar and clumsy, and they were treated with scorn and derision by representatives of polite metropolitan society in much the same way that provincials in Britain found themselves held up to ridicule and abuse.[8] Moreover, in a few areas where the general imprint of British culture was very faint, some elites either modified the gentlemanly ideal to a quite significant degree to meet the demands of local conditions or, alternatively, chose to abandon it altogether.[9] Thus, it is important that the genteel nature of elite colonial society is not overstated because local conditions, practical necessity and economic imperatives meant that codes of conduct and behaviour developed in metropolitan society simply could not always be applied in areas under British control. The pattern of everyday life in the West Indies and colonial America was repeatedly disrupted by warfare, natural disasters and fire in urban centres, while disease and poor health were serious ever-present problems for the white population.[10] Conditions were in many ways similar in the east. The British population in India was repeatedly devastated by illness (much of it related to intemperance), and large numbers of Britons died in service before they could return home.[11]

Life for many of the elite at the periphery was often very short, but it could also be nasty and brutish as well. Colonial life, particularly on the frontier, could be very harsh indeed as the small elite sought to preserve their often tenuous hold on their property and position. In order to do this, they presided over brutal and dehumanizing regimes which were designed to oppress and control vastly superior numbers of slaves or transitory white labourers.[12] Indeed, some who embraced metropolitan manners, attitudes and assumptions with some degree of enthusiasm were at the forefront of those perpetrating acts of violence and oppression in systematic attempts to protect their position within the population. Those who enjoyed the full benefits of English liberty and legal protection were not prepared to extend that liberty and protection beyond their own race, and this was reflected in the harsh nature of the slave codes drawn up and adhered to by local elites.[13] The case of William Byrd II of Virginia stands as an oft-cited example of an educated man who possessed cultured tastes and enjoyed a genteel lifestyle, but who regularly subjected his servants and slaves to beatings, brandings and whippings.[14] This type of behaviour might well have been condemned as barbaric and uncivilized by members of the metropolitan elite, yet some contemporaries were prepared to argue that the lot of the slave was in fact a happy and contented one.[15] Within the world in which he moved, Byrd was not considered to be a cruel man, but his treatment of slaves reflected the way in which the gentlemanly ideal had been adapted by aggressive members of the elite to the conditions prevailing in a planter society where such behaviour was regarded as a legitimate way of maintaining order and discipline. Not only were slaves regarded as a form of property, but they were perceived to be savages who were inferior to whites and had to be kept firmly in their place. The Evangelist George Whitefield believed that many southern plantation owners treated their dogs better than their slaves.[16] In the light of such attitudes, and despite the actions of some Christian reformers,[17] it is not surprising that slave populations and indigenous communities were seldom granted access to even the most basic fruits of European civilization. Indeed, from the beginnings of settlement, the elite usually sought to maintain a good distance between themselves and the rest of the population under their control.[18] Often the only features of the Old World to make themselves felt to the indigenous colonial population were the negative ones associated with disease, sickness, the destruction wrought by imported plants and livestock, and an enforced dependency upon imported goods, alcohol and weapons.[19]

NORTH AMERICAN ELITES

North American society was never static and the movement of people involved in westward expansion meant that the pace of economic and social development varied considerably from colony to colony. Even within a single colony there could be important subregional differences.[20] By 1750, however, several parts of the American colonies were well past the initial stage of pioneer settlement and some regions were beginning to experience developments which not only to gave them a greater social order and political stability, but also served to integrate them fully into the North Atlantic imperial and economic framework. In the words of Jack P. Greene, all colonies were moving closer together 'in the configurations of their socioeconomic life'.[21] As part of this process, colonial elites tended to adapt prominent features of metropolitan life to local conditions. In an urban context, towns such as Boston, Charles Town and Philadelphia took on the appearance of English towns as gardens, squares, exchanges and townhouses were built, and within this architectural framework cultural, economic and social life developed along lines similar to those in the provinces of Britain.[22] In the countryside, too, emerging elites ensured that both the landscape and architecture took on forms that were prominent in metropolitan society.[23] In many ways, this was part of a process of integration which affected the population of Lancashire and Cornwall in the same way that it touched the more distant parts of British settler communities. Recognition of this important trend, and an increasing willingness to use a comparative approach, has resulted in a large number of scholars emphasizing similarities rather than contrasts between British and colonial society. Indeed, it has been argued that in a North American context,

'Imperialism, in short, can be seen as an expression of the structure of British society.'[24] Awareness of this has led to historians stressing that, as the British North Atlantic economy grew to maturity, so the lifestyles of white colonial elites became increasingly similar to those of their metropolitan brethren.[25] Descriptions of the central elements of those elite lifestyles in colonial America often bear a striking resemblance to contemporary accounts of similar activities in Britain.[26]

Although the development of important aspects of genteel culture in North America was based upon a British pattern, it was often founded upon much more than simple imitation. As Richard Bushman has argued, cultural trends on both sides of the Atlantic belonged to a 'single integrated process' and colonists were able to respond almost as quickly as those in the British provinces to behavioural and material forces emanating from London.[27] Colonial elites kept up to date with the latest fashionable developments in British society through avid reading of genteel periodicals such as the *Tatler* and the *Spectator*,[28] and they were able to share common experiences with their metropolitan brethren as goods, styles, learning, information and ideas were imported from the mother country. This helped to weave the colonies into the imperial fabric. In urban centres, elites engaged in similar intellectual and cultural pursuits to their counterparts in British towns and cities, and their search for useful knowledge to assist progress and improvement reinforced their sense of common purpose. This homogeneity also found expression in the religious sphere where gentlemen in all colonies, as in Britain, developed strikingly similar forms of moderate, rational belief.[29]

All this is not to say, however, that the overseas elite became clones of the metropolitan elite, because they were capable of displaying an independence of mind and action in a wide variety of different contexts, and they were often prepared to condemn aspects of English culture that they considered inappropriate for their own particular environment.[30] Nevertheless, in most regions, they enthusiastically embraced many of the symbols of gentility and good taste paraded by the English gentry and this allowed them to define and consolidate their own position at the top of the colonial hierarchy.[31] Ian Steele, whose work has played a part in helping to focus scholarly attention on these matters,[32] has remarked that this allowed elites to display a 'fascinating ambivalence' towards Britain. Although they needed the many advantages that London bestowed upon them, in a political context they could at the same time demonstrate a deep suspicion and hostility towards key aspects of British economic and imperial policy.[33] Ultimately, however, one suspects that until the 1760s many of them would have felt that they had more in common with the metropolitan gentry than they did with their social inferiors in the colonies.[34] This meant that they could ill afford to oppose British interests.

Like their British counterparts, American colonists made an enthusiastic entry into the world of consumer goods that developed during the course of the eighteenth century, and their lifestyles altered accordingly.[35] As we saw in the previous chapter, necessity and trading arrangements played a key part in bringing the colonists and the British together as members of the same world of goods, but a powerful influence was also exerted by the need for colonists to emulate those in metropolitan society. Benjamin Franklin remarked on this to the House of Commons in 1766, when he declared that before the emergence of tensions in the relationship with the metropolitan authorities in 1764–5, the 'pride' of American colonists had been 'to indulge in the fashions of Great Britain'.[36] At all levels of society, patterns of consumption changed in response to vigorous advertising and increasingly sophisticated marketing techniques, and new types of goods flowed into North America. By 1740 this served to offer colonists a range of products way beyond those that had been available to previous generations.[37] Tea-drinking became a habit and social custom, initially within the elite, and, as in Britain, the accompanying rituals became an important part of the genteel colonial lifestyle.[38] This was noted by Joseph Bennett in 1740 when he visited Boston and observed that 'the ladies here visit, drink tea and indulge every little piece of gentility to the height of the mode and neglect the affairs of their families with as good grace as the finest ladies in London.'[39] Before tea-drinking could take its place in social life all the relevant luxury accessories needed to be purchased. Colonial demand for such items was so strong that Josiah Wedgwood, who supplied cheap tableware as well 'rich and costly wares' to the American and West Indian markets, could state quite emphatically in 1767 that home consumption of his products was 'quite trifling' when compared with what he sold to British North America.[40]

As new types of cloth, trimmings and furnishings became available in London, fashions were often transferred to well-to-do women in the colonies by merchants' wives who selected some of the new types of goods for dispatch in the ships that carried their husbands' cargoes.[41] In a few cases, female traders such as Frances Swallow of Charles Town and Catherine Rathell of Williamsburg even travelled to London to select and procure the latest fashionable goods for sale in their millinery shops.[42] The pace of change in elite fashion in the colonies was thus conditioned to a large extent by the way in which the metropolitan gentlemanly (and gentlewomanly) elite dictated style and patterns of consumption. Some commentators remarked on the extraordinary speed with which the well-to-do classes in the colonies were able to pick up and participate in the latest European purchasing trends.[43] In 1771, for example, a consignment of goods was ordered from the London merchant John Norton by Catherine Rathell. The invoice, which requested that Norton dispatch the goods 'with all possible speed', listed a wide range of trinkets, decorations, items of jewellery, and clothing, including '12 pairs of handsome new fashion gilt shoe . . . with knee to match but not very small', and 12 dozen of the 'neatest new fashion gentlemens sleeve buttons'. Not only did Norton have the difficult task of guessing the size of a 'not very small' pair of shoes, but he also had to decide on his colonial client's behalf what was new and fashionable in London.[44] In order to give themselves immediate access to the world of metropolitan fashion, many of the Virginia gentry built their houses, as the Reverend Hugh Jones remarked in 1724, 'near some landing-place; so that anything may be delivered to a gentleman there from London, Bristol, etc., with less trouble and cost, than to one living five miles in the country in England.'[45] Such indeed was the speed with which goods could be transported to North America by the 1770s that William Eddis was moved to declare that 'I am almost inclined to believe that a new fashion is adopted earlier by the polished and affluent Americans, than by many opulent persons in the great metropolis . . .'[46]

Contemporaries did not doubt that the planter elite of the tidewater Chesapeake bore a very close resemblance to the

English gentry. On the face of it, there were strong grounds to support this view and as historians have painstakingly re-created the lifestyles of this particular colonial elite they have drawn attention to a broad range of comparisons with metro-politan elites.[47] This elite, many of whom acquired wealth through commercial activity and speculation in land, began to emerge as the region moved beyond the initial pioneer settle-ment stage during the late seventeenth century. The families in question represented around 2 per cent of the landowning population; they owned about 50 per cent of the region's wealth; and they have been described by one historian as rep-resenting a 'nearly self-perpetuating oligarchy' by the 1730s.[48] Many of the behavioural patterns of this elite were closely modelled on those practised by the metropolitan gentry and, although many variants on the gentlemanly theme emerged, there can be little doubt that the upper echelons of Chesapeake society represented a relatively sophisticated genteel commu-nity by the early eighteenth century. Many planters, whatever their origins or lineage, sought to imitate key aspects of the lifestyle of the metropolitan gentry and this influenced the long-term development of economic, political, religious and social relationships within the region.[49] The Virginia gentry became the leaders of their community. They commanded local armed forces, acted as law interpretation and enforce-ment officers, and exercised political power in the Council. Indeed, in the political sphere, attention has been drawn to the homogeneous nature of the group of leaders who domin-ated the affairs of the Virginia House of Burgesses. This group has been shown to have been dominated by planters who of-ten engaged in other forms of economic activity. Many of them were connected through family links, and nearly all of them were of the Anglican faith and of English origin.[50]

The genteel lifestyle of the landed elite of the Chesapeake was often used by earlier generations of historians to reinforce caricatures of the great planters as a rural gentry or aristo-cracy. Modern detailed analyses of individual and family wealth have, however, revealed the full extent to which fortunes were often established and then developed through a combination of planting and a wide range of business enterprises, including money-lending, speculation, manufacturing, shipbuilding and commercial activity. Diversification not only moved individuals away from a dangerous dependency on the success of their tobacco crops, but it also played a key role in the accumulation of large fortunes.[51] One consequence of this is that it is difficult to make any straightforward comparisons between the lifestyle of elites in the Chesapeake and those in Britain. Because the planter elite of the region retained a close interest in the day-to-day running of their various enterprises, they were in fact quite different from the stereotypical leisured English landowners who, it was believed, provided them with a model for many of their social and cultural activities.[52] In particular, wealthy Virginia planters, unlike other landed elites, exercised close control over the productive process and took a deep interest in all aspects of the cultivation of the tobacco crop. In the words of one historian, this 'touched nearly every aspect of their existence' and it led to the creation of an all-pervasive 'tobacco mentality'.[53] Indeed, case-studies reveal that some local elites, such as the merchant-planters of Talbot County, Maryland, bore a close resemblance to metropolitan entrepreneurs of the type described in Chapter 3 because of the way in which they dedicated themselves to economic 'improvement' and to the diversification and development of their activities.[54] Elite families (including the Washingtons) throughout the Chesapeake were, through choice or necessity, increasingly to be found combining tobacco planting with speculation, trade and investment in industry.[55]

The Chesapeake elite might not have led an exclusively leisured existence, but they nevertheless displayed as deep a concern about the acquisition of the trappings of wealth and status as that exercised by any English landed gentleman. In a domestic context they built 'great houses' which followed many of the classical conventions of contemporary metropolitan style; they commissioned coats of arms and purchased luxurious furnishings from Europe; and they laid out parks and gardens in the English manner.[56] Moreover, social relationships were defined through an acceptance of metropolitan modes of behaviour. The gentry ate, drank and entertained in the English fashion; they met together in clubs and societies; and they followed gentlemanly sports and pastimes such as English-style horse-racing.[57] Above all, they practised good manners and adhered to codes of conduct and honour that at times were virtuous in the extreme. All of these factors helped to cast elite

Chesapeake society in a metropolitan mould and this served to define the hierarchy in the well-established areas of the region. In no context was this more clearly seen than in religion where elite adherence to Anglicanism and its rituals of service helped to reinforce notions of social order and organization.[58] Yet, as the range of their economic activities indicated, it would be wrong to think of the Virginia gentry as simple caricatures of rustic British squires. Like those within the innovating sections of metropolitan landed society, they were often dedicated to improvement in the personal as well as the public sphere. On the whole, they displayed a keen interest in education, books and learning. Although not all could afford to send their sons to English schools and universities, the influence of the mother country was strongly felt through the employment of English tutors and teachers who passed on the benefits of classical learning. The influence of the classics was further reinforced by a tendency for the great planters to stock their libraries with the works of Greek and Roman authors. Books might have been regarded as something of a luxury in the colony, but the focus of attention on traditional works played its part in helping to shape outlooks and assumptions.[59]

Of course, it must be stressed that members of elite families in Virginia such as the Beverlys, Byrds, Carters, Lees and Randolphs were not Englishmen abroad, and they belonged to a distinct form of Anglo-Virginian settler society. They had established themselves slowly over several generations and, unlike many West Indian planters, they had no desire to enjoy retirement in Britain. Yet, they had managed to carve out a position for themselves at the top of a socioeconomic hierarchy which spanned the entire Atlantic community and only in terms of slaveholding and political representation in Parliament did they differ from the British elite. Indeed, by the 1720s the Virginia gentry had become in some ways, as is so often the case, more English than the English themselves. The Reverend Hugh Jones made this point in his oft-quoted remark which neatly summarized the Virginians' disdain for those aspects of English life which did not conform to the notions of civility and good manners which had been defined for them by their cultural dependence on London. Jones wrote:

> The habits, life, customs, computations, etc. of the Virginians are much the same as about London, which they esteem

their home; and for the most part have contemptible notions of England, and wrong sentiments of Bristol and the other out-ports, which they entertain from seeing and hearing the common dealers, sailors, and servants that come from those towns, and the country places in England and Scotland, whose language and manners are strange to them . . .[60]

By 1740, the Virginia gentry dominated their colony but their position was not cast in stone and it would be wrong to depict them as belonging to the top tier of an unchanging *ancien régime* type of society. A number of modern historians have skilfully demonstrated that the position and status of the elite began to be threatened by changes to the economic system and by the emergence of powerful religious and political forces. Traditional assumptions about status, hierarchy, personal autonomy and authority were questioned in Virginia, leading to a crisis of confidence within the elite, while, on a broader scale, the very nature of the commercial and political relationship between the colony and Britain was gradually being recast. This posed some difficult questions for the gentry and, with one eye on the future, it obliged them to redefine many of their central social attitudes and ideals.[61]

As the Chesapeake gentry developed lifestyles based upon an ideal embraced by the English landed classes, other colonial elites began to follow patterns of development that were similar to those of elites in Britain. Some colonies saw the emergence of powerful commercial elites which bore a close resemblance to metropolitan merchants both in terms of lifestyle and the range of their economic activities. This was not surprising given transoceanic trading links and colonial integration into the Atlantic economy. These men sought the trappings and social status of the gentleman and, although they kept one foot in the world of work and another in trade, they were often to be found purchasing land for speculative purposes and the development of estates and country houses. On the other side of the coin, long-established landed families developed a close interest in trade and commerce, and their connections and involvement were often strengthened through marriage and family association. As in Britain, there was no firm line drawn between land and trade, and different colonial elites contained individuals drawn from a range of various economic backgrounds into relatively close-knit social alliances.

The commercial elite that emerged in New England during the second half of the seventeenth century based its economic rise on trade and land development, and their success was translated into political leadership which helped to erode the influence of powerful religious elements in the region. From the very first stages of development, the overseas merchants of New England had attempted to overcome the pressures exerted by the Puritan way of life in order to secure the same sort of social position enjoyed by their contemporaries in Britain. With varying degrees of success, speculative moves into landed property were accompanied by the improvement of estates, the building of country houses and the acquisition of all the trappings of gentlemanly status.[62] Levels of personal wealth within North American commercial elites did not reach the heights enjoyed by other colonial and metropolitan elites,[63] but the New England merchant elite were still able to establish a genteel lifestyle based upon patterns of behaviour and expenditure that they believed to be evident in polite British society. One English observer commented in 1720 that 'a gentleman from London would almost think himself at home in Boston. . . . In the concerns of civil life, as in their dress, tables and conversation they [the elite] affect to be as much English as possible.'[64] First and foremost, this served to shape the material life of the elite but, as elsewhere, it acted as a powerful agent in helping to determine social status and the region's hierarchy, even though many important aspects of the old pre-commercial socioreligious order remained intact. By the 1760s, New England had become 'far more demonstrably English than it had been during the decades immediately after its establishment', and there can be no doubting the fact that the emergence of an aggressive, innovative commercial elite had played a central part in this process.[65]

A similar intermingling of landed and commercial interests occurred within the elite of neighbouring New York. By the 1750s, the great landed dynasties such as the Schuylers, Livingstons, Crugers, Cuylers and Bayards had important branches of the family engaged in trade, commerce and industry. For its part, the merchant community had developed a genteel lifestyle with all the fashionable trappings enjoyed by members of the metropolitan elite. Accordingly, land was valued by all members of the elite not just for the speculative opportunities it offered to the investor but because it brought social status to the would-be gentleman. Even so, land did not capture the attention of entrepreneurs to the exclusion of everything else, and there was plenty of diversification into manufacturing, shipping, insurance, money-lending and privateering.[66] Further to the south, the forty or so wealthiest members of the merchant elite of Philadelphia also strove to combine involvement in trade with a genteel and landed lifestyle. At the same time, many of them sought, through choice or economic necessity, to diversify their range of business activities. Thus, there was, for example, a significant level of merchant involvement in the iron industry, even if that involvement was characterized by investment rather than by direct participation in the management of works.[67]

Elite culture was also defined by adherence to metropolitan ideas and standards in the lower southern colonies.[68] As South Carolina moved past the initial stage of pioneer settlement, an elite emerged who drew on English gentry values as they established their position. Patterns of education reveal that an ever-increasing number of Carolinians chose to send their children to school in England after 1750. Not only could they receive training as lawyers and medical practitioners, but it was hoped that they would also develop the social graces and manners appropriate for an English gentleman. This attitude began to change as the colonial period came to an end, but South Carolina's failure to establish its own educational establishments can in part be attributed to the strength of elite commitment to metropolitan values and standards. This commitment was also seen in the way elite lifestyles came to be based upon a somewhat idealized version of those adopted by the members of landed society in Britain. As elsewhere, members of different types of elite, most notably those involved in trade and commerce, were attracted to landownership, and it has been argued that there were few southern merchants who did not seek to channel their commercial profits into purchases of land.[69] As the *South Carolina Gazette* noted in 1773, 'Every tradesman is a merchant, every merchant is a gentleman, and every gentleman is a member of the noblesse. We are a country of gentry.'[70]

Land purchases often represented an important first step in the pursuit of the gentlemanly ideal in South Carolina, but others included the building of houses in the English style and participation in metropolitan forms of leisure activity, which included watching horse-racing on courses named after York and Newmarket.[71] The result was the development of a lifestyle for the elite that was at times both luxurious and extravagant, but this was not simply the result of straightforward imitation. It has been pointed out that other important influences were at work, not least of which was that South Carolina provided the least healthy environment in North America. Even the elite faced a precarious existence. Their lifestyles therefore reflected that life could be short, and consequently their wealth was often dedicated to conspicuous consumption. As a result, some sections of the elite resembled a caricature of the English gentry in which all the less appealing features of the leisured classes were accentuated. This provided plenty of ammunition to those such as the influential Methodist preacher George Whitefield and others who were critical of the materialistic nature of southern society, and who argued that the excesses of the Charles Town elite were far worse than those evident in London.[72] Other members of the elite, however, displayed many of the characteristics of the most innovative and enterprising groups in metropolitan society.[73] As such, they became important agents of growth and expansion in the region.

THE WEST INDIAN PLANTER ELITE

Integration into the broader English-speaking cultural world took place in the West Indies as British-held islands moved beyond the pioneering phases of settlement, and as relative stability replaced the turmoil and upheaval that had characterized the region during the second half of the seventeenth century. There had been little scope for the development of distinct regional elite cultures within the British Caribbean, despite the existence of different patterns of settlement and landholding on the various islands. Many settlers did not wish to see out their days in their new environment and they continued to lead a lifestyle based upon metropolitan patterns of behaviour. Yet although the lure of the metropolis exerted a strong influence on many of the planter elite, it would be wrong to suggest that they showed little interest in their local surroundings beyond that of straightforward economic exploitation. In recent years, the stereotypical view of the absentee planter has been modified and emphasis has been placed on the extent to which the Barbadian and Jamaican elite were committed to their islands.[74] By the mid-eighteenth century, they were investing heavily in improvements, developing modern urban social and cultural amenities, and playing an active part in political life in a way that compares quite favourably with their counterparts on the North American mainland.[75] In the urban sphere, the 1770s heralded the beginning of a process which saw the construction of a wide range of public buildings in Jamaica. Beyond forts and religious houses, a public hospital was built in Kingston in 1776, a theatre was built in Spanish Town in the same year, and botanical gardens were laid out in Gordon Town and St Andrew.[76] This commitment and investment played its part in helping to reinforce the anglicized nature of the world of the planter elite and, despite the creolization of Jamaican society that was taking place, these processes were reinforced by strong economic and cultural influences emanating from Britain. These developments helped to bring the island firmly into the English-speaking transatlantic community, a process greatly assisted by the way in which British West Indian elites, like their counterparts on the American mainland, had long been able to read locally produced newspapers such as the *Weekly Jamaican Courant* or the *Barbados Gazette* which reprinted news from London. This served to keep the focus of attention very much on what was happening in Britain, and the copies of periodicals, such as the *Gentleman's Magazine*, that were shipped into the Caribbean enabled the elite to keep abreast of metropolitan news, gossip, politics, and literary and philosophical developments.[77]

General rates of socioeconomic development had varied from island to island during the seventeenth century,[78] and land had been acquired and distributed in different ways and on different scales. By 1720, however, estates had been consolidated and Barbados, the Leewards and Jamaica were all dominated by elites comprising the wealthier members of the planter class. In Barbados the planter elite was formed by 175 individuals from 159 families, and this 6.9 per cent of all landholders owned 53.4 per cent of the island's land. In Jamaica, Britain's most valuable Atlantic colony, an elite of 50 or so sugar planters existed among the 198 individuals who had their property inventoried between 1674 and 1701.[79] Closely associated with these planters were leading merchants and professionals, many of whom also owned landed estates. These elites used metropolitan models to develop or recreate a social and political framework based upon English law, institutions and religion.[80] Militias, for example, were established along English lines, even to the extent that in Barbados they were clothed in traditional red-coated woollen uniforms.[81]

Imitation and replication played a similarly important role in the private sphere, and few of the elite were prepared to make many concessions to the local climate and conditions. This tendency had been evident from the time when the gentry had begun firmly to establish themselves, and the development of a comfortable lifestyle, together with the need to reinforce social status, continued to be based upon the importation of an extraordinarily wide range of British goods.[82] Consumption of food and drink, and the acquisition of clothing, furnishings and housing all followed prevailing trends in contemporary Britain. Those ordering goods from London repeatedly stressed the extent to which their colonial customers wished to keep abreast of the latest metropolitan styles and fashions.[83] This meant that the clothes worn by the elite were often heavy and uncomfortable, their diet was inappropriate and their houses, built on English lines, were not well suited to the tropical environment.[84] Even where necessity dictated that the homes of planters should remain basic and functional, elegant trappings were added wherever possible along lines dictated by what was believed to be fashionable in Britain.[85] Thus, as late as the 1790s one observer commented that even among the less wealthy white population of Jamaica it was not an 'uncommon thing to find, at the country habitations of the planters, a splendid side-board loaded with plate, and the choicest wines, a table covered with the finest damask, and a dinner of perhaps sixteen or twenty covers; and all this in a hovel not superior to an English barn.'[86] Even as the elite developed a distinctive vernacular building style, they still sought to stay firmly in touch with the world of metropolitan taste and standards. When, for example, Sir Charles Price built a mansion at the Decoy on Jamaica during the 1760s it was

designed and decorated in European style. It was surrounded
with elaborate walks and gardens, and the park appears to
have been stocked with imported deer.[87] Not surprisingly, many
accounts of the British Caribbean drew attention to similarities
rather than contrasts between local and metropolitan elites,
and contemporaries often described West Indian towns as being
closely akin to genteel British urban societies in miniature.[88]
These civilizing social trends meant that, even in islands where
distinct local identities were slowly emerging, the inhabitants
continued to emphasize their Englishness and attachment to
Britain.[89]

THE MERCHANT-GENTLEMEN OF BRITISH INDIA

Like permanent settlers in America and the West Indies, the
small transitory British community in India was shaped by
metropolitan gentry values, ideas and assumptions. This became increasingly marked after mid-century when Indian service became more attractive to recruits from the metropolitan
upper classes. Company servants and free merchants sought
to maintain a gentlemanly lifestyle, though some individuals
adopted Indian customs such as hookah smoking and the wearing of native clothing when indoors. In general, however, the
social and cultural contours of British settlements were defined and developed along metropolitan lines.[90] For the most
part, the British lived in isolation in communities where there
was only a limited Indian presence. There were few exchanges
between Britons and Indians other than those developed within
a business or administrative context, and there was little real
scope for social and cultural interaction. As elsewhere in the
overseas empire, the elite sought to recreate the type of society, amenities and institutions familiar to them and, again, the
strong imprint of metropolitan ideas and fashions was to be
found on everyday activities in British India.[91]

In Calcutta, the most noticeable outward signs of this process
were manifested in housebuilding in a European and English
style, as well as in the growth of a commercial community in
which a significant number of individuals were employed in
trades such as wig-making and pastry-cooking which catered
for gentlemanly habits and tastes.[92] Daily routines, amusement

and entertainment were all based upon metropolitan styles, and one female observer described a pattern of social life at Madras in the 1780s that was remarkably similar in form and structure to that experienced by members of the elite in Britain. Miss Humphries wrote to Lord Clive's widow in 1786 and told her about '... the hurry of pleasure in which our time is spent, a concert every fortnight and a meeting twice a week which is called the Rooms where people dance, play at cards, and sup, constant engagements to spend the evening out, never at home without company, and a great number of formal visits to receive and return ...'[93]

Beyond this frivolous world of light entertainment, other metropolitan forces helped the elite in India to retain close behavioural links with their counterparts in Britain. Inventories of personal possessions and the contents of libraries and book collections bear testimony to the extent to which the British in India continued to have their general outlook and lifestyle shaped by the intellectual and literary influences of the mother country.[94] Some Britons, most notably Warren Hastings, took a deep interest in indigenous culture, and they acted as patrons and sponsors for native and metropolitan scholars, painters and sculptors.[95] On the whole, however, this move towards a closer understanding of Indian society occurred after 1775, and before then the British restricted their interest in local culture to the collection of artefacts and curiosities for eventual shipment home. Individuals in India were also able to develop a range of individual economic activities that were broadly comparable to those pursued by their counterparts elsewhere in the empire. There were fewer potential business and investment openings for Britons in India, but a growing number of entrepreneurs nevertheless displayed a great willingness to experiment and diversify their activities. The wide range of industrial and mining projects developed by individuals in Bengal might not have borne much fruit in the form of financial reward, but they did indicate a strong desire to engage in private investment and enterprise.[96]

The anglicization of British Indian society was to some extent reinforced by the formal guidelines for behaviour and conduct that were laid down for the East India Company's servants by the metropolitan authorities.[97] The Company's directors, drawn almost exclusively from London's business and financial community, repeatedly sought to ensure that their representatives behaved as responsible and honourable English gentlemen. In 1769 they frowned upon 'Eastern' or 'Asiatic' practices, and declared that 'European simplicity is much more likely to engage the respect of the natives than an imitation of their manners.' Company employees, however, did not all subscribe to the view that simplicity was a guiding principle for their conduct in an environment where the climate was harsh, life was short, and the daily routine could be tedious and boring. This meant that the directors had to express concern that the English gentlemanly ideal was being corrupted by influences such as overindulgence and extravagance, to the point that they felt that 'luxury' rather than simplicity was becoming the main feature of everyday life during the 1760s. Thus, in seeking to define precisely what they meant by simplicity, the directors attempted to impose a set of 'sumptuary' guidelines on their employees based upon their own notions of self-discipline, moderation and sobriety. Having said that, they did recognize that senior Company servants on the spot were best placed to interpret whether or not their regulations were actually appropriate in the prevailing situation, and they left them free to apply the rules as they thought fit. Nevertheless, junior writers were singled out for particular attention so that a 'total change of manners' could be effected, the aim being to create 'a rising set of valuable servants' who could eventually replace those whose conduct was deemed to be unsatisfactory. Writers found that many of their 'gentlemanly' trappings were removed. They were no longer permitted to own a country house or a palanquin; they were not allowed to keep more than one servant other than a cook; dress was to be regulated in accordance with rank and status; and senior officials were to keep an eye on those whose drinking habits made them 'conspicuous in extravagance or intemperance'. That these guidelines were needed at all suggests that some Company servants were displaying unacceptable levels of overindulgence, and the directors' diagnosis of the problem was that writers were being given too much freedom and independence which allowed them to partake in what were described as 'youthful follies'. The cure was seen to be a much closer supervision of their activities, a clearer definition of their duties and a constant reminder of their responsibilities. It was hoped that in a well-regulated environment the best rather than the worst qualities of the English gentleman would be able to develop and flourish.

By 1750, elites at the core and the periphery of the British empire had been reasonably well integrated into a world of business, investment, goods, fashion, ideas and values that gave them a sense of common identity and belonging. With varying degrees of success, elites in different parts of the overseas empire had carved out an economic and social position for themselves that was similar to that of the metropolitan elite. The pursuit of the gentlemanly ideal had brought a sense of form and structure to the empire, and a commitment to enterprise and innovation had acted as an important dynamic within the various processes associated with economic and territorial expansion. In this sense, some of the central features of eighteenth-century British society had been clearly imprinted on the empire, and a truly transoceanic elite had been created. Yet, just at the moment that the main characteristics of this imperial elite were beginning to come sharply into focus, several powerful influences began to distort the picture in a number of ways. New economic, social and political forces were starting to transfigure the metropolis, and they were also brought to bear on the development of the empire. Any sociocultural stability and unity that may have existed within the empire was increasingly threatened by change and diversity, and the positions of elites were quite fundamentally altered in a number of different ways. At one level, the cohesion of elites everywhere was weakened by shifts in ethnic and cultural balances. At another level, there was a redefinition of the relationship between the core and the periphery of the empire. As this happened, the empire entered a period of sustained internal crisis and upheaval that was to threaten its future existence.

Part Four
A New Imperial Order, 1750–75

7 The End of the English Empire

In all its essential features, the British overseas empire that developed and expanded during the first half of the eighteenth century was an extension of the English empire that had been established during the course of the seventeenth century. Although, in a formal sense, colonists were now members of a British empire governed by a British Parliament in the name of a British sovereign, many of them still perceived themselves to be Englishmen, carrying English birthrights and belonging to an English empire. Some commentators and observers acknowledged the constitutional changes that had taken place since the Act of Union of 1707, and they chose their words with care and precision when they wrote and spoke about themselves and their contemporaries as British and Britons rather than English and Englishmen. Others used the words English and British interchangeably, but a large number of colonists continued to conduct constitutional and political discourse in terms dictated by membership of an unreconstructed English empire and polity.[1]

This state of affairs confirmed that in public and official life anglicization swept all before it, both at the core and the periphery, and this had created an extended empire given unity and coherence by English custom, language, law, liberty and traditions. At the same time, this had been reinforced in the private sphere by the way that England, and London in particular, dictated patterns of consumption, style, fashion, behaviour and conduct in the wider world. Yet, ironically, at the very time that this was happening, those of English ethnic origin within the overseas empire were gradually being overwhelmed in numerical terms by Celts and settlers of non-British origin. In Britain itself, not only did several elites become strikingly cosmopolitan in nature and composition, but also important centres of dynamic imperial activity began to develop well away from London and the south east of England. Increasingly, links between the core and the periphery of the empire were based upon multilateral ties rather than a single

Anglo-colonial connection dominated by English cultural values and the commercial and financial resources of the capital. By mid-century, cultural and ethnic diversity had become one of the main characteristics of the empire and, to all intents and purposes, the English empire had become a fiction. Slowly, almost imperceptibly, the empire had been transformed into a multinational business and military enterprise. Outwardly, the empire was still recognizably 'English' in shape and form, but many of its internal dynamic processes were characterized by contributions from powerful non-English influences.

THE RECONSTRUCTION OF THE IMPERIAL CORE

The expansion of trade and empire, union with Scotland and the institutional arrangements underpinning the making of the modern state had opened up England to an increasing number of outsiders. Access had not been denied in the past, but now an enormous range of opportunities were available to the non-English merchant, investor, soldier or sailor. Some of these outsiders sought to move to London on a permanent basis, some attempted to channel financial resources towards the City, and others endeavoured to find place or position in the institutions of state and empire. The effects of this can be quantified in any number of ways, from the increasing extent of foreign investment in the National Debt to the growth of Irish and Scottish representation in the officer corps of the armed forces.[2] All the time, at the very heart of the empire, the strength of English influence was being diluted as non-English cultural traditions and non-Anglican religious beliefs found a place within the dynamic processes of change and development.

This trend was perhaps most noticeable in the realm of trade and commerce. Indeed, one of the most striking features of the merchant community was the way in which its cosmopolitan complexion developed as the eighteenth century progressed. A recent calculation, based on figures compiled by the political economist Thomas Mortimer, suggests that by 1763 around three-quarters of London's merchants were of foreign origin or descent.[3] In part, this extraordinary figure stemmed from London having a long tradition of offering individuals a safe haven from religious persecution and becoming home to an international community of some size. Also, however, the growth of the capital as a financial and commercial centre after 1688 had fuelled an expansion in the numbers of denizens and naturalized foreigners who had made their homes in London. In particular, the disruption caused by warfare during the 1690s had prompted a foreign takeover of London's export trade to western Europe, and this had led to the merchant community becoming markedly more cosmopolitan over a short period of time.[4] Huguenots, Jews and the Dutch formed three influential ethnic groups within the merchant elite, and the presence of a large number of Scots also served to diminish English influence within the capital's commercial community. Joseph Addison conveyed something of the cosmopolitan nature of London's merchant community during the early eighteenth century when he wrote about his visits to the Royal Exchange and declared that 'It gives me secret satisfaction as an Englishman to see so rich an assembly of countrymen and foreigners making this metropolis a kind of emporium for the whole earth. Sometimes I am jostled by a body of Armenians, sometimes I am lost in a crowd of Jews or Dutchmen, sometimes Danes, Swedes or Frenchmen . . .'[5]

Leading members of London's permanent cosmopolitan merchant community moved into positions of considerable influence within the business world, and their resources played a key part in oiling the wheels of commerce and state finance. Yet, as these individuals found their way into the very heart of the commercial establishment, they retained their cultural identity and upheld their own religious and social traditions. This meant that even members of second- or third-generation immigrant families were often only partially assimilated into English society and, for example, a large number of merchants remained outside the Anglican religious community. One measure of this was to be found in the number and distribution of non-Anglican chapels and places of worship throughout London. This was of some importance, given that the political life of the City was so fundamentally influenced by religious divisions that one recent historian has characterized an important dimension of London politics as being the 'politics of belief' between 1688 and 1715.[6] In such a political atmosphere, strong links were forged between Whiggism and the Dissenting merchants who formed about a fifth of London's entire commercial community in 1695/6. These links played an important part in ensuring that about 60 per cent of Whig City leaders between 1688 and 1715 were overseas merchants.[7] At the same time, distinct merchant identities found expression in the establishment of powerful interest groups and marriage alliances, and this meant that trade and credit networks were often formed on the basis of ethnicity, kinship and religion.[8]

Membership of religious and ethnic groups was also an important factor in helping to determine the way in which commercial relationships were established between Britain and her overseas markets. Family, community and nationality links were extended from the core into the empire at large,[9] the best general example being provided by the Scots whose kinship connections were evident in most sectors of overseas trade. Other groups of individuals belonging to distinct ethnic and religious traditions were closely associated with particular regions or branches of trade, and they played a decisive part in reshaping and sustaining British commercial activity as a whole. Sephardi Jews belonging to London's Portuguese community, for example, helped to establish Britain's dominant position in the Iberian trade, and Jewish merchants were able to develop London into Europe's leading centre in the diamond trade.[10] Similarly, it is clear that merchants belonging to London's Dissenting community favoured involvement in certain trades, and during the 1690s there was a very strong and disproportionate link between Dissenters and the colonial sugar and tobacco trade.[11] Nowhere, however, was the cosmopolitan nature of English commercial activity more clearly evident than in the Anglo-Dutch commodity trade where, by the early years of the eighteenth century, English merchants accounted for only 30 per cent of all those involved. Huguenots comprised 28.5 per cent of the total, Jews 21 per cent, the Dutch 13 per cent and Germans 7.5 per cent. This situation had arisen, for a variety of reasons, from Dutch capital flowing into the English commodity trade, and this had helped to restructure the North Sea trade in general. Not only did this investment serve as a forerunner to later Dutch and Huguenot investment in the National Debt but, more importantly, it also helped to free English capital from the 'old' trade and allow for its redeployment in the Atlantic economy.[12] In this way, patterns of social and cultural diversification within the small merchant elite of London played a decisive part in the dynamic processes of expansion within the British overseas empire.

Beyond London, the diversification of economic enterprise, the broadening of commercial horizons, the growth of the outports and a shift of resources away from Europe to the wider world all combined to help the development of important links between British provinces and the overseas empire. Early on in the period, groups of landowners and merchants in Scotland combined in various projects designed to facilitate the establishment of overseas colonies. The ill-fated Darien Company venture to Central America together with settlement schemes in the Carolinas and East Jersey formed one strand in a broad innovative movement embracing agriculture, industry and trade, but they also represented an attempt to secure a Scottish presence in the wider world.[13] These colonizing ventures ultimately met with varying degrees of success, but they heralded the beginning of an enduring and broadly based Scottish interest in overseas investment and settlement. At the same time, Scottish merchants, like some of their provincial English counterparts, carved out a position of the greatest influence within the Atlantic trading world. Just as Bristol and Liverpool were more heavily committed to the slave trade than London was by the 1740s, so Glasgow was mounting a serious challenge to London as Britain's main centre of tobacco importation by the 1770s.[14] As this occurred, Scottish merchants brought their own distinct methods and forms of organization to British overseas trade.[15] London managed to maintain her position of overall commercial supremacy in Britain, but the rise of the outports demonstrated that more than one major commercial bridge had been built between the metropolis and the colonies by the mid-eighteenth century.

Provincial associations with overseas markets were not limited to commercial links between the outports and the Atlantic economy. They were based upon the development of a broad range of social and cultural connections between the core and the periphery of the empire. Trade was supplemented by the regular exchange of information, ideas and personnel, while the whole process was reinforced by family, kinship and religious ties. Thus, there are numerous examples of Scots at the periphery giving business to the merchant community of their

mother country.[16] Similarly, Quaker merchants operating out
of Bristol and Liverpool, as well as London, established important trading links with their religious brethren in North
America, most notably those who had settled in Pennsylvania.[17] This enabled them to develop a position of some importance in the transatlantic commercial world, and when Quaker
merchants from London and Bristol decided to emigrate many
of them were attracted to Philadelphia where they were able
to establish themselves with some success alongside their co-
religionists.[18] In sum, much of the trade carried out in Britain's name was developed and directed by individuals belonging
to one of several important non-English domestic merchant
communities.

The reconstruction of the imperial core has important implications for our understanding of the nature of the relationship between the metropolis and the overseas empire. All too
often, although much less so in recent years, the core of the
empire has been portrayed by imperial historians as displaying
the features of an homogeneous society and culture, with the
dominant and undiluted values and characteristics of the south
of England being held to be representative of the greater whole.
The processes underpinning the relationship between the core
and the periphery of the overseas empire are thus sometimes
seen largely as an extension of the processes defining the relationship between the core and the periphery of the British
Isles. The social and cultural forces emanating from London
are held to have affected the colonies in much the same way
as they affected the outlying provinces of Britain itself.[19] Yet
although, as we have seen, the process of anglicization was
indeed beginning to transcend ethnic and cultural boundaries
in Britain and beyond, distinct and powerful national and
regional characteristics and traditions still existed within metropolitan society. These were brought to bear on the imperial
process in a number of different ways, and they came to represent an important strand within British imperialism as the
provinces of the core began to establish their own direct links
with the overseas empire.[20] This ensured that diversity increasingly played its part in offsetting any uniformity that may have
existed within the social and cultural spheres of the British
imperial experience. It meant that instead of there being only
one significant core–periphery connection, that based upon

London's relationship with the wider world, there were multifarious links connecting different parts of the periphery to different parts of the core.[21]

The importance of relationships between metropolitan province and colonial province in helping to forge cultural links between the colonies and the mother country has recently been explored in a distinguished contribution to the debate about the development of identity within the wider British imperium during the eighteenth century. Ned C. Landsman has drawn attention to the way in which positive aspects of life in the provinces (in this case Scotland) were seen in some quarters as embodying 'piety, virtue (in several senses of that term), and Reformed religion, as well as liberty, innovation, and growth'. The (English) metropolis, on the other hand, was often depicted as being corrupt and stagnant, and the provinces could at times be identified as the 'moral centre and the most dynamic sector of the British empire'. This enabled those living, working and thinking in Scotland to develop their own outlook on matters related to commerce, empire and identity. It was an outlook that was both provincial and transatlantic in scope, and it manifested itself in the development of distinct strands of thought related to the expansion, improvement and organization of the British empire.[22]

Such thought was often brought directly to bear on some of the overseas societies developing within the Atlantic empire. In Philadelphia, for example, commercial connections facilitated the export of books, journals, newspapers and people from Scotland. Scottish teaching had a direct influence on the development of education in the city, and plenty of Philadelphians visited Scotland or were educated there. This illustrated that some of the key elements of Scottish Enlightenment thought were enthusiastically embraced by members of the Philadelphia elite who were attracted by notions of improvement, moderation and modernity.[23] Other distinct, and quite different, forms of Scottish thought were strongly represented within the constellation of British attitudes that were developing towards the empire and imperialism in general.[24] Bearing this in mind, it is important to stress that metropolitan attitudes towards the empire did not represent a set of monolithic ideas, values and assumptions. Of course, this had never been the case, but the opening up of the empire to individuals drawn from across Britain, and beyond, increasingly meant that British imperialism was a construction based upon much more than ideas developed within a narrow English political and social context. Overseas activity helped to give expression to several different strands of thought and tradition, and it reflected all the complexities and cross-currents evident in British society itself. By 1750, not all British connections with the wider world were passing through a social and cultural filter provided by London and the south east of England. During the course of the first half of the century, there had been a shift away from London as the all-powerful engine of commercial and imperial growth and, as other centres of dynamic activity had emerged, they had brought their own methods, ideas and cultural traditions to bear on the process of imperial expansion.

DIVERSITY AT THE PERIPHERY

Alongside the various processes of anglicization occurring in all of Britain's overseas communities there were a number of powerful forces which were simultaneously serving to reduce the strength of Englishness at the periphery of the empire. These demographic and cultural forces not only redefined the worlds in which the overseas elite moved, but they also helped to open up the highest echelons of colonial hierarchies to individuals drawn from across Great Britain and beyond. Linda Colley has noted that Celtic elites were playing a full part in the making of the 'unified and genuinely British ruling class' that emerged in Britain after 1760. These individuals were also becoming increasingly prominent at the periphery of the empire. Irish, Welsh and, most notably, Scottish adventurers and men of talent were still often denied opportunity and advancement at home, but they were able to make their way with conspicuous success at the outer margins of the empire.[25]

This opening up of the empire to those drawn from across Great Britain was to a large extent born out of necessity. In the economic sphere, for example, the labour needs of the Atlantic colonies could only be met by large numbers of migrants and imported slaves. At the same time, a state under military threat, as Britain was throughout the eighteenth century, cannot afford to be selective about the nationality of those enlisted for armed service. P.J. Marshall has recently outlined the extent to which, by 1760, the British armed forces had become dependent upon Highlanders and the Irish, not to mention colonial Americans, American Germans and vast numbers of Indian sepoys.[26] The creation of this multinational military organization not only helped to play a part in bringing the Celtic nations into the British state by drawing them together in joint overseas enterprises against a common enemy, but it also superimposed a form of British identity over those national and regional loyalties which had hitherto served only to highlight division and conflict within British society. As this process occurred, the empire ceased to be an English empire and it became more fully a British empire.

Beyond the context provided by those undertaking short-term service at the periphery of the empire, it is also clear that changing patterns of migration and settlement helped to alter the ethnic composition of the societies in all Britain's overseas colonies during the eighteenth century. At the most basic of levels, the empire ceased to be dominated in numerical terms by those of English origin, and the Scots, Irish and Welsh made their mark in all quarters. The American colonies, for example, became far more cosmopolitan because of a move away from a pattern of immigration that in its first stages had been based largely upon settlers from England. In particular, the development of the Middle Colonies (Delaware, New Jersey, New York and Pennsylvania) and the Lower South (North and South Carolina) after 1650 was shaped by an influx of settlers from a wide range of ethnic backgrounds, which gave them a cultural and social diversity unknown in New England and the Chesapeake.[27] This trend continued into the eighteenth century.

Even when reproduction became the dominant factor for population expansion in the American colonies, the influx of newcomers still played a central role in determining the distribution and composition of society in different regions.[28] The most recent detailed calculations suggest that between 1700 and 1775 about 585,000 immigrants found their way to the thirteen North American colonies, with just under half that number coming from Africa as slaves.[29] There were 84,500 immigrants from Germany, and those from Ireland amounted to 108,600.[30] The pattern of immigration from mainland Britain showed quite a marked change from that evident during the seventeenth century, with settlers from England (44,100) representing a minority of 40.7 per cent. Scottish and Welsh settlers (perhaps as many as 35,500 and 29,000 respectively) made up the total. The rates of immigration from Scotland, slow and uneven before 1763, quickened significantly towards the end of the period, with over 20,000 colonists leaving their homeland for North America between 1768 and 1775. In cultural terms, the steady and increasing stream of new arrivals led to change in even long-established areas of English settlement where alternative forms of language, religion and tradition were introduced. These alternatives did increasingly have to be acknowledged and, as Bailyn has observed, the process of 'hybridization' was evident 'everywhere south of New England – and in New England too, to a lesser extent, after the mid-eighteenth century'.[31]

Of course, colonists of British origin did have some basic common characteristics because most of them used the English language, belonged to Protestant religious orders and adhered to British notions of law, liberty and justice. This should not be taken, however, to mean that a uniform set of values, ideas and assumptions were being bequeathed to the colonies by the mother country. For, as scholars such as Bernard Bailyn, David Hackett Fischer and Jack Greene have recently pointed out in different ways, patterns of emigration and settlement exerted a fundamental influence on the development of important regional differences within North American society.[32] In particular, movements of people from different parts of the mother country continued to have a considerable effect upon the making and remaking of all colonial societies during the eighteenth century.

Through adopting a long-term perspective, identifying four waves of immigration between 1620 and 1775 and linking each movement of people to an exodus from a particular region of Britain, David Hackett Fischer has attempted to demonstrate that by 1775 cultures had been established in Massachusetts, Virginia, the Delaware Valley and the Appalachian backcountry that were quite distinct. Not only did the inhabitants display different attitudes towards religion, social status and wealth, but they spoke their own dialects, built their houses in different styles and conducted their everyday lives in different ways. Although Fischer has been criticized for seeking out contrasts rather than similarities between colonial societies, and for understating the hybrid nature of many communities, his work serves as a useful reminder that the environment in which elites settled and developed varied quite significantly from region to region. His work also illustrates that immigrants were drawn from a wide range of social and cultural backgrounds in Britain. For, like Bailyn in his detailed studies of immigration between 1773 and 1776, he has emphasized the extent to which groups of settlers drawn from different regional backgrounds and cultural traditions in Britain moved into particular American colonies or regions. This meant that no simple, uniform pattern of settlement and expansion developed, but it also ensured that very different types of regional elites came into being during the various stages of the settlement process. These elites then attempted to replicate the social and cultural arrangements that had prevailed in their particular part of the mother country in their new surroundings. Thus, the gentleman planters of the Virginia tidewater area, whose origins were often to be found in the upper ranks of society in the south and west of England, were quite distinct in many respects from the Quaker elite of the Delaware Valley who belonged to, or were descended from, the wave of immigrants who arrived from the North Midlands and Wales between 1675 and 1725. The Quaker elite in turn had little in common with the 'North British' elite who established a cultural and political ascendancy in the backcountry in the wake of the great wave of immigration from Scotland, Ireland and the North of England between 1725 and 1775. These important differences and distinctions suggest that, whether one agrees with Fischer or not on the central issue of the successful replication of metropolitan regional cultures in the colonies, it can no longer be tenable to use only the term 'anglicization' to characterize the transfer of cultural and social values from the mother country to North America during the course of the eighteenth century. The process of transferance from core to periphery embraced an infinite variety of metropolitan cultural forms, and a wide range of interactions with indigenous and other European cultures helped to produce a colonial society of immense diversity and complexity.[33] Pursuit of the gentlemanly ideal bestowed some common characteristics upon elites in all colonies, but the ideal proved sufficiently flexible to allow for the development of distinct features within the upper echelons of different regional societies. At one level, individuals often displayed some of the defining qualities of the English gentleman, while at another level they retained important elements from their social and cultural backgrounds.

THE CELTIC DIASPORA AND SCOTTISH ENTRY INTO THE OVERSEAS ELITE

Changing patterns of immigration and settlement affected the ethnic composition of elites in all Britain's overseas colonies during the course of the eighteenth century. Indeed, by the 1760s overseas elites were no more 'English' than were many metropolitan elites, and those governing, directing and defending the empire at the periphery had developed into a remarkably diverse and cosmopolitan range of individuals. In part, this weakening of English cultural hegemony within the upper echelons of overseas societies occurred because of the ongoing process of creolization that was taking place in the colonies. At the same, continued emigration from Britain ensured that the base of colonial elites was progressively extended during the course of the century before 1775.

During the early days of settlement, the process of immigration helped to create and renew founding elites in North America.[34] Later on, newcomers could acquire wealth, status and political power in such a way that they could move quite rapidly to the highest echelons of colonial society in even long-established regions. A study of 91 Philadelphia merchants during the third quarter of the eighteenth century has revealed, for example, that a third were immigrants. Their presence in the city was reinforced by second- or third-generation settlers who had been successful enough to carve out a position for themselves within the city's political and social elite.[35] Even in some parts of the Chesapeake, where inheritance and marriage played an important part in creating tight-knit elites based on wealth accumulated over several generations, about one-sixth of the richest men were immigrants in both 1733 and 1776.[36] Rapid upward social mobility was possible in most

American colonies, and incomers, from other colonies as well as the mother country, posed a wide range of challenges to existing elites through their different outlooks, attitudes and assumptions.[37]

Celts, and Scots in particular, were at the forefront of those seeking to move into the upper echelons of colonial societies. As far as the Scots were concerned, this was part of the general trend which saw large numbers of them taking advantage of the opportunities for career advancement that had presented themselves in England and the wider world after the Act of Union.[38] As Linda Colley has recently pointed out, it was still quite difficult as late as 1780 for Scots to find their way into the offices of state in London, but the army and the empire offered them plenty of openings.[39] Thus many Scots, unlike their English counterparts, saw overseas service and settlement as a means of escape from limited prospects and harsh economic conditions at home.[40] During the 1720s, Daniel Defoe had drawn attention to the extent to which such an escape was taking place, and he had offered the opinion that if it continued for much longer a colony such as Virginia 'may rather be called a Scots than an English plantation'. As the detailed figures reveal, there was more than a grain of truth in this comment. Defoe believed that this extraordinary concentration of Scots in the British North American colonies was partly because Scots made much better settlers than the English. He also pointed out that the general attitude towards emigration was quite different north of the border. In Scotland there was no need for those operating settlement schemes to rely upon 'the scandalous art of kidnapping, making drunk, wheedling, betraying, and the like', as was the case in England. Instead Defoe could point to 'the poor people offering themselves fast enough, and thinking it their advantage to go; as indeed it is, to those who go with sober resolutions, namely, to serve out their times [as indentured servants], and then become diligent planters for themselves'.[41] For those drawn from the middling and upper ranks of Scottish society, the empire presented opportunities for them to secure the fortune that could make them comfortable and secure. Some would enjoy this comfort at the periphery, but many others sought to use their careers in the colonies as a means to improve their position and standing in the Old World.[42] By enthusiastically taking up the challenges posed by emigration and overseas service, the Scots were able to find a place for themselves within the wider British community, and within the wider British elite. In doing this, they brought their own distinct blend of culture, tradition, education and outlook to the British overseas elite.

Details of entry into colonial elites by immigrants in general, and by Celtic immigrants in particular, suggest that luck and marriage played an important part, but settlers also took advantage of established commercial, family and kinship networks of their fellow countrymen.[43] Newcomers with some wealth and good connections often first established.themselves in overseas communities in a professional capacity, and from there they were then able to move into landed society when a suitable opportunity presented itself. For the most successful, rewards could be forthcoming in the form of wealth, influence, high office and even titles.[44] In material possessions alone, though, few Celtic immigrants could match the success of Charles Carroll in Maryland. Following his arrival from Ireland in 1688, he was appointed (albeit briefly) to the middle-ranking post of attorney-general under the patronage of the Proprietor, Lord Baltimore. Although as a Catholic he was then deprived of his post following the Protestant revolt, Coode's Rebellion, in 1689, he managed to make the transition to landowner through marriage in the same year. Following the death of his wife in childbirth in 1690, he remarried to good effect in 1693/4 when he took the hand of the daughter of the colony's most influential Catholic, Colonel Henry Darnall. At his death in 1720, Carroll was not only the most powerful Catholic in the colony and the most significant money-lender, but was also the greatest landowner. He possessed 47,777 acres in total, and the pattern of its acquisition is quite instructive: 26,413 acres were acquired by patent, 13,026 acres through purchase and 12,249 acres through mortgage foreclosure.[45]

Celtic immigrants were also able to climb to the top of the social and political ladder in the West Indies where the ravages of warfare and disease, together with the consequences of further territorial expansion, had combined to produce significant alterations in both the structure and distribution of the white population during the second half of the seventeenth century. Some of the older colonies such as Barbados, St Christopher and Nevis suffered depopulation as conditions took their toll and people sought resettlement in other Caribbean islands and on the American mainland.[46] This meant that in general the West Indies continued to offer plenty of opportunities to migrants from Britain and the Caribbean itself.

Patterns of entry by Celtic immigrants into West Indian elite societies are clearly illustrated by the case of Walter Tullideph who was able to establish himself in landowning circles on the island of Antigua. Like many Scots, he entered Caribbean landed society by first establishing himself in a profession.[47] He began his career in the West Indies in *c.*1726 as a doctor, but later branched out into commercial activity through trading and acting as a correspondent for his uncle, William Dunbar, a sugar factor in London. On the strength of this, he became a money-lender who borrowed at 5 per cent in London and lent locally at 8–10 per cent. His breakthrough into landed society did not come, however, until he acquired an estate of 127 acres when he married a young widow. From there, he embarked on an expansion of his estate which was based upon a variety of financial strategies and, although the scale of his operation was modest in comparison to that of Charles Carroll of Maryland, his plantation had reached 536 acres of land by 1757. Six years later it was valued at £30,000.[48]

Tullideph was not alone in establishing himself as a Scottish landowner in Antigua. Scots represented by far the most important group to establish new landed dynasties on the island after 1707, and they eventually comprised 13 of the 65 leading 'gentry' families that have been identified on the island.[49] Scots also made their mark on St Kitts, but it was Jamaica which provided them with the greatest opportunities. It has been calculated that 485 Scotsmen constituted a quarter of all landholders by 1754, and they owned about the same amount of taxable land on the island. Analysis of personal property inventories reveals that Scots held 40.4 per cent of the value of all goods recorded between 1771 and 1775, and, if the holdings of other nationalities are added to this figure, it appears that English personal property accounted for something less than half the total.[50] Of course, many other less wealthy Scotsmen were also to be found in the Caribbean, and the evidence suggests that they came from a wide variety of backgrounds. They all brought with them, as did the Irish, distinct qualities, characteristics and traditions, and contemporary observers who commented on their industry and education noted that they were in some ways quite different from their English counterparts.[51]

The Scots also made their mark in the east where large numbers of them found their way to India as private traders and servants of the East India Company. Detailed studies of Company appointments reveal a trend in which Scots formed a very high proportion among those entering areas of service which required a 'gentry' family background.[52] Moreover, this was not, as was thought at the time, simply something which coincided with Henry Dundas's appointment as President of the Board of Control in 1785. Although Dundas's position gave him access to a great deal of influence over East India Company appointments, there was a relative decline in benefit to his fellow countrymen after 1784. The Bengal establishment of 1772 illustrated just how large the Scottish contingent within the Company had become. While few Scots found their way, or wanted to find their way, into the Company's army as ordinary soldiers, just under half of those serving as officers or civil servants were from well-to-do Scottish backgrounds. Such figures support the general view that Scots were at the forefront of the members of the British elite who were seeking to make their way in India, and subsequent appointments served only to reinforce this trend. Between 1775 and 1785, 47 per cent of those appointed as writers, 49 per cent of those given cadetships, 60 per cent of those licensed as free merchants and 52 per cent of those who became assistant surgeons in Bengal were Scots. In view of these figures and the continuing Scotophobia that was evident in England, it is hardly surprising that when Edmund Burke sought to inflame public and political opinion against Warren Hastings during the impeachment proceedings, he made much of the fact that Hastings had favoured Scots with appointments during his time in India.

There were a number of reasons for this concentration of Scotsmen in India, and in Bengal in particular. Many of them, like their English counterparts, were attracted by the possibility of amassing a personal fortune in a short length of time. There were relatively few opportunities for members of large Scottish families to support themselves on the land, and it was possible for only a limited number of them to make their way into commerce and trade in Edinburgh and Glasgow where both connections and capital were required. Attention was thus focused on London and the wider world. The East India Company proved itself to be a suitable vehicle for personal advancement because it was free from a number of the constraints and prejudices imposed on Scots by many English institutions. Although, of course, connection and patronage were required for access to the military and civil sections of the Company's service, commissions in the Indian army were free. This factor, together with the military tradition of Highland gentry families, made a career in the Company's army an attractive and realistic proposition for many Scotsmen. Moreover, those seeking entry into the officer corps were assisted after mid-century by the development of a network of Scottish connections within the Company's administrative hierarchy in London. Once the Scottish presence in India had been established, an extended web of patronage, connection and clan obligation was also developed at the periphery, and this operated so successfully that even Scots themselves became conscious of the fact that they might be overexploiting the situation.[53]

THE SCOTS AND THE WELSH: CELTIC IDENTITIES IN THE WIDER WORLD

That Scots retained a strong sense of their own cultural identity at the periphery during the eighteenth century is beyond doubt, but much often depended on the extent to which they managed to remain as a coherent socioeconomic unit within the wider British community. This process was aided by the way in which connections and family ties created networks of patronage and support, which in turn served to draw new settlers and transitory residents to particular regions and colonies. In Canada, there were concentrated areas of Scottish settlement, such as that on Prince Edward Island, which grew from schemes promoted by Scottish landowners such as Sir James Montgomery and Lord Selkirk. Similarly, the establishment of the colony of East Jersey by Scottish investors during the 1690s led to a permanent concentration of settlers from Scotland in the region. This had a profound and distinct effect upon patterns of development in the region and, despite subsequent resettlement and movements of people, those of

Scottish descent represented over a fifth of the population of New Jersey and parts of the middle colonies by 1750.[54] Naturally enough, later migrants were attracted to areas where fellow countrymen had already established a foothold and thus, for example, hundreds of Scots with commercial backgrounds settled in Halifax, Nova Scotia, where a thriving merchant community developed after the 1760s. In such circumstances tight-knit business groups were developed and renewed from the mother country, and it was in this way that a distinct Scottish presence was established in different parts of Canada. A similar pattern developed in the Caribbean, and in Jamaica the Scots were heavily concentrated in particular parishes in the north of the island.[55]

During the early days of colonization, there was of course no single composite form of Scottish identity in the wider world. Distinct characteristics displayed by migrants drawn from different parts of Scotland meant that they adopted different patterns of behaviour from one another when they settled overseas. Those from the Highlands had little in common with those whose roots were in the Lowlands, and diversity within developing metropolitan Scottish societies was reflected in the nature of Scottish overseas communities. In the long term, however, the bringing together of a large number of Scots drawn from a wide variety of backgrounds in a colonial environment could result in the development of a sense of common identity. Such was the case, for example, in central New Jersey where settlers were first unified through political conflict with English colonists and were then drawn together in the 1730s and 1740s through increasing membership of Presbyterian churches.[56] As one authority has argued, many Scots at the periphery, unlike those living in Scotland, found themselves brought into close contact with the English and because of this 'they became more self-consciously Scottish than their countrymen back home.'[57] One manifestation of this was to be found in the way that Scotsmen in all Britain's overseas colonies gravitated towards one another socially, and this played its part in reinforcing their sense of identity and difference. They formed societies such as the North British Society established at Halifax, Nova Scotia, in 1768; they offered a welcome, a safe haven and contacts for new arrivals; they celebrated St Andrew's Day; and they remained loyal to their own educational and, occasionally, linguistic traditions.[58] Not all Scots went as far as the newspaper publisher Robert Wells of South Carolina who during the 1760s, as his son later recalled, 'obliged me to wear a tartan coat, and a blue Scotch bonnet, hoping by these means to make me consider myself a Scotchman.'[59] Nevertheless, a sense of clannishness and common cultural heritage helped to keep Scottishness alive at the periphery.

At times, these close ties based upon kinship and ethnicity helped to make life difficult for Scottish colonists. This was the case in a number of the thirteen colonies, particularly in the Chesapeake where by the eve of the War for Independence Scottish traders had gained an economic stranglehold over the tobacco trade.[60] Many planters found themselves deeply indebted to Glasgow tobacco firms, and they were also dependent upon them for the supply of goods. This fuelled considerable resentment towards Scottish factors, storekeepers and merchants. Although economic dependence was the primary cause of this hostility, Scottish methods and business efficiency, which were seen as being national characteristics, were such that one commentator represented them in bitter terms in the 1770s as 'something like the stinking and troublesome weed we call in Virginia wild onion. Whenever *one* is permitted to fix, the number soon increases so fast, that it is extremely difficult to eradicate them, and they poison the ground so that no wholesome plant can thrive.'[61] One Scot remarked in 1775 that 'A man's being a Scotchman is sufficient to condemn him upon the slightest information. They being looked upon as the greatest enemies to America.'[62] Such sentiment, which in some ways was an extension of mid-century metropolitan prejudice against North Britons, had long manifested itself in outbreaks of tension and conflict between Scots and other ethnic groups at the periphery of the empire, and this only helped to reinforce a general sense of Scottish identity and separateness.

The defining characteristics of Scottish identity at the periphery were not fixed in stone when particular settlers arrived in overseas communities. Rather, the Scottish social and cultural presence in the wider world was subjected to a process of ongoing renewal and reorientation through the numerous commercial, family and religious connections that existed between Scotland and the wider world. Such links kept settlers in touch with their homeland, and they also meant that many

Scottish colonists had limited first-hand contact with England, Englishmen and the various agents of English influence. This is precisely what the founders of the Scottish colony of East Jersey had tried to ensure in the 1690s,[63] and Scots everywhere during the eighteenth century retained contact, to varying degrees, with a metropolitan province rather than with the imperial core. This meant that colonists often lived in a cultural, economic and social environment that was shaped by patterns of development extended from a Scottish society that contained sectors and regions that were both innovative and dynamic. That society might in itself have been shaped by anglicization, but it nevertheless exerted upon the colonies influences that were often quite different from those emanating from south of the border. In the realms of commerce, education, medicine, political thought and religion, the Scottish connection between the core and the periphery of the British empire brought distinct patterns of development to bear on colonial societies.[64]

Unlike the Scots, the Welsh did not make a mark in India during the eighteenth century. A few individuals such as Sir William Jones, the distinguished linguist who founded the Asiatic Society of Bengal in 1784, became important figures, but on the whole the Welsh concentrated their energies and attention on the Atlantic empire, and on North America in particular.[65] In North America, Welsh settlers, like their Dutch and German contemporaries, were not able to resist the pressures which brought them into contact with the English-speaking world in the public sphere. The settlers in the Welsh Tract of Pennsylvania were, for example, unable to realize their dream of being left alone to 'decide all controversies and debates amongst ourselves in a gospel order, and not to entangle ourselves with laws in an unknown tongue.' They protested that officialdom denied them the cultural and linguistic freedoms they had enjoyed in Wales where 'all causes, quarrels, crimes, and tithes were tried and wholly determined by officers, magistrates, [and] juries of our own language, which were our equals.'[66] But although the colonial authorities decreed that many Welsh-speakers would be obliged to become entangled with the 'unknown tongue' of the English, some monoglot Welsh communities survived well into the eighteenth century.

The use of Welsh was preserved through everyday talk in the home and, in response to demand from congregations, religious services continued to be conducted in Welsh.[67] In addition, many settlers of Welsh origin were to some extent able to stay in touch with their homeland, and this meant that, like Scottish settlers, they were connected with a province of the metropolis and not with the English imperial core. This was particularly the case with those Baptists and Quakers who, like Scottish Presbyterians, belonged to religious communities which had strong roots in the mother country from where a steady stream of ministers and preachers crossed the ocean to promote spiritual and cultural renewal among the exiles. Other settlers, especially those who had become well established and reasonably affluent, came under the metropolitan influence of the first Cymmrodorion Society. Although the Society was located in London, and therefore operated in a context one step removed from the Principality, it nevertheless endeavoured between 1751 and 1787 to strengthen cultural ties between Wales and America. In the colonies themselves, the need among settlers to retain a sense of distinct identity was also met by organized groups. In Philadelphia, where a few Welsh-language books were published, the Society of Ancient Britons was established in 1729 and St David's Day was celebrated at an annual banquet at The Tun tavern.[68] This helped to provide an important cultural focal point for the sizeable number of Welsh settlers in the region. That such efforts to sustain Welsh identity in the colonies met with at least some degree of success may be inferred from the comment of one observer in 1763 who spoke of the need to anglicize the Pennsylvanian Germans in order to prevent them 'from becoming a separate body and using a separate language, like the Welsh'.[69]

The Scottish and Welsh presence in the British overseas empire underlined the extent to which that empire had become markedly more diverse in ethnic and cultural terms during the course of the eighteenth century. The provinces of the British mainland had managed to establish positions of varying degrees of influence within the dynamic processes of settlement and expansion in all areas of overseas activity. But the bringing to bear of distinct Celtic traditions and patterns of behaviour on the development of the empire did not mean that Scotsmen and Welshmen perceived their long-term interests to be any different from their English neighbours'. As the American colonies moved towards independence, a wide variety of factors determined loyalty or opposition to the Crown, but separation from England in the cultural or economic sphere did not lead necessarily to separation in political terms. Indeed, many Scots in North America proved to be fiercely loyal towards the established metropolitan order when it was threatened after 1775. Although Scottish merchants in the colonies were at the forefront of those seeking conciliation between Britain and America during the 1760s and 1770s, many Scots at both the core and periphery joined those defending the established imperial order when armed conflict eventually broke out in 1775. In a sense, of course, they had little choice because they perceived that their economic interests were threatened by American independence, but, in an atmosphere of mounting hostility towards them, their loyalty to the Crown also reflected that the empire had helped them to secure a prominent place for themselves within the wider British elite. This needed to be defended and protected.[70]

The main characteristics of the empire – religious toleration, political liberty, economic diversity and opportunity, the establishment of dual identities, and the elite social cohesiveness provided by the gentlemanly ideal – were all flexible enough to allow for the relatively smooth development of the empire into a multinational, multicultural entity during the first half of the eighteenth century. The empire could mean all things to all (white) men, and no one was excluded, even at the highest levels. This was of the greatest importance as a new imperial order emerged, and as Britishness replaced Englishness as the empire's central defining characteristic. By 1760, the cultural, ethnic and social contours of the overseas empire were, like those of the mother country itself, quite different from the ones that had existed in 1688.

8 Enterprise and Expansion: Drawing a Line

For much of the half-century or so before 1750, strong bonds of common interest and identity existed between various elites within different parts of the British empire. There are numerous examples of colonists falling out with their metropolitan brethren over a wide range of economic and political issues, but it is nevertheless clear that many attitudes, assumptions and ideals at the periphery were broadly similar to those in the metropolis. This played an important part in acting as a cement within the social and economic structures that held the empire together. Gradually at first and then with gathering pace, however, the relationships between elites were redefined. As this happened, individuals at the core and the periphery began to reappraise their position within the broader imperial scheme of things, and this inevitably affected their sense of identity, loyalty and self-interest. These shifts in position played an important part in fuelling the general crisis that afflicted the empire during the 1760s and 1770s. This crisis, which all too often is located in a narrow North American context, had several defining characteristics which affected British India as well as the Atlantic empire. The existence of two parallel chronologies of crisis is not a coincidence because they belonged within the same broad developmental framework. What happened in North America between 1763 and 1776 had its own distinct political and constitutional agenda, but many of the general issues were much the same as those that underlaid the problems that beset the Anglo-Indian imperial relationship at almost precisely the same time.

ENTERPRISE AND LIBERTY

Imperial expansion, the development of government finance and the creation of the modern state had opened up a broad

171

range of opportunities to individuals at both the core and the periphery of the empire. Those with an enterprising spirit and eye for the main chance had been swift to take advantage of these opportunities. Elites everywhere had used British activity in the wider world to diversify and extend the range of their economic endeavours, and their lifestyles and patterns of behaviour were defined to a considerable degree by a commitment to improvement and expansion. For the most part, and notwithstanding their place within broad systems of regulated trade, these developments had been allowed to follow a course which had seldom been determined by effective statutory control, regulation, government intervention or metropolitan supervision. As far as most individuals were concerned, the hands of the authorities played little part in restraining business, commerce and investment.

Metropolitan commentators often argued that the empire had developed under a loose rein, and that to adjust this state of affairs would run the risk of threatening future peace and tranquillity.[1] Indeed, political liberty and flourishing commerce were held to be synonymous with one another, and before the middle of the eighteenth century it was widely feared that any coercion or use of arbitrary power by the metropolitan authorities would threaten the growth and prosperity of the colonies.[2] These fears translated themselves into a general belief, deeply rooted in 'country' ideology, that colonists should be able to enjoy the liberties of Englishmen, and in practical terms this meant that they should be allowed freedom in both a constitutional and an economic sense. Parliament displayed a willingness to legislate on a wide range of colonial matters during the first half of the century, but most of this action was designed to reinforce the position of the mother country within the broader imperial economy.[3] Within the economic framework provided by these measures and the earlier Navigation Acts, colonies were able to determine the course of their own economic growth and development. There was very little routine interference from the authorities in London, and it was left to colonial governments to take the lead in providing the conditions necessary for the promotion of private enterprise and economic expansion.[4] The same applied in the Asian sphere of British operations. The state had created and developed the East India Company in an institutional sense, but little attention had been paid to how the Company conducted its overseas affairs. In practice, Company servants were not answerable to anyone other than directors and stockholders, and the way in which the British conducted themselves in India was not subjected to review and supervision by the political authorities in London.

From a metropolitan perspective, these arrangements meant that although the growth of the empire was ultimately being directed towards serving Britain's needs and interests, those at the periphery were at liberty to exercise considerable control over their own individual and collective destinies. In the Atlantic empire, this relationship was reflected in the way that Parliament dealt with issues of general concern, while colonial legislatures exercised control over local matters. This state of affairs suited the mother country and the colonies themselves and, although there were problems and crises from time to time, the political relationships between Britain and her Atlantic colonies were largely based on consent and cooperation. This, however, was essentially a practical arrangement born out of the necessity of making the empire work in everyone's interests, and it had not been codified or defined in a formal sense. As has been pointed out by Jack P. Greene, there was no fully formed, widely recognized 'imperial constitution' to give a sense of permanent shape and form to the empire. Instead, colonists found themselves located in a political and economic situation that was in effect determined by the existence of three different and overlapping sets of constitutional arrangements: one was provided by the mother country, one had been established by individual colonies and one was slowly emerging within a broad imperial context.[5] This was acceptable and workable at a time when British ministers displayed little interest in imperial affairs, but it was to prove to be a source of great tension and misunderstanding when attempts were made to redefine, or define for the first time, the precise nature of the relationship between the colonies and the mother country during the 1760s.

In some ways, a British imperial economy based upon loose central control over enterprise, diversification, innovation, risk taking and speculation contained the seeds of its own destruction. The expansion that formed an integral part of that enterprise culture could only go so far before it began to threaten the broader interests of the state that had spawned it in the first place. When this point was reached there would almost inevitably have to be a reassessment of the direction that was being taken by British overseas activity. That point was reached during the years following the end of the Seven Years' War when the opening up of new imperial horizons obliged many to give serious thought for the first time to lines of future imperial development. Most informed contemporaries were agreed that the old prewar scheme of arrangement was entirely unsuited to the nation's postwar imperial concerns and needs.

CHANGING PERCEPTIONS OF EMPIRE

The restructuring of relationships between Britain and her colonies that occurred during the 1760s and 1770s was prompted by significant changes in metropolitan attitudes towards the overseas empire. A growing awareness of the empire and the nation's role in the wider world, together with a much better understanding of the dynamics of Britain's rise to great power status, helped to focus an increasing amount of attention on the direction being taken by British overseas activity. As this happened, it became clear to many in Britain that it was no longer appropriate for imperial endeavour to be conducted within a loose and ill-defined framework of operations. Indeed, such a state of affairs was not only held to pose a serious threat to the future stability and security of the empire, but it also seemed likely to undermine the status and position of the mother country itself. The informal ties that had held the empire together during the first half of the century were no longer deemed to be a sufficient representation of the imperial relationship, and a wide range of metropolitan policy initiatives sought for the first time to bring shape and structure to key areas of British overseas activity.

Warfare in the 1740s, success in North America and growing command of the seas had all acted as catalysts within the processes which served to draw together and develop a far-reaching imperial ideology in Britain. This ideology was based in large part upon the notion that Britain's interests were best served by detachment from Europe and the adoption of what one historian has aptly described as 'aggressive commercial expansion'.[6] The colonies, and the trade and resources they brought to the nation, were increasingly identified as key elements within the factors that had contributed to the making of Britain as a great power. In the early part of the century, the importance of the empire had been defined primarily in terms of the military and strategic benefits it brought to the nation, but by the 1750s commercial considerations had assumed a much greater significance in the eyes of many observers.[7]

The web of imperial trade and finance had become such a tangled one, and Britain's overseas possessions contributed so much to national wealth, that it was widely believed that the consequences of the loss of any of those possessions would now be disastrous. As the Earl of Halifax remarked in the House of Lords in 1755, if North America was 'exposed to the ravages of the French, a national bankruptcy would probably in a very few years ensue'.[8] In the event, war against France in America did not bankrupt the nation, but the prosecution of a successful global campaign against the French during the Seven Years' War did serve to increase the National Debt from £74 million in 1756 to £133 million in 1763.[9] Although the nation was able to cope with the financial strains of war, the impact that crisis in the overseas empire might have on the City of London was still widely feared, as the London merchant Barlow Trecothick reminded the House of Commons in 1766. When asked in Committee to speculate on the effect that the loss of North America would have on the stock market, he answered in blunt terms: 'A very fatal one.'[10] Such fears were realized three years later when the misreporting of a series of events in India led to the widespread belief that the East India Company had suffered a series of damaging reverses at the hands of the French and Haidar Ali of Mysore. Speculators and stockjobbers took advantage of this reversal of imperial fortunes by fuelling a panic in the financial markets which led to the collapse of East India Company stock prices and the ruination of many prominent investors. Some contemporaries likened the events of May 1769 to the bursting of the South Sea Bubble in 1720 and, while there is no doubt that events were manipulated by unscrupulous elements in the City, the episode served to illustrate the extent to which domestic financial stability now depended upon peace and good order at the periphery. Ministers and politicians now recognized that they could ignore the empire at their peril.

Not only was there a steady general advance in the importance attached by contemporaries to the possession of colonies, but there were also significant changes in the way Britons viewed different parts of their overseas empire. Most notably, the 1740s and 1750s saw marked changes in British perceptions of North America. The context for this change was provided by war against France, and several historians have commented on the extent to which the press represented the capture of Louisbourg and the acquisition of Cape Breton in 1745 as a golden commercial opportunity that could not be ignored.[11] Indeed, some historians have argued that the events of 1745 represent a key moment in the development of British attitudes towards their overseas possessions because they led to a decisive shift in the focus of overseas attention from the West Indies to North America.[12] Thereafter, the French threat ensured that the American colonies remained uppermost in the minds of those with an interest in overseas affairs, and the fact that North America became an important sphere of military operations between 1754 and 1763 meant that this continued to be the case.[13] As one authority has remarked, the 'single most important' result of the Seven Years' War was 'the vivid enhancement of awareness on both sides of the Atlantic of the crucial significance of the [American] colonies to Britain both economically and strategically.'[14] Members of Parliament who tackled the problems of empire might have had little detailed knowledge of life and conditions in British America,[15] but few informed contemporaries could have doubted that great wealth and other advantages were being brought to the mother country by the possession of overseas colonies.[16]

British activity in India took rather longer to impress itself on metropolitan consciousness. When it did, the fears and emotions that were aroused served to call into question the role and purpose of the East India Company in its administrative and political capacity on the subcontinent. Britons spent much more time pondering about the nature and purpose of the British activity in India than they ever did about North America or the West Indies. It has been argued that the Third Mysore War (1789–92) can be seen as the first occasion when the defeat of an Indian opponent (Tipu Sultan) by the British was seen as a 'national' objective,[17] but for some time before that well-informed sections of metropolitan society had been rejoicing at the steady advance of British influence and power on the subcontinent. Although successes such as Clive's victory at the Battle of Plassey in 1757 were barely noticed by the London press, things changed quite markedly during the mid-1760s. The press, politicians, Company officials and speculators in India stock all recognized the potential financial benefits that might be forthcoming in the wake of British military and political advances. Beyond the tight-knit political and financial world of London, there were also those who were happy to rejoice about the fact that British superiority had been asserted over European and Indian rivals alike. They celebrated the fact that there had been a significant improvement in the national wealth and an enhancement of Britain's standing in the world.[18]

As awareness of British activity in the wider world started to permeate through the nation's political and print culture, observers began to try and bring a sense of order and coherence to the patterns of advance and expansion they saw occurring in different quarters of the globe. This was not an easy task, not least because British imperialism took several different institutional and organizational forms. Moreover, there were few direct links between the Atlantic empire and the empire of the east. However, as more individuals diversified their interests and became involved in activities in different geographical regions, they became increasingly aware of the need to address issues and problems that transcended imperial boundaries and frontiers. Answers to difficult questions related to sovereignty, trade and revenue set in particular regional contexts were found to have implications for developments in other areas. Metropolitan lawyers grappling with questions related to territorial rights found themselves addressing similar problems in different parts of the overseas empire. Not surprisingly, solutions formulated in one context were later applied in cases that arose elsewhere.[19] In the economic sphere, attempts to stimulate sales of East India Company tea were based to some degree upon the development of a market for the product in North America. As is well known, the consequences of this were disastrous because Company tea was eventually dumped into Boston harbour by disaffected colonists, but the strategy illustrated how different parts of the empire might in certain in circumstances be brought into play to serve Britain's broader imperial interests. In the words of the Chairman of the East India Company, Sir George Colebrooke, a 'connexion' could be established between east and west in order to establish one system of trade.[20] This was by no means a universally accepted view, and most problems continued to be dealt with on a short-term *ad hoc* basis, but there were nevertheless several clear signs by the 1760s that the empire was beginning to be perceived in some quarters as an integrated global whole rather than as a series of unconnected administrative or economic units.

EXPANSION, AUTHORITY AND CONTROL

In the world of opportunity and enterprise that had existed before 1750, the metropolitan elite and the overseas elite had for the most part marched to the same general tune. Thereafter, they increasingly began to fall out of step with one another. Part of the reason for this was the same in all areas of British overseas activity: fears about further expansion at the periphery prompted moves towards tighter imperial control from the centre. This caused bitterness and resentment when many of those who operated in the wider world realized that their interests were being threatened and their ambitions thwarted by the actions of the authorities in London. This is not to suggest that Britain's imperial crisis stemmed simply from a clash of economic interests of the type once described by older generations of American Progressive historians, but rather to point to the fact that British imperial activity was reordered in such a way that it threatened to destroy the common outlook and assumptions that had hitherto embraced elites at the core and the periphery of the empire. Many individuals found that for the first time the scope of their interests was being determined by something other than ambition and resources. As the authorities intervened to prescribe areas of activity and fields of endeavour, they weakened the cohesion and unity of the empire they were trying to preserve.

Problems associated with territorial conquest and expansion were not new in 1763, but British success in the Seven Years'

War brought them to the top of the political agenda. Before the 1750s, overseas expansion had been relatively modest in terms of territorial acquisition and control. Of course, the area of North America under British control had grown steadily, if imperceptibly to metropolitan eyes, as settlement and development had pushed back western and southern frontiers, and several peace treaties had bestowed new overseas possessions upon Britain. Nevertheless, any contemporary who coloured in British territory on the world map would have had little sketching of note to do before the 1760s. Extensive territory is not necessarily synonymous with wealth and resources, but although Britain had plenty of valuable possessions scattered around the globe before 1750 she did not have to administer and defend large tracts of land. This state of affairs reflected the fact that, unlike many members of the public, those in positions of authority in London had long sought to avoid territorial acquisition on the grounds that it brought increased costs and responsibilities to bear upon the home government. Ministers were often lambasted by the public for their unwillingness to commit resources to aggressive or expansionist campaigns during times of war, preferring instead to develop a limited 'maritime empire' in which the securing of new possessions in the wider world was determined first and foremost by consideration of the nation's commercial and strategic needs.[21] As Daniel Baugh has recently remarked, 'the controlling idea in Whitehall before 1750 was to hold the costs of imperial defence and administration to a minimum, to keep transoceanic military activity overseas confined, and to fight with and for maritime advantages.'[22]

A decisive move away from a commitment to a limited territorial empire came during the 1760s. First, as part of the Peace of Paris, Britain acquired Canada, and then in 1765 the East India Company was granted control over a large part of northern India. Britain's ability to wage warfare on a global scale, and the success of ministers in organizing the state in such a way that it could cope with the demands of protracted struggle, had been rewarded with two important territorial prizes. In some quarters in Britain, however, the fruits of war were greeted with considerable unease about what the future would hold for the imperial nation. The decision to retain Canada at the peace settlement in 1763 had been preceded and accompanied by a vigorous political and public debate which had focused attention on the whole general question of territorial expansion, imperial security and the relative worth of recent overseas acquisitions.[23] Ultimately, the decision to keep Canada in preference to the Caribbean island of Guadeloupe represented much more than a simple choice between trade or land. Those on all sides were obliged to give careful thought to the complex consequences of the general extension of British influence into new spheres of activity, all of which would, in whatever form they took, have a profound impact on the domestic economy. These issues were kept alive during the postwar years, and discussion took on a new form as reports of the East India Company's military successes of 1763 and 1764 filtered back to Britain. The benefits of conquest and annexation continued to be discussed, but now they were increasingly linked to a range of detailed practical questions related to the subjects of sovereignty, trade and revenue.[24]

Some individuals were carried away by Britain's military success and now saw the nation as being capable of advancing its territorial empire even further. This was the case with some within the East India Company who advocated the seizure of the province of Awadh, and one observer warned that the directors might even be tempted to sanction the conquest of China.[25] Others took the high-minded view that further conquests should be made, in both Asia and North America, in order to extend the benefits of British government and religion to yet more people.[26] Those with a firmer grip on economic and strategic realities saw things quite differently. For although the removal of the threat from Bourbon and native powers had opened up new horizons for individuals who were keen to expand and develop their business interests at, or even beyond, the redrawn frontiers, the same circumstances prompted deep concern among those who recognized the problems associated with the need to administer, control and defend more territory. With the nation staggering under the burden of debt incurred during the recent war, retrenchment was uppermost in the minds of many politicians and officials. For them, one of the most important aspects of the imperial problem was the question of determining how the expansionist process could be halted so that Britain's new position could be consolidated and reinforced. With this process under way, attention could then be devoted to ensuring that the benefits of empire could be brought to bear on the domestic economy. Like many of his contemporaries, Sir George Colebrooke had learned the lessons of ancient history, and he reminded the House of Commons in 1769 that 'By extension of territory the Roman empire was dissolved.' He argued that territorial consolidation was the immediate priority in the nation's overseas affairs, and he urged MPs and ministers 'to try to give a permanency to these acquisitions, and by doing so secure the prosperity of Great Britain.'[27] It was this search for permanency which lay at the heart of British imperial concerns during the 1760s and 1770s. Whereas permanency had previously been based upon informal associations and relationships, there was now perceived to be a need for a new and formal set of regulations to give shape and structure to the overseas empire.

Territorial expansion also raised concern about the types of societies that were now being brought under British control, because a large number of alien people had been drawn into the imperial fold during the 1750s and 1760s. In conjunction with immigration from the Celtic nations, mainland Europe and Africa, this helped further to weaken the numerical position of Englishmen at the periphery. The addition of large numbers of Bengalis and French Canadians served only to confirm to many contemporaries that the empire was no longer composed primarily of free-born, free-living, Protestant Englishmen.[28] This prompted widespread fears that English ideals and attitudes would be corrupted and the body politic would become tainted. Consequently, discussions of Oriental despotism, luxury and vice loomed large in the analyses of those who saw dangers ahead for an ever-expanding imperial Britain.

Fears about the wide-ranging effects of territorial expansion did not of course represent the only area of metropolitan concern about the empire. Issues related to defence, trade, revenue and sovereignty all became interwoven with the land question to form a patchwork of ideas about the nature of the relationship between Britain and her overseas possessions. If few of these ideas were in themselves new, what was new was the fact that during the 1760s they were interconnected in such a way as to produce a distinct general metropolitan stance on imperial affairs. With Britain's imperial position transformed, with perceptions of the empire changing, and with domestic politics in a state of turmoil both inside and outside Parliament, there was a decisive move away from traditional attitudes towards the colonies and overseas possessions. A much harder line was adopted, and arguments which had long stressed liberty and a loose rein for the colonies were replaced by calls for Britain to exert direct supervision and much closer control over the periphery, both in the national economic interest and to prevent the spread of political disorder throughout the Atlantic empire. Contemporaries began to adhere to a much more authoritarian concept of empire, and politicians of different persuasions and backgrounds became convinced of the need for Britain to assert her supremacy. In particular, there was increasingly a refusal to regard the American colonists as anything other than inferior subjects who needed to be kept in their proper subordinate position within the imperial order.[29]

Authoritarian views had, of course, surfaced from time to time in the past, and attempts had been made to secure greater central control over the empire. Many policy initiatives, even if they were rather half-hearted, had emanated from the Lords of Trade in the 1690s and from the Board of Trade in the 1740s and 1750s.[30] Most of these proposed measures for better regulation of British overseas territory and for the centralization of authority had not been translated into action. Nevertheless, they did allow policy guidelines to be drawn up, and precedents to be established, and it was this fund of ideas and proposals that politicians drew on in the 1760s when they attempted to redefine the nature of the economic and constitutional relationship between the colonies and the mother country. In the area of exerting general control over the expansionist process, however, politicians had little or no experience and they could not base action on precedent. Although in the past they had always attempted to avoid the acquisition of territory at the peace table, and although they had regularly warned colonial authorities about the formal annexation of new land, they had never become deeply involved in the precise definition of areas of settlement or trading activity. When they did begin to do this, they encountered stiff opposition from within Britain as well as from within the colonies, and the issue threatened to undermine any emergent authoritarian consensus view on the empire. In attempting to call a halt to expansion, ministers were seeking to control the very forces that had brought growth and prosperity to the empire in the first place, and they were curbing the activities and interests of many of those who had committed finance and resources to British activity in the wider world.

CONTROLLING THE EXPANSIONIST PROCESS: INDIA AND NORTH AMERICA

Developments in India during the 1750s and 1760s highlighted particular concerns among observers who were worried about the unregulated and uncontrolled expansion of British overseas influence. In Company circles, many of those in London argued that the realization of profits for stockholders had become dependent upon an urgent need to promote a programme of consolidation and retrenchment in all areas of overseas activity. Further expansion would jeopardize this by diverting resources away from trade and revenue collection, and this fundamental point was stressed in dispatch after dispatch sent out to India by the Company's directors during the 1760s. Many of those operating at the periphery were, however, attempting to improve their private fortunes with little regard for broader British interests. In doing so, they repeatedly sought out opportunities and took risks in such a way that they were drawn into new areas of activity which sometimes threatened the Company's stability and security. At all times, therefore, there was a need to strike a fine balance between the consolidation of territory and the expansion of trade.

These differences of opinion about the nature and scope of British activity on the subcontinent fed into the debate about the conduct of Company servants in India. The need for moderation and good order in India was repeatedly stressed by those who feared for the Company's future, and 'nabobs' were portrayed as aggressive and greedy individuals whose self-seeking activities not only threatened the Company's well-being but also brought the name of Britain into disrepute. Indeed, such was the general level of concern in Britain about corruption and immorality among the Company's overseas servants that, when the Company proved to be incapable of implementing its own programme of reform, the government was obliged to intervene in order to put a stop to some of the more obvious abuses. In the wake of the House of Commons inquiry of 1773 into Lord Clive's affairs, Parliament decreed that Company servants would no longer be permitted to lend money to, or receive presents from, members of the local population. Most important of all, the involvement of Company servants in private trading activity was prohibited by Lord North's Regulating Act.

The action taken by Parliament against errant East India Company servants represented only one of the areas of Company affairs that the state found itself drawn into during the 1760s and 1770s. The Regulating Act of 1773 was a bold attempt to bring order to the Company's internal affairs, and the reform and regulation of corporate administrative and political procedures formed a central part of a process in which the relationship between the state and the Company was gradually redefined.[31] At the same time, ministers were also trying to develop a much closer supervision of the Company's external affairs in India. In some government quarters, there was deep unease about the fact that the state might be drawn into conflict and war if ambitious British advances in India were reversed and long-standing commercial interests were threatened. India represented a potential weak link in the British imperial system, and ministers could not afford to allow the Company to threaten what had become an important part of the national interest by making rash or injudicious decisions. With the Company making annual payments of £400,000 to the Treasury after the first parliamentary foray into East Indian affairs in 1767, the government had to take a more active role in helping to protect this important source of revenue.

At one level, these concerns manifested themselves in the way ministers responded to the Company's attempts to establish a commercial presence off the coast of north-east Borneo.[32] When the Company dispatched a ship to take possession of the island of Balambangan, the ministry intervened and told the directors in no uncertain terms that such an action was inappropriate because it did not take national strategic considerations into account. At another level, ministers began to exercise a much closer supervision of Company relations with the representatives of other European nations and, as they did this, the lines between foreign and imperial policy became rather blurred. The French, in particular, were held to represent an ever-present threat to the British position in India, and it was believed that they could well disrupt the flow of tribute from India to Britain. Hence, on several occasions during the late 1760s ministers deemed it necessary to remind the Company about the need to keep a very careful eye on French activity in Bengal. Indeed, repeated French attempts to reinforce their position in India culminated in a flurry of diplomatic activity in London and Paris, and caused a brief crisis in Anglo-French relations in 1770.[33]

Ministerial concern about several aspects of the Company's conduct of its external affairs was such that during 1769 Lord Weymouth, the Secretary of State for the South, secured the appointment of a 'ministerial voice' to represent the British Crown in India. The appointment of Sir John Lindsay as Plenipotentiary provoked fierce resistance from the Company who saw, quite rightly, that this would end their diplomatic and political monopoly in the east. In the broader scheme of things, however, Weymouth's actions reflected official concern about the way in which an unregulated commercial organization pursuing expansionist policies might ultimately draw Crown forces into conflict with Asian or other European powers. In view of the the stakes now at risk, such a state of affairs could no longer be tolerated, and the East Indian events of the late 1760s serve to illustrate the depth of concern that had developed about the way in which the expansionist process had developed a momentum of its own in recent years. For the first time, ministers circumvented the Company in order to try and exercise some direct influence on the development of British interests at the periphery, and this marked a small but significant parting of the ways between Crown and Company.

Tension between expansionists and consolidators was also evident in British North America during the 1760s and early 1770s. As far as expansionists were concerned, British success in the war against France had presented them with a wide range of new land-settlement and speculative opportunities in North America. The governor of Massachusetts, Thomas Hutchinson, recalled that before the war 'speculative men had figured in their minds an American empire . . . but in such distant ages that nobody then living could expect to see it . . . But as soon as [the French] were removed, a new scene opened.' With North America dominated by the British after 1763, Hutchinson continued, 'The prospect was greatly enlarged. There was nothing to obstruct a gradual progress of settlement, through a vast continent, from the Atlantic to the Pacific Ocean . . .'[34] Such developments, changing attitudes and extending horizons helped to quicken the pace of land purchase to the point that a leading authority on transatlantic emigration and settlement has written of a 'speculative fever' gripping the Anglo-American world after 1763.[35]

At precisely the same time, however, a wide range of arguments were being deployed against further settlement and colonization in the west. In the early 1760s these arguments held sway to the extent that in 1763, in the wake of the Indian war known as the Pontiac rising, the Grenville ministry moved to prohibit expansion into the interior. It was believed that new areas of settlement would be difficult and expensive to defend and, as had recently been seen, colonists would be drawn into disputes with the local Indian population that could well escalate into war. More generally, it was feared that the growth of new colonies would serve to undermine British economic strength in a number of different ways. Not only would emigration to the colonies depopulate the mother country, but the development of commerce and manufacturing capacity in areas beyond the reach of the metropolitan authorities would weaken Britain's industrial and trading position. Such thoughts lay behind the Royal Proclamation of 7 October 1763 which sought, on a temporary basis, to restrict settlement beyond the watershed of the Appalachian mountains.[36]

Having devised a policy for the west, ministers had to ensure that the new frontier was policed. At the same time, they had also to resist continued pressure for expansion. This was far from easy, not simply because of the need to reduce military costs, but because opinion in Britain and the colonies remained divided over whether or not expansion was a good and desirable thing. This division reached into high political circles and, for much of the time between 1763 and 1775, the policy for the American interior failed to unite cabinets in which individual ministers were often pursuing their own economic interests. Thus, in 1767–8 strong pressure for westward expansion and the establishment of new inland colonies was being exerted from some ministerial quarters, and this was only resisted when the Board of Trade rehearsed some of the long-standing arguments in favour of the limited possession of coastal colonies to support the nation's commercial and strategic needs.[37]

Whatever principles determined the making of official policy in London, ministers could not exercise much direct control over the continued acquisition of inland territory in North America by colonists or anyone else. This problem was no better illustrated than in 1768 when the Superintendent of Indian Affairs, Sir William Johnson, who was deeply involved in land-speculation schemes, negotiated a settlement with Indians, embodied in the treaty of Fort Stanwix, which took the Ohio boundary 400 miles beyond the one that had been authorized by the Board of Trade. This action threatened the proposed withdrawal of army units from the interior, a measure that had been designed as a means of securing economies in military expenditure in the region. However, in a development which neatly illustrated the complexities and cross-currents involved in the question of territorial expansion, cabinet opinion flew in the face of official policy and ministers were reported to have approved Johnson's negotiations, despite strong objections from the American Secretary, Lord Hillsborough.[38]

It was difficult to apply the brake to expansion when forward initiatives came from within the colonies themselves. Those, such as Hillsborough, who were deeply concerned about the acquisition of new territory could do little when presented with a *fait accompli* which was then endorsed by colleagues who took a close personal interest in developments at the frontier. These difficulties were again illustrated when a well-organized group of speculators set about cultivating contacts in high political circles in order to secure support for the Grand Ohio Company which, under the direction of Philadelphia businessman Samuel Wharton, sought to establish the new colony of Vandalia in the Ohio Valley. Wharton's consortium of interested parties represented a powerful alliance between leading public figures in both Britain and the colonies. The weight of opinion behind the project was such that it eventually provoked the resignation of Hillsborough in 1772 after the Privy Council ignored a report from the Board of Trade which had reaffirmed recent official policy on the prohibition of settlement in the interior.[39] In the end, the Vandalia project fell victim to the developing political crisis over general unrest in the colonies, but the fact that ministers had endorsed a scheme which ran counter to the government's policy for the west illustrated the continuing division within metropolitan opinion on the question of expansion. It also illustrated one aspect of the ways in which a wide range of businessmen and entrepreneurs increasingly, and successfully, sought to influence imperial policy-making through extensive lobbying and petitioning activity.[40]

By 1773 official attempts to regulate expansion at the frontier had foundered in the face of considerable pressure from speculators and business interests. This stemmed from the fact that some in London recognized that it was simply not possible to prevent movement into the interior, while others feared that a fixed boundary would reduce scope for speculative and commercial activity at the frontier. In the end, these concerns, which in many cases were fuelled by self-interest, undoubtedly helped to overcome metropolitan unease about the consequences of further territorial expansion in the west. As the American crisis began to break in 1773, investors were preparing to finance another decisive move into the interior, and in doing this they had the approval of a majority of those in positions of political power and influence. Attempts to control the expansionist process had to all intents and purposes been abandoned.

At the same time that some politicians were trying, and failing, to restrict movement into the American interior, they were also attempting to tackle the closely related problem of stemming the flow of people from Britain to the new lands in the west. From a metropolitan perspective, the granting of large tracts of American land to speculators acted as a powerful dynamic in the emigration process, and one Scot wrote of the 'American madness' sweeping the land as the movement of people to new areas of settlement gathered pace. He was not alone, and a wide range of writers and observers, including Dr Johnson, voiced their fears about the 'epidemick' of emigration that was taking place. Although it could be argued that emigration might ultimately help to further the growth of colonial markets for British goods, it was thought, on balance, to have a number of debilitating effects on the domestic economy. Not only was the labour force depleted as agricultural and skilled workers left the country, but those seeking a new life in the colonies took capital with them when they went and many feared that this would help to promote the growth of colonial manufacturing capacity. Emigration had a particularly severe effect in Ireland and Scotland, and even in London itself the weavers of Spitalfields were thought to be leaving in droves for America. Politicians such as Hillsborough were increasingly fearful about the effects that emigration was having upon the domestic economy and society, but they were confronted by a wide range of influential interest and lobby groups who were pressing for official endorsement of ambitious land-settlement schemes which were bound to attract increasing numbers of settlers from Britain.

Again, leading policy-makers often found that their responses to imperial problems were determined to a considerable degree by their own private interests. Hillsborough, for example, was deeply concerned about the depopulation of his own estates in Ireland. On the other hand, his successor as American Secretary, Lord Dartmouth, also expressed concern about the condition of British estates but was one of the most active players in the game of North American land speculation. By 1773, and in spite of conflicting pressures, the issue of depopulation could no longer be ignored. In April, the Privy Council recognized the direct causal link between territorial grants in America and emigration from Britain, and it prohibited the granting of new land while a policy was devised to tackle the problem. The policy that finally emerged in 1774 did fundamentally reshape the way land was distributed, and grants were replaced by public auctions, but at the same time very little could be done to prevent emigrants leaving Britain and the rates of departure from British ports remained little changed.[41] Again, territorial expansion had raised issues and posed questions that metropolitan politicians were unable or unwilling to address in any meaningful way. In practice, the growth of the empire in the west, both in terms of acreage and population, remained largely unchecked.

As attempts to regulate movement into the American interior indicated, there was no straightforward division between metropolitan consolidators and expansionists who operated at the frontiers of the British empire. Many in Britain were divided over the question of territorial expansion, and those pursuing private business interests often clashed with those who were attempting to formulate policy in the wider national interest. There were similar divisions among the overseas elite. In all colonies, and in all spheres of activity, members of the elite held different visions of the future. In North America, some sought to take swift advantage of the opportunities laid before them by Britain's military success. Others feared the consequences of unregulated advances into the interior. They were much more cautious, and saw the development of the colonies taking place within a framework provided by a British empire established on traditional limited territorial lines.[42] Similarly, some in the east saw the East India Company's military and political success as opening the way forward to new areas of individual commercial enterprise, while others, such as Clive, had an eye on the need to maximize corporate trade and revenue collection. They reinforced the directors' concerns about the need to consolidate British interests within limited, and easily defended, frontiers.[43]

Whatever stances individuals adopted on these important issues, few could deny that the metropolitan authorities were no longer prepared to give free rein to those on the spot. There were perceived to be increasing levels of interference in local affairs from the centre, and this ran counter to the long-established tradition by which the metropolis left the conduct of internal matters to individual colonies or, as in the case of India, to trading companies. What had changed was that unregulated enterprise and expansion was now threatening the security and stability of the greater imperial whole. However, this argument cut little ice with those who had long been free to pursue their own business interests in a manner of their own choosing. Not surprisingly, as hardline metropolitan attitudes toward the empire found expression in new policy initiatives, they caused resentment at the periphery and this contributed to the restructuring of relationships between elites that occurred during the 1760s and 1770s.

In the east, the metropolitan authorities had for the most part turned a blind eye to the private business activities of Company servants and military personnel before the 1760s. Private trade and the acceptance of 'presents' from Indians had formed a key element in the making of private fortunes, and this made East Indian service an attractive proposition for many individuals. During the late 1760s and early 1770s, however, the changing climate of opinion in Britain meant that leading figures such as Clive were called to account for activities that had not raised any questions when they had first occurred over a decade earlier. At the same time, much tighter regulation was imposed on those who were on the Company's payroll, first by the Company itself and then by the state.[44] Not only were many observers outraged by the wealth accumulated by 'nabobs', but concern was also expressed about the way in which unfettered enterprise was leading to the 'oppression' of Indians and drawing Britain into new and unwanted areas of activity. These issues provoked fierce debate and a great deal of recrimination as those responsible for shaping the British presence in India found their private affairs being subjected to the closest public and parliamentary scrutiny. Individuals who had once been fêted as heroes were obliged to justify themselves before a political audience whose perceptions of empire had changed and who were no longer prepared to let imperial development take an uncontrolled course.

In a different economic and geographical context, the restrictions on land settlement imposed in North America during the 1760s had an obvious impact on those who were seeking to extend their activities into new areas. Although restrictions were difficult to enforce, and although ministers did not always adhere to their stated policy, several colonists found that their territorial ambitions were thwarted by the new mood of retrenchment and consolidation that held sway in official circles. Hopes were raised in 1763, only to be dashed when it became clear that the metropolitan authorities were not prepared to sanction any scramble for land in the interior. Restrictive British policies could have quite a profound effect upon ambitious individuals, and in some cases thwarted commercial hopes played a part in transforming those loyal to the Crown into leading Patriots. This happened with William Henry Drayton whose plans for land purchases in the interior were rejected by the Council of South Carolina following the intervention of John Stuart, the Superintendent of Indian Affairs.[45] Something similar occurred with Jonathan Bryan in Georgia.[46] Having established an extensive 'plantation empire' in South Carolina and Georgia during the 1750s and 1760s, Bryan's attempts to develop land in territory ceded to Britain by Spain foundered in the face of British refusal to settle disputes in the region. Bryan's frustrations were channelled into efforts to secure land beyond the Proclamation Line in Florida. This represented a challenge to the British authorities, and it helped to draw him towards the Patriot movement after 1769. Like many land-hungry speculators, Bryan refused to accept metropolitan restrictions on his economic activities and he now began to implement different strategies to ensure the continued growth of his interests. Above all, he began to question whether or not membership of the empire was still appropriate for the colonies and men like himself. These cases do not by themselves constitute a cause of the movement towards colonial independence, but they do illustrate the way in which a much more assertive metropolitan policy could alienate individuals who had hitherto been quite prepared to work within a loose business and commercial framework imposed upon them by the British imperial authorities.

Adherence to gentlemanly ideals were to continue to shape the lifestyles of North American elites long after the War for Independence had come to an end, but political and economic circumstances during the 1760s caused resistance to some of the forces promoting anglicization within the colonies. In particular, wide-ranging government policy initiatives raised constitutional fears and prompted considerable political unrest.[47] As a result, colonial protests against metropolitan attempts to establish a new imperial order were expressed in a number of different ways, from boycotts of British goods to attempts to prevent the establishment of an Anglican bishopric in the colonies. Each form of action weakened the informal ties that had previously bound the periphery to the core of the empire, and, at the same time, misunderstanding and suspicion ensured the erosion of any lingering sense of common purpose and identity that might still have existed within the transoceanic elite. As the colonies moved towards independence during the early 1770s, elites increasingly splintered and divided along lines determined by loyalty to the Crown and empire. Events were to demonstrate that broadly similar cultural, economic and social outlooks within different elites were not by themselves enough to prevent political and religious conflict leading to the dissolution of the North American empire.

The expansion of overseas activity had raised fears in Britain which manifested themselves in various attempts to establish a new imperial order based upon the assertion of metropolitan authority. This was seen in several different geographical contexts but, because Britain did not have the means at her disposal to impose her will at the periphery, the establishment of the new order met with mixed results. Not only was it impossible to regulate territorial frontiers effectively, but opposition to these and other financial, political and strategic measures alienated elites and caused general overseas dissatisfaction with the prevailing state of imperial relations and structures. Individuals in all parts of the empire, from North America to India, resisted control from the centre, raised the cry of 'liberty', and proclaimed their rights as free-born Englishmen or Britons. The peculiar nature of the British presence in India was such that the metropolitan authorities were eventually able to bring errant individuals to heel by imposing some degree of legislative control over the East India Company's affairs at home and abroad, although events later in the century were to demonstrate that they could still do little to prevent further territorial expansion at the periphery. No such control could be exerted over the American colonies, however, and Britain found that not even the deployment of considerable military force could keep the colonies within the empire. Attempts to integrate the empire and bind overseas territories more tightly to Britain had thus strengthened control over India but had also played their part in prompting the loss of the American colonies. The efforts that had been made to reinforce informal imperial ties with those of a more formal nature had not been a great success, and the rather clumsy nature of those efforts reveal that there were many in positions of authority in Britain who misunderstood, or perhaps had forgotten, what had given the overseas empire its great inner strength during the first half of the eighteenth century.

Afterword

Although the North American empire collapsed in on itself between 1775 and 1782, the calamitous loss of the thirteen colonies did not signal the end of a particular phase of British imperial development. If anything, such a phase had ended during the 1760s when, for the first time, serious attempts had been made to bring the expansionist process under control from the centre. Of course, the importance of the loss of America cannot be understated because it shook Britain to its foundations and had a profound effect upon economic and political life. However, this trauma did not lead to the emergence of a radically different set of ideas and assumptions about the overseas empire. Instead, lines of development that had become clear in the 1760s were extended and sharpened in the new conditions that prevailed during the 1780s and 1790s. In particular, the authoritarian legacy of the 1760s ensured that the late eighteenth century was characterized by repeated and ever more ambitious attempts to assert government authority over key areas of imperial activity through the 'creation of new institutions of control, coercion, and audit'.[1] Thus, although the development of many of these institutions might be attributed to the consequences of the growth of Britain's imperial power during the French Wars (1793–1815),[2] their lineage can be traced back to the 1760s and 1770s when politicians sought to reorganize the empire without being in possession of the will, expertise and specialist knowledge that was necessary for the translation of authoritarian ideas into effective action. If Britain did ultimately make a decisive move into a 'new imperial age' during the 1790s,[3] this followed the half-hearted and damaging false start that had been made during the 1760s.

Attempts to develop control from the centre represented one of the most important imperial continuities during the period between 1760 and 1820, and another was provided by the further growth and diversification of British business activity in the wider world. Of course, the issue of unregulated private commercial enterprise, which had first prompted the deep concern about territorial expansion that had emerged in the 1760s, still posed a threat to national interests during the 1780s and 1790s. In response to this, politicians endeavoured to curb activities, notably in India, which were likely to lead to serious political and military consequences. Nevertheless, such actions were not allowed to stifle the further development of legitimate private business and commercial activity. In part, this was because it was widely recognized that, thus far, private enterprise had provided much of the inner strength within the processes that had prompted the growth of the overseas empire. Indeed, the central characteristics of the enterprise culture that had been established since 1688 had provided Britain, unlike her European rivals, with the capacity to absorb the loss of an important part of her overseas empire. Some Britons already perceived the empire as a global empire, and a significant number of individuals operated in several different sectors and regions. During the 1780s and 1790s they were well aware of the range of empire-related business and commercial opportunities that were still open to them both in Britain and the wider world. The long-standing willingness of these businessmen to innovate, take risks and develop broad portfolios of investment stood them in good stead as they came to terms with the need to reshape Britain's commercial and imperial system during the final quarter of the eighteenth century.

In the event, Britain managed to retain, and indeed strengthen, many of her business links with North America and the West Indies after 1782 but at the same time new areas of commercial interest and activity were opened up in India, the Middle East, China, Indonesia and South America.[4] Developments at the periphery ensured that the structure and form of the overseas empire would long continue to bear testimony to the strength and flexibility of the gentlemanly ideal and the enterprise culture that had been created in Britain after 1688. At the same time, changes in attitude at home reflected the gathering strength and influence of those who sought to open up the whole of the overseas empire to the full force of private trade and enterprise. Outmoded mercantilist assumptions about the organization and purpose of overseas trade were called into question as the inefficiencies and shortcomings of monopoly trading arrangements were revealed for all to see. The East India Company, which was struggling with its attempts to combine new administrative responsibility with revenue collection

and commercial activity, found that its status and position was
increasingly undermined by those merchants and manufac-
turers from London and the provinces who wished to break its
monopoly in order to gain access to the India trade. By 1813,
the battle was lost and the Charter Act of that year confirmed
the strength of opinion in favour of regulated private enterprise by opening up the Indian (though not the China) trade
to licensed British merchants. Such a development was not
only in tune with the prevailing economic and political thought
of the period, but it also marked a logical extension of the
business conditions and culture that had been established in
Britain and the rest of the overseas empire after 1688.

The crisis of the 1760s and 1770s is usually, and rightly, depicted as exposing many of the weaknesses of the eighteenth-
century British imperial system, particularly those of a political
and constitutional nature located in a context provided by the
North American colonies. Yet the crisis and its aftermath also
revealed the enduring strength of the empire that had been
built before 1760. The empire had already shown that it was
well able to come to terms with significant and potentially
destabilizing shifts in its internal cultural and ethnic balances.
Now it was able to demonstrate that it was also flexible and
durable enough to cope with serious political and military
setbacks. One of the most important reasons for this was that
members of all domestic elites were swift to reveal the full
extent of their commitment to the empire through their refusal to withdraw from overseas activity after 1782. This was
perhaps to be expected in view of their deployment of considerable resources to the periphery of the empire but, although
there was much despair and anguish, there were fews signs of
a sustained crisis of imperial confidence and virtually no voices
were raised against future commitment to national involvement in overseas endeavour. Part of the empire might have
collapsed, but the metropolitan elites who had established the
original structure would now set about using the same foundations and many of the same basic materials to build a new and
rather different imperial edifice.

Notes

The following abbreviations have been used in the notes and bibliography

BH	*Business History*
Econ. Hist. Rev.	*Economic History Review*
HJ	*Historical Journal*
JICH	*Journal of Imperial and Commonwealth History*
WMQ	*William and Mary Quarterly*

Unless otherwise stated, London is the place of publication for all works cited.

CHAPTER 1   HISTORIANS AND THE EIGHTEENTH-CENTURY EMPIRE

1. There is a vast literature detailing the expansion of the empire before 1776. For two recent surveys which examine the Atlantic empire and the empire of the east see Anthony McFarlane, *The British in the Americas, 1480–1815* (1994), pp. 9–251 and Philip Lawson, *The East India Company. A history* (1993), pp. 1–125. For Britain's position in relation to other competing European imperial powers see J.H. Parry, *Trade and dominion. The European overseas empires in the eighteenth century* (1971).
2. See, for example, Lewis Namier, *England in the age of the American Revolution* (2nd edn, 1961), pp. 29–35. The question of stability in its broad political context is discussed in Paul Langford, *A polite and commercial people. England, 1727–1783* (Oxford, 1989), pp. 683–92.
3. B. Bailyn and P.D. Morgan (eds), *Strangers within the realm: cultural margins of the first British empire* (Chapel Hill, 1991), p. 30. See also the similar comments made in P.J. Cain and A.G. Hopkins, *British imperialism: innovation and expansion, 1688–1914* (1993), p. 55.
4. In a purely commercial context see Jacob M. Price, 'What did merchants do? Reflections on British overseas trade, 1660–1760', *Journal of European Economic History*, XLIX (1989), 277. This theme has been pursued by Kenneth Morgan, *Bristol and the Atlantic trade in the eighteenth century* (Cambridge, 1993), pp. 6, 9. For a detailed case-study of a North American region which stresses the importance of the transatlantic dimension in colonial commercial and political life see Richard R. Johnson, *Adjustment to empire. The New England colonies, 1675–1715* (Leicester, 1981).
5. Bailyn and Morgan (eds), *Strangers within the realm*, pp. 8–10. Bailyn and Morgan do not themselves make this claim, but they draw attention (p. 9) to those such as T.H. Breen who do. They also draw attention to an impressive volume of recent work in this area (p. 9, n. 10).

6.   Linda Colley, *Britons. Forging the nation, 1707–1837* (New Haven, 1992).

7.   John Clive and Bernard Bailyn, 'England's cultural provinces: Scotland and America', *WMQ*, third series, XI (1954), 200–13.

8.   See Richard L. Bushman, 'American high-style and vernacular cultures', in Jack P. Greene and J.R. Pole (eds), *Colonial British America. Essays in the new history of the early modern era* (Baltimore, 1984), pp. 345–83. For a detailed elaboration of this theme see idem., *The refinement of America. Persons, houses, cities* (New York, 1992).

9.   The outlines of this important debate can be followed through the following exchanges: Stephen Saunders Webb, 'Army and empire: English garrison government in Britain and America, 1569–1763', *WMQ*, third series, XXXIV (1977), 1–31; Richard R. Johnson, 'The imperial Webb: the thesis of garrison government in early America considered', ibid., XLIII (1986), 408–30; Stephen Saunders Webb, 'The data and theory of Restoration empire', ibid., pp. 431–59.

10. For discussion and references see Chapters 5 and 6.

11. Jack P. Greene, *Pursuits of Happiness. The social development of early modern British colonies and the formation of American culture* (Chapel Hill, 1988), passim (quotation on p. 171). For parallels between the development of British settler communities in Ireland and those in the wider Atlantic world see Nicholas Canny, *Kingdom and colony. Ireland in the Atlantic world, 1560–1800* (Baltimore, 1988), pp. 105–6, 113–14, 124–7.

12. Reflecting this important historiographical trend, these themes were discussed at the 63rd Anglo-American Conference of Historians at the Institute of Historical Research, University of London in July 1994. The conference was devoted to consideration of 'The formation of the United Kingdom'.

13. Colley, *Britons*. For the integration of imperial themes into domestic culture and political ideology see Kathleen Wilson, 'Empire of virtue: the imperial project and Hanoverian culture, *c.*1720–1785', in Lawrence Stone (ed.), *An imperial state at war. Britain from 1689 to 1815* (1994), pp. 128–64.

14. J.C.D. Clark, *The language of liberty, 1660–1832. Political discourse and social dynamics in the Anglo-American world* (Cambridge, 1994), pp. 10–13.

15. See, for example, Bailyn and Morgan (eds), *Strangers within the realm*, pp. 30–1.

16. This point has been made recently by Cain and Hopkins, *Innovation and expansion*, pp. 54–5.

17. Ibid., pp. 318–19.

18. See pp. 59–60, 98–100.

19. This theme is explored in Nancy F. Koehn, *The power of commerce. Economy and governance in the first British empire* (Ithaca, 1994).

20. For a recent important study of this period see C.A. Bayly, *Imperial meridian. The British empire and the world, 1780–1830* (1989). See in particular the remarks on the historiographical tradition on pp. 7–10.

21. Vincent T. Harlow, *The founding of the second British empire, 1763–1793* (2 vols, 1952 and 1964).

22. For discussion of Harlow's work and the conceptual problems it raised see P. Marshall, 'The first and second British empire. A question of

demarcation', *History*, XLIX (1964), 13–23; R. Hyam, 'British imperial expansion in the late eighteenth century', *HJ*, X (1967), 113–31; Frederick Madden with David Fieldhouse (eds), *Select documents on the constitutional history of the British empire and commonwealth, vol. III: Imperial reconstruction, 1763–1840. The evolution of alternative systems of colonial government* (Westport, Conn., 1987), xxii–xxvi; Cain and Hopkins, *Innovation and expansion*, pp. 55–7. For a recent overview of the eighteenth-century empire which stresses that while colonial 'policy' did not change in the 1760s, 'a new sense of empire seems clearly perceptible' see P.J. Marshall, 'The eighteenth-century empire' in Jeremy Black (ed.), *British politics and society from Walpole to Pitt, 1742–1789* (1990), pp. 177–200 (quotation on p. 200).

23. Cain and Hopkins, *Innovation and expansion*, pp. 57–8.
24. Ibid., p. 55.
25. For a discussion of these developments in a context provided by British imperialism in the eighteenth and early nineteenth century see ibid., pp. 58–104.
26. John Brewer, *The sinews of power. War, money and the English state, 1688–1783* (1989).
27. For a detailed study see P.G.M. Dickson, *The financial revolution in England. A study in the development of public credit 1688–1756* (1967).
28. In an American context see, most notably, Jack M. Sosin, *Whitehall and the wilderness. The Middle West in British colonial policy, 1760–1775* (Lincoln, Nebraska, 1961) and Franklin B. Wickwire, *British subministers and colonial America, 1763–1783* (Princeton, 1966).
29. H.V. Bowen, *Revenue and reform. The Indian problem in British politics, 1757–1773* (Cambridge, 1991).
30. For a recent study see Alison Gilbert Olson, *Making the empire work. London and American interest groups, 1690–1790* (Cambridge, Mass., 1992). See also Jack M. Sosin, *Agents and merchants. British colonial policy and the origins of the American revolution, 1763–1775* (Lincoln, Nebraska, 1965) and Michael G. Kammen, *A rope of sand. The colonial agents, British politics, and the American Revolution* (Ithaca, 1968).
31. K.N. Chaudhuri, *The trading world of Asia and the English East India Company, 1660–1760* (Cambridge, 1978). For general histories of the Company see John Keay, *The honourable company. A history of the English East India Company* (1991) and Lawson, *East India Company*.
32. Bowen, *Revenue and reform*; L.S. Sutherland, *The East India Company in eighteenth-century politics* (Oxford, 1952).
33. See the trilogy of works by P.D.G. Thomas: *British politics and the Stamp Act crisis. The first phase of the American Revolution, 1763–1767* (Oxford, 1975); *The Townshend duties crisis. The second phase of the American Revolution, 1767–1773* (Oxford, 1987); *Tea party to independence. The third phase of the American Revolution, 1773–1776* (Oxford, 1991). For Canadian issues see Philip Lawson, *The imperial challenge. Quebec and Britain in the age of the American Revolution* (Montreal, 1989).
34. See, for example, P.J. Marshall, 'Empire and authority in the later eighteenth century', *JICH*, XV (1987), 105–22; Koehn, *The power of commerce*.
35. J.R. Seeley, *The expansion of England. Two courses of lectures* (1883), p. 10.

As Cain and Hopkins have noted, Seeley's book is generally regarded as the starting-point for serious historical study of British overseas activity (*Innovation and expansion*, p. 4, n. 1.), but of course political economists and sociologists had been endeavouring to explain modern imperialism since the middle of the eighteenth century. For a recent analysis of the development of the study of imperialism see Bernard Semmel, *The liberal ideal and the demons of empire. Theories of imperialism from Adam Smith to Lenin* (Baltimore, 1993).

36.   P.J. Cain and A.G. Hopkins, 'The political economy of British expansion overseas, 1750–1914', *Econ. Hist. Rev.*, second series, XXXIII (1980), 463–90; 'Gentlemanly capitalism and British expansion overseas I. The colonial system, 1688–1850', ibid., XXXIX (1986), 501–25; 'Gentlemanly capitalism and British expansion overseas II. New imperialism, 1850–1945', ibid., XL (1987), 1–26; *Innovation and expansion*; *British imperialism. Crisis and deconstruction, 1914–1990* (1993).

37.   *Innovation and expansion*, pp. 13–17.

38.   The rest of this paragraph is based on Semmel, *Liberal ideal*, passim.

39.   In the main, reviews and criticisms of the gentlemanly capitalist thesis have been located in a context provided by nineteenth-century imperialism and socioeconomic development. See, for example, the brief comments and citations in Maxine Berg and Pat Hudson, 'Rehabilitating the industrial revolution', *Econ. Hist. Rev.*, second series, XLV (1992), 43–4.

40.   Andrew Porter, '"Gentlemanly capitalism" and empire. The British experience since 1750?', *JICH*, XVIII (1990), esp. 269–72, 289. In spite of the use of the date '1750' in the title of his article cited above, Porter's criticisms of gentlemanly capitalism focus mainly on issues relating to a historiographical agenda determined by dominant nineteenth-century themes and issues. His observations, however, do help to provide a general framework for discussion of the imperialist process in the eighteenth century.

41.   Cain and Hopkins, *Innovation and expansion*, pp. 48–51.

42.   As with Porter's article cited above, the review article written by D.K. Fieldhouse, 'Gentlemen, capitalists, and the British Empire', *JICH*, XXII (1994), 531–41 discusses gentlemanly capitalism, imperial policy, and the causes of expansion almost exclusively in terms of the empire as it existed in the nineteenth century, and in this case attention is focused very much on the period after 1850. In part, this reflects the fact that much of Cain and Hopkin's work deals with the nineteenth-century empire (see p. 46), but it also illustrates the extent to which general scholarly debate about the British empire and British imperialism tends to neglect the eighteenth-century dimension.

43.   These two key areas are explored in Cain and Hopkins, 'Gentlemanly capitalism I', 517–19. The overseas dimension is explored at greater length in an eighteenth-century context in *Innovation and expansion*, pp. 84–96.

44.   Cain and Hopkins, *Innovation and expansion*, p. 86. This comment was made in response to my observation that there is little evidence of the landed interest committing much investment capital to the City in the

eighteenth century (H.V. Bowen, 'Investment and empire in the later eighteenth century. East India stockholding, 1756–1791', *Econ. Hist. Rev.*, second series, XLII (1989), 195–6). On this issue see, pp. 54–6.

45. As Fieldhouse has put it, 'should gentlemanly capitalism be regarded as merely an "organising principle" . . . , or does it offer a genuinely explanatory model?' ('Gentlemen, capitalists and the British empire', p. 536).

46. Review by Keith Robbins, *Times Higher Education Supplement*, 30 July 1993.

47. Cain and Hopkins, 'Political economy', 466.

CHAPTER 2   THE DYNAMICS OF EXPANSION

1. For the long-term continuities evident in the development of the British position in India see Chaudhuri, *Trading world of Asia*, pp. 41–4.

2. The colonial dimension to European wars is conveniently outlined in McFarlane, *The British in the Americas*, pp. 220–5.

3. See, for example, John Shy, *Toward Lexington. The role of the British army in the coming of the American Revolution* (Princeton, 1965), pp. 28, 30, 34, 36–8.

4. For a brief summary of the development of the relationship between merchants and the state in Britain see M.N. Pearson, 'Merchants and states', in J.D. Tracy (ed.), *The political economy of merchant empires* (Cambridge, 1991), pp. 87–94.

5. For a recent interpretation of the assumptions behind the introduction of the Navigation Acts of 1651 and 1660 see Daniel A. Baugh, 'Maritime strength and Atlantic commerce. The uses of a "grand marine empire"', in Stone (ed.), *Imperial state at war*, pp. 191–2. Baugh sees the Act of 1660 as being drawn up with the 'urgent needs of the state in view'. For the Navigation Acts see also pp. 32–3.

6. The deployment of regular troops in the Atlantic empire before the Seven Years' War is examined in Shy, *Toward Lexington*, pp. 19–35. London was not so responsive to requests for help from colonies such as Georgia and South Carolina (see pp. 31–33).

7. D. Crossley and R. Saville (eds), *The Fuller letters, 1728–1755. Guns, slaves, and finance* (Lewes, 1991), p. xxvi.

8. For a vigorous and wide-ranging reexamination of the expedition of 1740–2 see Richard Harding, *Amphibious warfare in the eighteenth century. The British expedition to the West Indies, 1740–1742* (Woodbridge, 1991).

9. The development of these bases is charted in Daniel A. Baugh, *British naval administration in the age of Walpole* (Princeton, 1965), pp. 347–55.

10. P.J. Marshall, 'British expansion in India in the eighteenth century: a historical revision', *History*, LX (1975), 39.

11. P. Crowhurst, *The defence of British trade, 1689–1815* (Folkestone, 1977), esp. pp. 43–80.

12. See, for example, the case of British activity in Asia as outlined in P.J. Marshall, 'Western arms in maritime Asia in the early phases of

expansion', *Modern Asian Studies*, XIV (1980), 24; and idem, 'British expansion in India', 38–40.

13. Wilson, 'Empire of virtue', pp. 144–5, 152.
14. Marc Egnal, *A mighty empire. The origins of the American Revolution* (Ithaca, 1988), pp. 92–100. See also Robert D. Mitchell, *Commercialism and frontier. Perspectives on the early Shenandoah Valley* (Charlottesville, 1977), pp. 59–60, 80. For a study with a maritime perspective on the interactions between the British, French and Spanish empires in the North Atlantic and the Caribbean see John Robert McNeill, *Atlantic empires of France and Spain. Louisbourg and Havana, 1700–1763* (Chapel Hill, 1985).
15. Baugh, 'Maritime strength and Atlantic commerce', pp. 201–3.
16. The problems related to the 'western lands' from a British point of view are discussed in Thomas, *British politics and the Stamp Act crisis*, pp. 41–3 and idem, *The Townshend duties crisis*, pp. 51–75.
17. See the examples taken from the 1760s cited in Philip Lawson, '"The Irishman's prize". Views of Canada from the British press, 1760–1774', *HJ*, XXVIII (1985), 585. For a discussion of this issue see pp. 179–81.
18. S. Das, 'British reactions to the French bugbear in India, 1763–83', *European History Quarterly*, XXII (1992), 41.
19. These matters are discussed in detail in ibid., passim. For a case-study see Nicholas Tracy, 'Parry of a threat to India, 1768–1774', *Mariner's Mirror*, LIX (1973), 35–48. For the broad context see M.E. Yapp, *Strategies of British India. Britain, Iran, and Afghanistan, 1798–1850* (Oxford, 1980), pp. 158–9. See pp. 184–5.
20. See references cited above p. 198, n. 9.
21. See, for example, the case of the southern frontier of the American colonies in Alan Gallay, *The formation of a planter elite. Jonathan Bryan and the southern colonial frontier* (Athens, Ga., 1989), pp. 17, 72. Shy, *Toward Lexington*, p. 285.
22. Shy, *Toward Lexington*, p. 43. For accounts of the development of the militia which stress regional diversity and the differences between defence forces and the volunteer forces used for offensive expeditions see ibid., pp. 6–19 and John Shy, 'A new look at the colonial militia', in John Shy, *A people numerous and armed. Reflections on the military struggle for American independence* (Oxford, 1976), pp. 22–33.
23. Carl Bridenbaugh and Roberta Bridenbaugh, *No peace beyond the line. The English in the Caribbean, 1624–1690* (New York, 1971), pp. 171–2.
24. Edward Brathwaite, *The development of creole society in Jamaica, 1770–1820* (Oxford, 1971), pp. 26–31.
25. Shy, *Toward Lexington*, pp. 41–3.
26. Michael Craton, 'Reluctant creoles. The planters' world in the British West Indies', in Bailyn and Morgan (eds), *Strangers within the realm*, pp. 324–7.
27. For a detailed discussion of the relationship between trade and force see Chaudhuri, *Trading world of Asia*, pp. 109–20.
28. Ibid., pp. 50–1.
29. The part played by the Company's army in maintaining law and order in Bengal is explored in G.J. Bryant, 'Pacification in the early British raj, 1755–85', *JICH*, XIII (1985), 4–19.

30. P.J. Marshall, 'The Company and coolies. Labour in early Calcutta', in Pradip Sinha (ed.), *The urban experience: Calcutta. Essays in honour of Nisith R. Ray* (Calcutta, 1987), pp. 23–38.

31. Douglas M. Peers, 'Contours of the garrison state: the army and the historiography of early nineteenth-century India', in N.G. Cassels (ed.), *Orientalism, evangelicalism, and the military cantonment in early nineteenth-century India. An historiographical overview* (Lampeter, 1991), pp. 89–124.

32. Marshall, 'British expansion in India', 40–2. For the general military context see idem, 'Western arms in maritime Asia'.

33. This and the next paragraph are based upon Bowen, *Revenue and reform*, pp. 5–15, 103–18.

34. Quoted in ibid., p. 105.

35. Namier, *England in the age of the American revolution*, p. 35. For the central importance of trade to the development of the British state and empire see Colley, *Britons*, pp. 56–71.

36. For the pattern and growth of English trade in the seventeenth century see D.W. Jones, *War and economy in the age of William III and Marlborough* (Oxford, 1988), pp. 43–52.

37. Kathleen Wilson, 'Empire, trade, and popular politics in mid-Hanoverian Britain. The case of Admiral Vernon', *Past and present*, CXXII (1988), 98–101.

38. Marcus Rediker, *Between the devil and the deep blue sea. Merchant seamen, pirates, and the Anglo-American maritime world, 1700–1750* (Cambridge, 1987), p. 21.

39. There has been considerable scholarly debate over the forces which influenced the making of the Navigation Acts. For a convenient review which strikes a balance between different interpretations see McFarlane, *The British in the Americas*, pp. 98–102. For concise details of the Navigation Acts see Ralph Davis, *The rise of the English shipping industry in the seventeenth and eighteenth centuries* (1962), pp. 306–9.

40. In 1775, 32 per cent of 'English' shipping was colonial-built (Price, 'What did merchants do?', p. 271).

41. Jones, *War and economy*, pp. 49–51 (quotation from p. 50).

42. Baugh, 'Maritime strength and Atlantic commerce', pp. 192–3.

43. *Trade and dominion*, pp. 273–9.

44. Bowen, *Revenue and reform*, pp. 68–9. See also Chaudhuri, *Trading world of Asia*, pp. 55–6.

45. Baugh, 'Maritime strength and Atlantic commerce', pp. 201–3.

46. Ibid. Baugh's essay is devoted to a detailed assessment of the Atlantic empire and the assumptions that underpinned its development. For a different perspective which emphasizes Britain's long-standing concern with the need for territorial sovereignty as well as trade to form the basis of empire see John Robertson, 'Union, state, and empire. The Britain of 1707 in its European setting', in Stone (ed.), *Imperial state at war*, pp. 224–57. Much of the focus of Robertson's essay is, however, on Ireland and Scotland and, like Baugh, he argues that it was only after 1763 that ministers began to follow public opinion and became 'aggressively territorial' (p. 248) in North America.

47. For the general context provided by the development of the Atlantic

economies see Ralph Davis, *The rise of the Atlantic colonies* (Ithaca, 1973). For the central importance of the slave trade in helping to establish commercial links between America and Europe see Barbara L. Solow, 'Slavery and colonization', in Barbara L. Solow (ed.), *Slavery and the rise of the Atlantic system* (Cambridge, 1991), pp. 21–42.

48. Ralph Davis, *The industrial revolution and British overseas trade* (Leicester, 1979), pp. 13–14. For the importance of the North American and West Indian colonial markets to the development of London's economy in particular see Nuala Zahedieh, 'London and the colonial consumer in the late seventeenth century', *Econ. Hist. Rev.*, second series, XLVII (1994), 239–61. For a general overview of the expansion of British trade which identifies a number of factors promoting growth see Price, 'What did merchants do?', esp. p. 277.

49. Figures based upon Ralph Davis, 'English foreign trade, 1700–1774', *Econ. Hist. Rev.*, second series, XV (1962), 285–303. For longer term trends which illustrate the further displacement of Europe as a destination for domestic exports see Davis, *The industrial revolution and overseas trade*, pp. 14–35. For the North American context in particular see also Jacob M. Price, 'New time series for Scotland's and Britain's trade with the thirteen colonies and states, 1740–91', *WMQ*, third series, XXXII (1975), 307–25.

50. An Act of 1705 granted subsidies for the importation of these goods (Price, 'What did merchants do?', p. 275). For the view that northern Europe continued to be the main source of British naval stores see Baugh, 'Maritime strength and Atlantic commerce', p. 199.

51. For contemporary perceptions of the mid-eighteenth-century empire see Bowen, *Revenue and reform*, pp. 16–29.

52. For attempts to develop English interests in the Pacific during this period see Glyndwr Williams, '"The inexhaustible fountain of gold": English projects and ventures in the South Seas, 1670–1750', in John E. Flint and Glyndwr Williams (eds), *Perspectives of empire. Essays presented to Gerald S. Graham* (1973), pp. 27–53. This essay stands as a corrective to the view that the British only developed an interest in the Pacific after 1763.

53. See pp. 116–18.

54. Davis, *The industrial revolution and British overseas trade*. Davis was at pains to stress that overseas trade did not have a direct role to play in the initial stage of Britain's industrial development (ibid., pp. 9–10, 63–4). In recent years, there has been considerable debate over the part played by overseas trade in the development of the domestic economy in the eighteenth century. For an interpretation which stresses the importance of overseas trade see P.K. O'Brien and S.L. Engerman, 'Exports and the growth of the British economy from the Glorious Revolution to the Peace of Amiens', in Solow (ed.), *Slavery and the rise of the Atlantic system*, pp. 177–209. For an alternative view which argues that 'At no time did the gains from trade revolutionise the economic strength of the nation' see R.P. Thomas and D.N. McCloskey, 'Overseas trade and empire, 1700–1860', in Roderick Floud and Donald McCloskey (eds), *The economic history of Britain since 1700. Volume*

1: 1700–1860 (Cambridge, 1981), pp. 87–102 (quotation from p. 102).

55. This is not to say that those involved in the slave trade did not play a part in helping to sustain and strengthen the process of industrialization once it was under way.

56. J.R. Ward, 'The industrial revolution and British imperialism, 1750–1850', *Econ. Hist. Rev.*, second series, XLVII, (1994), 44–65. The following two paragraphs are based on this source.

57. Bowen, *Revenue and reform*, pp. 107–8.

58. Ward, 'Industrial revolution and imperialism', pp. 51–5.

59. For detailed annual figures for Company tea sales see B.W. Labaree, *The Boston Tea Party* (Oxford, 1964), p. 334.

60. For full details of the tea problem see Bowen, *Revenue and reform*, pp. 121–5, 151–3.

61. Carole Shammas, *The pre-industrial consumer in England and America* (Oxford, 1990), pp. 76–86.

62. This general theme has recently been explored by P.J. Marshall, 'Empire and opportunity, 1763–75', *Transactions of the Royal Historical Society* (forthcoming). I am grateful to Professor Marshall for allowing me to read his paper prior to publication.

63. For a detailed case study see Julian Gwyn, *The enterprising admiral. The personal fortune of Admiral Sir Peter Warren* (Montreal, 1974). A successful officer such as Warren was able to acquire an enormous fortune of £127,405 from prizes between 1739–48 and this enabled him to engage in land speculation and money-lending on a grand scale, in both America and Britain.

64. Shy, *Toward Lexington*, pp. 332–8.

65. See Chapter 4.

66. The links between speculation and settlement are explored in general terms in Bernard Bailyn, *The peopling of British North America. An introduction* (1987) pp. 65–86 and in more detail in Bernard Bailyn with the assistance of Barbara De Wolfe, *Voyagers to the west. Emigration from Britain to North America on the eve of the Revolution* (1986), pp. 335–637. For detailed case-studies see Mitchell, *Commercialism and frontier*, pp. 15–58 and Charles E. Clark, *The eastern frontier. The settlement of northern New England, 1610–1763* (New York, 1970), pp. 169–79.

67. Washington to Captain John Posey, 24 June 1767, quoted in T.H. Breen, *Tobacco culture. The mentality of the great tidewater planters on the eve of revolution* (Princeton, 1986), p. 184.

68. Shy, *Toward Lexington*, p. 357. Examples are to be found on pp. 357–8. For examples of colonial governments making similar grants to veterans of their armed forces see Mitchell, *Commercialism and frontier*, p. 83.

69. For examples of this as it applies to Scottish soldiers in New York in the 1760s and Georgia in the 1730s see W.R. Brock, *Scotus Americanus. A survey of the sources for the links between Scotland and America in the eighteenth century* (Edinburgh, 1982), pp. 72, 79.

70. Gary B. Nash, 'The early merchants of Philadelphia. The formation and disintegration of a founding elite', in Richard S. Dunn and Mary

Maples Dunn (eds), *The world of William Penn* (Philadelphia, 1986), pp. 340–2, 344–5.

71. Carl Bridenbaugh, *Cities in the wilderness. The first century of urban life in America, 1625–1742* (second edition, New York, 1955), p. 148.

72. Richard S. Dunn, 'Penny wise and pound foolish. Penn as a businessman', in Dunn and Dunn (eds), *The world of William Penn*, pp. 45–8.

73. Nash, 'Early merchants', p. 346.

74. Brian Levy, 'From "dark corners" to American domesticity. The British social context of the Welsh and Cheshire Quakers' familial revolution in Pennsylvania, 1657–85', in Dunn and Dunn (eds), *The world of William Penn*, p. 234.

75. For examples see Bridenbaugh, *No peace beyond the line*, pp. 319–25, 367–9.

76. Robert C. Ritchie, *Captain Kidd and the war against the pirates* (Cambridge, Mass., 1986), pp. 26, 37–9.

77. Kidd's career as a upstanding member of New York society was short-lived. See ibid., pp. 36, 39–40. For his connection with leading politicians see ibid., pp. 52–4. For the general economic and social benefits that stemmed from privateering see the examples cited in Carl Bridenbaugh, *Cities in revolt. Urban life in America, 1743–1776* (New York, 1955), pp. 61–4, 335. For the contribution of American privateers to the British war effort in the mid-eighteenth century see Carl E. Swanson, 'American privateering and imperial warfare, 1739–1748', *WMQ*, third series, XLII (1985).

78. Nuala Zahedieh, 'Trade, plunder, and economic development in early English Jamaica, 1655–89', *Econ. Hist. Rev.*, second series, XXXIX (1986), 205–22.

79. W.J. Eccles, 'The fur trade and eighteenth-century imperialism', *WMQ*, third series, XL (1983), 341–62.

80. For examples of several such episodes in the southern frontier region see Alan Gallay, *The formation of a planter elite*, pp. 3, 11–14, 127–52 (esp. 129).

81. Shy, *Toward Lexington*, pp. 60–2.

82. Bowen, *Revenue and reform*, pp. 67–72.

83. P.J. Marshall, 'Private British investment in eighteenth-century Bengal', *Bengal Past and Present*, LXXXVI (1967), 52–67. This theme is developed in more detail in P.J. Marshall, *East Indian fortunes. The British in Bengal in the eighteenth century* (Oxford, 1976). For the development of private trade in western India in the mid-eighteenth century see Pamela Nightingale, *Trade and empire in western India, 1784–1806* (Cambridge, 1970), pp. 16–23. See also I.B. Watson, *Foundations for empire: English private trade in India, 1659–1760* (New Delhi, 1980). For the substantial involvement of English private traders in inter-Asian trade, the 'country' trade, see P.J. Marshall, 'Private British traders in the Indian Ocean before 1800', in Ashin Das Gupta and M.N. Pearson (eds), *India and the Indian Ocean 1500–1800* (Calcutta, 1987), 276–300.

84. See, for example, the case of expansion into Awadh after 1764 in P.J. Marshall, 'Economic and political expansion. The case of Oudh', *Modern Asian Studies*, IX (1975), 465–82.

CHAPTER 3 GENTLEMEN AND ENTREPRENUERS: LANDOWNERS, MERCHANTS AND BANKERS

1. Richard Pares, 'The economic factors in the history of the empire', *Econ. Hist. Rev.*, first series, VII (1937), 120.
2. Lawrence Stone, 'Introduction', in Stone (ed.), *An imperial state at war*, p. 6.
3. For the importance of London in this context see Colley, *Britons*, p. 64.
4. Paul Langford, *Public life and the propertied Englishman, 1689–1798* (Oxford, 1991), Ch.1. See also Namier, *England in the age of the American Revolution*, pp. 18–26.
5. For a concise summary of this debate and a detailed discussion of the issues involved see J.A. Cannon, *Aristocratic century. The peerage of eighteenth-century England* (Cambridge, 1984), pp. 1–33.
6. N.F.R. Crafts, *British economic growth during the Industrial Revolution* (Oxford, 1985), p. 13. Crafts has tabulated information derived from the important cautionary article by P.H. Lindert and Jeffrey G. Williamson, 'Revising England's social tables 1688–1812', *Explorations in Economic History*, 19 (1982), 385–408.
7. G.E. Mingay, *English landed society in the eighteenth century* (1963), pp. 3–26.
8. Cannon, *Aristocratic society*, pp. 31–3.
9. Ibid., pp. 93–118.
10. Langford, *Public life*, pp. 289–94. See, for example, the six members for Hertfordshire returned in 1761 and cited by Namier in *England in the age of the American Revolution*, pp. 12–13.
11. For political and social divisions within the landed elite see Cannon, *Aristocratic century*, pp. 123–4, 126–7.
12. Ibid., pp. 34–70
13. Langford, *A polite and commercial people*, p. 71.
14. Mingay, *English landed society*, p. 105.
15. For a general discussion of this process see G.E. Mingay, *The gentry. The rise and fall of a ruling class* (1976), pp. 90–104.
16. Mingay, *The gentry*, pp. 38–9; W.A. Speck, 'Conflict in society', in Geoffrey Holmes (ed.), *Britain after the Glorious Revolution, 1689–1714* (1969), pp. 142–4.
17. For details of the part played by landowners in industrial development see Mingay, *English landed society*, pp. 189–201. For a detailed case study of the involvement of the Lowthers of west Cumberland in mining and trade see J.V. Beckett, *Coal and tobacco. The Lowthers and the economic development of West Cumberland, 1660–1760* (Cambridge, 1981), passim. For South Wales see Philip Jenkins, *The making of a ruling class. The Glamorgan gentry, 1640–1790* (Cambridge, 1983), pp. 57–62 and D.W. Howell, *Patriarchs and parasites. The gentry of south-west Wales in the eighteenth century* (Cardiff, 1986); for Scotland see S.G. Checkland, *Scottish banking. A history, 1695–1973* (Glasgow, 1975), pp. 112, 124–5, 131–3.
18. See, for example, the case of the Coke family in R.A.C Parker, *Coke of*

Norfolk: a financial and agricultural study, 1717–1842 (Oxford, 1975), p. 134.

19.   Langford, *Public life*, p. 62. For a detailed study of the family's fortunes and a collection of letters which amplify the information given by Langford and reveal the full extent of their financial activities see Crossley and Saville (eds), *The Fuller letters.*

20.   Gill Simmons, 'Buckler's Hard. Warship building on the Montagu estate at Beaulieu', *New Arcadian Journal,* 35/36 (1993), 24–47 (esp. 24–34).

21.   See, for example, the detailed study of Sir James Lowther (1673–1755) of West Cumberland (Beckett, *Coal and tobacco,* pp. 211–19).

22.   Cannon, *Aristocratic century,* p. 127.

23.   Jenkins, *Making of a ruling class,* p. 62.

24.   See, for example, J.V. Beckett, *The aristocracy in England, 1660–1914* (Oxford, 1986), pp. 84–6.

25.   F.T. Melton, *Sir Robert Clayton and the origins of English deposit banking, 1658–1685* (Cambridge, 1986), pp. 12, 36.

26.   M.G. Davies, 'Country gentry and payments to London, 1650–1714', *Econ. Hist. Rev.,* second series, XXIV (1971), 15–36; Henry Roseveare, *The financial revolution 1660–1760* (1991), pp. 19–20.

27.   L.S. Pressnell, *Country banking in the industrial revolution* (Oxford, 1956). Some regions, however, still directed few resources towards the City. Investment in London from Lancashire, for example, was almost non-existent in the first half of the century (B.L. Anderson, 'Provincial aspects of the financial revolution of the eighteenth century', *BH,* XI (1970), 21–2).

28.   D.M. Joslin, 'London private bankers, 1720–1785', *Econ. Hist. Rev.,* second series, VII (1954), pp. 176–9.

29.   See, for example, the case of Richard Grenville, later Earl Temple, whose timely acquisition and sale of stock allowed him to transform his position as a landowner. See J.V. Beckett, *The rise and fall of the Grenvilles, Dukes of Buckingham and Chandos, 1710–1921* (Manchester, 1994), pp. 33–8, 50–1.

30.   See pp. 90–1.

31.   Wyndham Beawes, *Lex mercatoria rediviva. Or the merchants' directory* (1752, 4th edn., 1783), p. 31.

32.   For the importance of merchants within London's political elite see Gary Stuart de Krey, *A fractured society. The politics of London in the first age of party, 1688–1715* (Oxford, 1985), p. 125. The political domination of Glasgow by the merchant elite is noted in T.M. Devine, *The tobacco lords. A study of the tobacco merchants of Glasgow and their trading activities, c.1740–1790* (Edinburgh, 1975), pp. 103, 124. For the civic position of West India merchants in Bristol see Morgan, *Bristol and the Atlantic,* pp. 186–7 and 'Bristol West India merchants', pp. 201–2. For the economic and political dominance of Liverpool's small merchant eilte see Paul G.E. Clemens, 'The rise of Liverpool, 1665–1750', *Econ. Hist. Rev.,* second series, XXIX (1976), 216–17.

33.   Wilson, 'Empire, trade, and popular politics', pp. 100–1; James Raven, *Judging new wealth. Popular publishing and responses to commerce in England, 1750–1880* (Oxford, 1992), p. 256.

34. For business diversifaction among the Bristol merchant elite see Morgan, 'Bristol West India merchants', p. 201, and for 'fairly common' industrial investment among Glasgow merchants see T.M. Devine, 'The colonial trades and industrial investment in Scotland, *c.*1700–1815', *Econ. Hist. Rev.*, second series, XXIX (1976), 1–13. For other examples of merchant involvement in industry see A.H. John, *The industrial development of South Wales, 1750–1850* (Cardiff, 1950), pp. 24–5; M. Atkinson and C. Baber, *The growth and decline of the South Wales iron industry, 1760–1880* (Cardiff, 1987), pp. 48–9; Beckett, *Coal and tobacco*, pp. 114–15, 119–55.

35. Morgan, *Bristol and the Atlantic trade*, pp. 95–6.

36. For an example of the scale of merchant losses in the war years of 1694–5 see Jones, *War and economy*, p. 158.

37. Stanley Chapman, *Merchant enterprise in Britain from the industrial revolution to World War I* (Cambridge, 1992), pp. 22–9. J. Hoppit, *Risk and failure in English business, 1700–1800* (Cambridge, 1987), pp. 98–103. Jacob M. Price, *Capital and credit in British overseas trade. The view from the Chesapeake* (Cambridge, Mass., 1980), Ch. 6.

38. Chapman, *Merchant enterprise*, p. 27; Price, *Capital and credit*, p. 38. For details of the capital requirements of some English provincial merchants trading abroad see R.G. Wilson, *Gentlemen merchants. The merchant community in Leeds, 1700–1830* (Manchester, 1971), pp. 66–9 and Morgan, *Bristol and the Atlantic trade*, pp. 161–2. The difficulties associated with trying to trade on a small capital are described in Brock, *Scotus Americanus*, pp. 61–2.

39. J. Hoppit, *Risk and failure*, p. 96. For examples of bankruptcies among large Glasgow firms involved in the West Indies trade see T.M. Devine, 'An eighteenth-century business elite. Glasgow-West India merchants, *c.*1750–1815', *Scottish Historical Review*, 57 (1978), 50–1.

40. For the five main groups of firms who dominated the London Chesapeake trade see Jacob M. Price (ed.), *Joshua Johnson's letterbook, 1771–1774. Letters from a merchant in London to his partners in Maryland* (1979), pp. xi–xii, and for the Glasgow–West Indies trade see Devine, 'Eighteenth-century business elite', pp. 42–3.

41. Cannon, *Aristocratic century*, p. 131.

42. Morgan, *Bristol and the Atlantic trade*, p. 186. For the similar size of some fortunes of Whitehaven merchants see Beckett, *Coal and tobacco*, p. 113.

43. Peter Earle, *The making of the English middle class. Business, society and family life in London, 1660–1730* (1989), p. 35.

44. This was an issue that vexed many contemporary commentators as they strove to define the merchant community (Hoppit, *Risk and failure*, p. 4).

45. Peter Mathias, 'The social structure in the eighteenth century. A calculation by Joseph Massie', *Econ. Hist. Rev.*, second series, X (1957), 43. Lindert and Williamson find these figures acceptable ('Revising England's social tables', pp. 388, 393, 396).

46. For London in the 1690s see Jones, *War and economy*, pp. 262, 272. See also De Krey, *Fractured society*, pp. 101, 128. For a detailed profile and analysis of London's merchant community in the 1690s see ibid., pp.

136–56. For London in 1763 see Chapman, *Merchant enterprise*, p. 23. See also Earle, *Making of the English middle class*, pp. 34–5. For Bristol see Morgan, *Bristol and the Atlantic trade*, p. 93. For the figure of 2900 'eminent merchants' in England in 1773 see Sosin, *Agents and merchants*, p. 1.

47.   For the position of London see Christopher J. French '"Crowded with traders and a great commerce". London's domination of English overseas trade, 1700–1775', *London Journal*, XVII (1992), 27–35. As the century progressed, Bristol increasingly focused its attention on sugar, Liverpool committed itself to the slave trade and Glasgow concentrated on tobacco. For Bristol see Morgan, *Bristol and the Atlantic trade*; for Glasgow see Jacob M. Price, 'The rise of Glasgow in the Chesapeake tobacco trade, 1707–1775', *WMQ*, third series, XI (1954), 179–99; for Liverpool see Clemens, 'Rise of Liverpool'; and for Whitehaven see J.E. Williams, 'Whitehaven in the eighteenth century', *Econ. Hist. Rev.*, second series, VIII (1956), 393–404 and Beckett, *Coal and tobacco*, pp. 102–18.

48.   For the increasingly cosmopolitan nature of the merchant community see pp. 150–3.

49.   For a detailed study of this important trend in its North American context see Jacob M. Price and Paul G.E. Clemens, 'A revolution of scale in overseas trade. British firms in the Chesapeake trade, 1675–1775', *Journal of Economic History*, XLVII (1987), 1–43. For a reduction in the number of importers in the Bristol tobacco and sugar trades between 1700 and the 1770s see Morgan, *Bristol and the Atlantic trade*, pp. 158–60, 180. For the small number of merchants involved in Whitehaven's considerable tobacco trade with the Chesapeake during the 1740s see Beckett, *Coal and tobacco*, pp. 112–13.

50.   Price, *Capital and credit*, pp. 25–9.

51.   Chapman, *Merchant enterprise*, pp. 26–9; Earle, *Making of the English middle class*, pp. 37–8.

52.   On the specialization and diversification of the London merchant community in the late seventeenth century see Jones, *War and economy*, pp. 260–72.

53.   Olson, *Making the empire work*, p. 16.

54.   De Krey, *Fractured society*, p. 139; Jones, *War and economy*, pp. 263–4.

55.   For a detailed case study of Hall see Conrad Gill, *Merchants and mariners of the eighteenth century* (1961).

56.   Ian K. Steele, 'A London trader and the Atlantic empire. Joseph Cruttenden, apothecary, 1710 to 1717', *WMQ*, third series, XXXIV (1977), 289.

57.   Morgan, *Bristol and the Atlantic trade*, pp. 95, 160.

58.   Eric Kerridge, *Trade and banking in early modern England* (Manchester, 1988).

59.   See, for example, Morgan, *Bristol and the Atlantic trade*, pp. 2, 162, 186.

60.   Jones, *War and economy*, pp. 278–88. For a detailed case study of a merchant who broadened the scope of his investment to incorporate a wide range of ventures during the final quarter of the seventeenth century see Richard Grassby, *The English gentleman in trade. The life and works of Sir Dudley North, 1641–1691* (Oxford, 1994), pp. 17–120.

61. Dickson, *Financial revolution*, pp. 29–30.
62. David Hancock, '"Domestic bubbling". Eighteenth-century London merchants and individual investment in the Funds', *Econ. Hist. Rev.*, second series, XLVII (1994), 679–702.
63. For a detailed study of Braund see L.S. Sutherland, *A London merchant 1695–1774* (Oxford, 1933).
64. J.H. Clapham, *The Bank of England. A history* (2 vols, Cambridge, 1944), Vol. I, p. 14.
65. Checkland, *Scottish banking*, pp. 69–70, 97–108.
66. For a good general discussion of the development of banking in the seventeenth century see Melton, *Sir Robert Clayton*, pp. 16–39.
67. De Krey, *Fractured society*, pp. 156–65.
68. The classic study of the Bank is Clapham, *Bank of England*.
69. For private banking see Joslin, 'London private bankers', and Price, *Capital and credit*, pp. 63–95. See also F.T. Melton, 'Deposit banking in London, 1700–90', *BH*, XXVIII (1986), 40–50. For provincial banking see Pressnell, *Country banking in the industrial revolution*. For the development of banking in Scotland see Checkland, *Scottish banking*, and C.W. Munn, *The Scottish provincial banking companies, 1747–1864* (Edinburgh, 1981); and for Wales see R.O. Roberts, 'Financial developments in early modern Wales and the emergence of the first banks', *Welsh History Review*, XVI (1993), 291–307.
70. Rondo Cameron, *Banking in the early stages of industrialization. A study of comparative economic history* (New York, 1967), p. 23. For the relationships between provincial banks and the London money market see Pressnell, *Country banking in the industrial revolution*, pp. 75–125.
71. This paragraph is based upon Joslin, 'London private bankers', and Price, *Capital and credit*, pp. 63–95.
72. Beawes, *Lex mercatoria rediviva*, p. 399.
73. For a study of stockbroking and speculation in the eighteenth century see H.V. Bowen, '"The pests of human society". Stockbrokers, jobbers, and speculators in mid-eighteenth-century Britain', *History*, LXXVIII (1993), 38–53.
74. See pp. 16–17.
75. For a classic formulation of the long-standing tensions between the landed interest and the commercial classes in Britain written during the middle of the nineteenth century see the description of W.E.H. Lecky's analysis in Semmel, *Liberal ideal*, pp. 51–2. For a modern study of the early years of the eighteenth century which stresses conflict between a monied interest who 'were involved in the machinery of public credit' and a landed interest who 'lived exclusively from their rents' see W.A. Speck, 'Conflict in society' in Holmes (ed.), *Britain after the Glorious Revolution*, pp. 135–54. Such was the intensity of this conflict, Speck concludes, that it 'threatened to melt the foundations of the political nation' (p. 152).
76. H.T. Dickinson, *Liberty and property. Political ideology in eighteenth-century Britain* (1977), pp. 163–92. For attacks on the monied interest and stockjobbers see Dickson, *Financial revolution*, pp. 26–9, 249–51, and Bowen, '"The pests of human society"'.
77. Raven, *Judging new wealth*, p. 89.

78. Brewer, *Sinews of power*, p. 210.
79. H.V. Bowen, 'The Bank of England during the long eighteenth century, 1694–1820', in Richard Roberts and David Kynaston (eds), *The Bank of England. Money, power and influence, 1694–1994* (Oxford, 1995).
80. For hostility towards returned East India Company servants or 'nabobs' see Philip Lawson and Jim Phillips, '"Our execrable banditti". Perceptions of nabobs in mid-eighteenth-century Britain', *Albion*, XVI (1984), 225–41.
81. Bowen, '"The pests of human society"', pp. 48–51. For a detailed study of attitudes (most of which were favourable) towards trade and merchants see Raven, *Judging new wealth*, esp. Ch. 5.
82. Nicholas Rogers, *Whigs and cities. Popular politics in the age of Walpole and Pitt* (Oxford, 1989), p. 129
83. Wilson, 'Empire of virtue', pp. 145–8.
84. For an assessment which stresses the diminishing general levels of tension between the landed interest and the financial interest but which does not deny that from time to time there were outbursts of hostility and antipathy towards the monied men see Brewer, *Sinews of power*, pp. 199–210.
85. Colley, *Britons*, pp. 56–71 (esp. p. 71).
86. Cannon, *Aristocratic century*, pp. 178–9. See also Langford, *A polite and commercial people*, pp. 75–6.
87. Wilson, 'Empire, trade, and popular politics', pp. 78–80, 97–8.
88. Brewer, *Sinews of power*, pp. 202–3 (quote from p. 203). See also Namier, *England in the age of the American Revolution*, pp. 13–18, 29–35.
89. Quoted in J.H. Soltow, 'Scottish traders in Virginia, 1750–1775', *Econ. Hist. Rev.*, second series, XII (1959), 98.
90. Of course, as Wilson has noted, groups pressing particular concerns could well hoist the flag of 'national interest' in order to mobilize support for their cause (Wilson, 'Empire, trade, and popular politics', p. 95).
91. Langford, *Public life*, p. 309.
92. Alison Vickery, 'Golden age to separate spheres? A review of the categories and chronologies of English women's history', *HJ*, XXXVI (1993), 395–7. For the general nature of the relationship between land and finance see Langford, *Public life*, pp. 305–15.
93. Beckett, *The aristocracy in England*, pp. 71–9. On this theme see the analysis of the real estate owned by the London business community during the early part of the eighteenth century in Earle, *Making of the English middle class*, pp. 155–7. Earle concludes that it was unusual for Londoners to try and 'transform themselves and their descendants into landed gentry.'
94. Ibid., p. 229. For examples of this see John Brooke, *History of Parliament. The House of Commons, 1754–1790. Introductory survey* (Oxford, 1964), p. 195; Langford, *Public life*, p. 61; Mingay, *English landed society*, pp. 102–5; Gill, *Merchants and mariners*, Ch. 12.
95. Devine, *Tobacco lords*, pp. 18–30. The situation was much the same among the Glasgow–West India merchants. See idem, 'Eighteenth-century business elite', pp. 43–5. For the general relationship between

land and the merchant community see idem, 'Glasgow colonial merchants and land, 1700–1815', in J.T. Ward and R.G. Wilson (eds), *Land and industry. The landed estate and the industrial revolution* (1971), 205–35.

96. Raven, *Judging new wealth*, Ch. 5; Namier, *England in the age of the American Revolution*, pp. 8–9. For the popularity and elasticity of the word 'gentleman' see P.J. Corfield, 'Class by name and number in eighteenth-century Britain', *History*, 72 (1987), 38–61, and idem, 'The democratic history of the English gentleman', *History Today* (December 1992), 40–7. See also Langford, *A polite and commercial people*, pp. 65–6. For 'the unity of polite society' see ibid., pp. 116–21.

97. De Krey, *Fractured society*, p. 2; Langford, *Public life*, p. 71.

98. For the development of fashion consciousness in general and the influence of London fashions throughout England see E. Robinson, 'Matthew Boulton and Josiah Wedgwood, apostles of fashion', *BH*, XXXVIII (1986), 98–114. The dissemination of metropolitan ideals did not occur at a uniform pace even within England, and the author of a detailed case study has concluded that centres such as York which had long attracted the gentry imitated London fashions and trends much more quickly than did places such as Leeds (J. Jefferson Looney, 'Cultural life in the provinces. Leeds and York, 1720–1820', in A.L. Beier, David Cannadine and James M. Rosenheim (eds), *The first modern society. Essays in honour of Lawrence Stone* (Cambridge, 1989), p. 507). For brief comments on Scotland see Clive and Bailyn, 'England's cultural provinces', p. 209. For these trends as they affected the Welsh landowning elite see Geraint H. Jenkins, *The foundations of modern Wales. Wales, 1642–1780* (Oxford, 1987), pp. 239–71, and Howell, *Patriarchs and parasites*, pp. 171–93.

99. Jacob M. Price, 'Who cared about the colonies? The impact of the thirteen colonies on British society and politics, circa 1714–1775', in Bailyn and Morgan (eds), *Strangers within the realm*, pp. 395–436.

100. Wilson, 'Empire of virtue'.

101. Davis, *The rise of the English shipping industry*, p. 323.

102. For a detailed development of this argument see Zahedieh, 'London and the colonial consumer'. For a general overview of the debate about the importance of overseas colonies to the domestic economy see John J. McCusker and Russell R. Menard, *The economy of British America, 1607–1789* (Chapel Hill, 1985), pp. 39–45. For contemporary recognition of the importance of the relationship between the expansion of colonial markets and employment in the domestic economy see Koehn, *Power of commerce*, pp. 91–3.

103. Davis, *Rise of the English shipping industry*, pp. 66–8.

104. John E. Wills, Jr, 'European consumption and Asian production in the seventeenth and eighteenth centuries', in John Brewer and Roy Porter (eds), *Consumption and the world of goods* (1993), pp. 136–7 (quotation on p. 136).

105. For good examples of the way in which these products found their way into the homes of the well-to-do see Jenkins, *Making of a ruling class*, pp. 251–2.

106. For details and figures on the importation of groceries into England and Wales from 1550 to 1800, and for the ensuing changes in patterns of food consumption and household expenditure see Shammas, *Pre-industrial consumer*, pp. 77–86, 121–56.
107. Hoh-Cheung Mui and Lorna H. Mui, *The management of monopoly. A study of the English East India Company's conduct of its tea trade, 1784–1833* (Vancouver, 1984), p. 16. For some brief comments on eighteenth-century advertising strategies see John Styles, 'Manufacturing, consumption and design in eighteenth-century England', in Brewer and Porter (eds), *Consumption and the world of goods*, pp. 540–2.
108. Jones, *War and economy*, p. 140.
109. Bowen, *Revenue and reform*, pp. 8–9, 13–15, 22–5, 48–66.
110. D.H. Murdoch, 'Land policy in the eighteenth-century British empire. The sale of crown lands in the Ceded Islands, 1763–1783', *HJ*, 27 (1984), 549–74.
111. Wilson, 'Empires of virtue', pp. 132–6 (for the press) and pp. 136–43 (for the theatre).
112. On travel literature in general see P.J. Marshall and Glyndwr Williams, *The great map of mankind. British perceptions of the world in the age of enlightenment* (1982), pp. 45–63.
113. For the contents of provincial newspapers see G.A. Cranfield, *The development of the provincial newspaper, 1700–1760* (Oxford, 1962), pp. 65–116. For the contents of the press in general see Jeremy Black, *The English press in the eighteenth century* (1987), esp. pp. 25–86, 197–244. Neither Cranfield nor Black draw much attention to items about imperial affairs or Britain's colonies. Instead, they tend to focus on foreign news in a narrowly defined European context. Wilson, however, makes it clear that widespread interest in the colonies was expressed by provincial and London newspapers and periodicals by the 1740s and 1750s ('Empire of virtue', p. 133) See also Robert Harris, *A patriot press. National politics and the London press in the 1740s* (Oxford, 1993). For a general discussion of imperial themes in the press see Philip Lawson, '"Arts and empire equally extend". Tradition, prejudice and assumption in the eighteenth century press coverage of empire', *Studies in History and Politics*, VII (1989), 119–46.
114. Philip Lawson, 'The Irishman's prize', pp. 575–6, 585–7.
115. Marshall and Williams, *Great map of mankind*, pp. 74–8.
116. For an examination of nabobs which draws on a large amount of evidence taken from the press see Lawson and Phillips, '"Our execrable banditti"'.
117. Bruce Lenman, *Integration, enlightenment, and industrialization. Scotland, 1746–1832* (1981), p. 60.
118. For the late 1730s and early 1740s see Wilson, 'Empire, trade, and popular politics', pp. 81–8, and for the 1760s see Bowen, *Revenue and reform*, pp. 16–17.
119. The next two paragraphs are based upon Patrick Eyres, 'Neoclassicism on active service. Commemoration of the Seven Years' War in the English landscape garden', *New Arcadian Journal*, 35/6 (1994), 62–123. See also the same author's 'Fleets, forests, and follies. Supremacy of the seas and of the eye', *ibid.*, pp. 8–22.

CHAPTER 4 INVESTMENT IN EMPIRE

1. Lance E. Davis and Robert A. Huttenback, *Mammon and the pursuit of Empire: the political economy of British imperialism, 1860–1912* (Cambridge, 1987).
2. Nuala Zahedieh, 'Trade, plunder, and economic development in early English Jamaica'.
3. Julian Gwyn, 'British government spending and the North American colonies, 1740–1775', *JICH*, VIII (1980), 77. P.D.G. Thomas has calculated that the average amount paid out for the British army in America between 1763 and 1775 was £389,752. This figure was a little higher than the annual costs actually recorded by the army because it included outstanding payment for some expenses incurred during the Seven Years' War (P.D.G. Thomas, 'The cost of the British army in North America, 1763–1775', *WMQ*, third series, XLV (1988), 510–16). For the impact of military expenditure on the colonial economy between 1768 and 1774 see Shy, *Toward Lexington*, pp. 338–40. Zahedieh has argued that the cost to the metropolis of defending and administering Jamaica in the late-seventeenth century was 'nominal' (Zahedieh, 'Trade, plunder, and development', p. 222).
4. Richard B. Sheridan, *Sugar and slavery: an economic history of the British West Indies, 1623–1775* (Baltimore, 1973), pp. 282–305, 467–73; McCusker and Menard, *The economy of British America*, pp. 80–4; Greene, *Pursuits of happiness*, pp. 181–4.
5. McCusker and Menard, *The economy of British America*, p. 354.
6. Richard Pares, *Merchants and planters* (Cambridge, 1960), p. 50.
7. The definitive study of the growth of public credit is Dickson, *Financial revolution*.
8. Brewer, *Sinews of power*, p. 40.
9. Ibid., pp. 89–91, 126–34. For a concise summary of the debate about tax levels in Britain and Europe as it affected the landed classes see Cannon, *Aristocratic century*, pp. 141–3. The structure and incidence of taxation in the eighteenth century is discussed in detail in Patrick O'Brien, 'The political economy of British taxation, 1660–1815', *Econ. Hist. Rev.*, second series, XLI (1988), 1–32.
10. Brewer, *Sinews of power*, pp. 40, 89.
11. Dickson, *Financial revolution*, p. 9.
12. Ibid., pp. 10–11; Brewer, *Sinews of power*, pp. 30, 40, 95–8, 114.
13. Brewer, *Sinews of power*, pp. 199–210. Unless otherwise stated the next paragraph is also based on this source. For changes in the relationship between direct and indirect taxation see J.V. Beckett and Michael Turner, 'Taxation and economic growth in eighteenth-century England', *Econ. Hist. Rev.*, second series, XVLIII (1990), 378–9 and O'Brien, 'Political economy of British taxation', pp. 8–17.
14. Dickson, *Financial revolution*, pp. 256–60, 265–7, 294, 296–7, 302.
15. Ibid., pp. 300–1. The decline in provincial investment was not, however, mirrored by a decline in investment by the peerage (p. 302).
16. Ibid., pp. 27–8; Bowen '"Pests of human society"', p. 39.
17. See, in general, Dickinson, *Liberty and property*, pp. 163–92.
18. See Dickson, *Financial revolution*, pp. 278–80, 286–90 for details of the

'relatively small circle of London financiers [who] were essential to the success of government loans' (p. 290).

19. Brewer, *Sinews of power*, p. 209.
20. Dickson, *Financial revolution*, pp. 301–3.
21. Foreign and overseas public creditors are analysed in detail in ibid., pp. 304–37.
22. Cain and Hopkins, 'Gentlemanly capitalism I', p. 518.
23. K.G. Davies, *The Royal African Company* (1957), p. 346.
24. H.V. Bowen, 'The "little parliament". The General Court of the East India Company, 1750–1784', *HJ*, XXXIV (1991), 857–72.
25. Bowen, 'Investment and empire'.
26. Dickson, *Financial revolution*, pp. 407–14.
27. Bowen, 'Investment and empire'.
28. Melton, *Sir Robert Clayton*, p. 91.
29. H.V. Bowen, 'Lord Clive and speculation in East India Company stock, 1766', *HJ*, XXX (1987), 905–20; idem, *Revenue and reform*, pp. 7–14, 76–7, 103–32; Sutherland, *East India Company*, pp. 191–3, 209–12.
30. Morgan, *Bristol and the overseas trade*, p. 160; John Bezis Selfa, 'Planter industrialists and iron oligarchs. A comparative prosopography of early Anglo-American ironmasters', *Business and Economic History*, XXIII (1994), 66; Gwyn, *Enterprising admiral*, p. 95.
31. For a detailed examination of the development, structure and operation of the store system see Soltow, 'Scottish traders in Virginia'. The development of the British-Chesapeake trade is explored in detail by Price, *Capital and credit*, passim.
32. Jacob M. Price, 'Buchanan & Simson, 1759–1763. A different kind of Glasgow firm trading to the Chesapeake', *WMQ*, third series, XL (1983), 3–41.
33. It has recently been noted that as far as Bristol was concerned the consignment system was gradually giving way to the direct purchase system and more Bristol tobacco merchants used the latter system than was once thought (Morgan, *Bristol and the Atlantic trade*, pp. 167–75).
34. For a description of the trading systems from the Virginian point of view see Rhys Isaac, *The transformation of Virginia, 1740–1790* (Chapel Hill, 1982), pp. 24–30. For a brief summary of the differences between the systems see Morgan, *Bristol and the Atlantic trade*, pp. 165–6.
35. Morgan, *Bristol and the Atlantic trade*, pp. 160, 186.
36. Ibid., 193–6; Morgan has calculated that 29 out of 50 Bristol West India merchants were owners of plantations (Kenneth Morgan, 'Bristol West India merchants in the eighteenth century', *Transactions of the Royal Historical Society*, sixth series, III (1993), 194–5).
37. Devine, *Tobacco lords*, pp. 55–68. For a detailed account of the shipping arrangements used in the tobacco trade see Ian K. Steele, *The English Atlantic 1675–1740. An exploration of communication and community* (New York, 1986), pp. 41–56.
38. Soltow, 'Scottish merchants in Virginia', p. 85. See also T.M. Devine, 'Sources of capital for the Glasgow tobacco trade, c.1740–1780', *BH*, XVI (1974), 116–17. For brief details of capital investment in goods

and stores by merchants from other ports see Morgan, *Bristol and the Atlantic trade*, p. 173.

39. Beckett, *Coal and tobacco*, p. 113.
40. Devine, *Tobacco Lords*, pp. 10, 72–80.
41. Ibid., pp. 89–98; Soltow, 'Scottish traders in Virginia', 95.
42. Bailyn, *The peopling of British North America*, p. 65. See, in general, T.P. Abernethy, *Western lands and the American Revolution* (New York, 1937).
43. Bailyn, *Voyagers to the west*, p. 356; David Hackett Fischer, *Albion's seed. Four British folkways in America* (Oxford, 1989), pp. 748–9.
44. Bailyn, *Voyagers to the west*, pp. 365–7, 398, 435–7, 440, 471.
45. Ibid., p. 440; Namier, *England in the Age of the American Revolution*, pp. 271–2; Thomas, *The Townshend duties crisis*, pp. 66–70. For a list of the five peers and 17 MPs who purchased shares in the Grand Ohio Company see Price, 'Who cared about the colonies?', p. 403, n. 18.
46. Bailyn, *Voyagers to the west*, pp. 604–37.
47. See, for example, Allan Kulikoff, *Tobacco and slaves. The development of southern cultures in the Chesapeake, 1680–1800* (Chapel Hill, 1986), pp. 122–7. For a colourful contemporary view of the importance of credit in helping the Virginian elite to develop luxurious lifestyles see Egnal, *Mighty empire*, p. 127.
48. Gwyn, *Enterprising Admiral*, pp. 95–126. Warren had begun to lend money (including some in South Carolina) while serving as a naval officer in North America during the 1730s and 1740s and, via agents, he continued to supervise his colonial investments after his return to Britain.
49. The remainder of this paragraph is based upon David Hancock, ' "Capital and credit with approved security". Financial markets in Montserrat and South Carolina, 1748–1775', *Business and Economic History*, XXIII (1994), 61–84.
50. For a good individual example, see the case of Walter Tullideph of Antigua in Sheridan, *Sugar and slavery*, p. 197. He borrowed at 5 per cent from London and then lent locally at 8–10 per cent, offering both mortgages and bonds. In Virginia, small planters often secured credit from larger planters who in turn were in debt to metropolitan merchants (T.H. Breen, *Tobacco culture*, p. 94). For the sources of local credit in colonial America see McCusker and Menard, *The economy of British America*, pp. 334–7, and for the local credit market in the West Indies see Sheridan, *Sugar and slavery*, pp. 294–5 and Pares, *Merchants and planters*, p. 47. We must be careful not to tie all credit networks to Britain. In some cases internal credit markets played a key role during the very earliest phases of development when metropolitan creditors were reluctant to deploy resources at the periphery. For Jamaica see Zahedieh, 'Trade, plunder, and development', p. 213.
51. Egnal, *Mighty empire*, Ch. 7, looks at the whole question of colonial debt and the effect of the depression of the 1760s on North America.
52. Price, *Capital and credit*, pp. 6–15. For the development of indebtedness in Virginia see also Emory G. Evans, 'Planter indebtedness and the coming of the Revolution in Virginia', *WMQ*, third series, XIX (1962), 511–33. For early examples of colonial debt in the London–

Chesapeake trade of the 1690s and 1700s see Jacob M. Price, 'Sheffield v. Starke. Institutional experimentation in the London–Maryland trade *c.*1696–1706', *BH*, XVIII (1986), 19–39.

53. Quoted in Price, *Capital and credit*, p. 6.
54. The calculation was made by the merchant Barlow Trecothick in the House of Commons on 11 February 1766 (R.C. Simmons and P.D.G. Thomas (eds), *Proceedings and debates of the British Parliament respecting North America, 1754–1783* (6 vols, 1982–6), Vol. II, p. 185).
55. Robert E. and B. Katherine Brown, *Virginia 1705-1786. Democracy or aristocracy?* (East Lansing, 1956), p. 97.
56. Thomas, *British politics and the Stamp Act crisis*, pp. 218–19.
57. Morgan, *Bristol and the Atlantic trade*, pp. 110–15. Reeve was owed over £150,000 in the mid-1760s and Cruger nearly £100,00 in 1772.
58. Price, 'Buchanan & Simson', 4.
59. Katherine A. Kellock, 'London merchants and the pre-1776 American debts', *Guildhall Studies in London History*, I (1974), 109–149. This article gives a breakdown of individual firms and their claims.
60. Devine, *Tobacco lords*, pp. 114–15.
61. Ibid., p. 124.
62. This estimate was made by the Jamaica merchant Thomas Collett in the House of Commons on 6 May 1766 (Simmons and Thomas, *Proceedings*, Vol. II, p. 384).
63. Sheridan, *Sugar and slavery*, pp. 463–5.
64. Richard B. Sheridan, 'The British credit crisis of 1772 and the American colonies', *Journal of Economic History*, XX (1960), 161–86.
65. Devine, 'Eighteenth-century business elite', p. 43. For the Bank of England becoming a reluctant owner of sugar estates in such circumstances during the 1770s see Clapham, *Bank of England*, Vol. I, p. 249.
66. Quoted in R.B. Sheridan, 'The commercial and financial organization of the British slave trade, 1750–1807', *Econ. Hist. Rev.*, second series, XI (1958), 258.
67. Price, *Capital and credit*, pp. 63–95.
68. Ibid., pp. 142–3. Warehousemen and other wholesalers were themselves an important link in the credit chain because they often bought goods on short credit and them sold them for export on long credit to overseas merchants (Price, 'What did merchants do?', pp. 273–4).
69. Devine, *The tobacco lords*, pp. 93–5; Price, *Capital and credit*, pp. 44–62. For the raising of working capital in Bristol see Morgan, *Bristol and the Atlantic trade*, pp. 162–3.
70. Price, *Capital and credit*, pp. 18–19.
71. Anderson, 'Provincial aspects of the industrial revolution', pp. 21–2.
72. The general causes of West Indian indebtedness after mid-century are examined in Pares, *Merchants and planters*, pp. 38–44.
73. Sheridan, 'Commercial and financial organization', pp. 249–63. For the part played by credit in the functioning of the eighteenth-century slave trade see Jacob M. Price, 'Credit in the slave trade and plantation economies', in Solow (ed.), *Slavery and the rise of the Atlantic system*, pp. 293–339.
74. The next two paragraphs are based on Marshall, *East Indian fortunes*, pp. 29–50.

75. The relationship between the British and their banians is explored in P.J. Marshall, 'Masters and banians in eighteenth-century Calcutta', in B.B. King and M.N. Pearson (eds), *The age of partnership. Europeans in Asia before dominion* (Honolulu, 1979), pp. 191–213.

76. Nightingale, *Trade and empire in western India*, pp. 12–35. See also Ward, 'Industrial revolution and empire', pp. 46–51.

77. See pp. 59–60.

78. Marshall, 'First and second British empire', p. 21.

79. Ritchie, *Captain Kidd and the war against the pirates*, pp. 66–7.

80. Jacob M. Price, 'One family's empire. The Russell–Lee–Clerk connection in Maryland, Britain, and India, 1707–1857', *Maryland Historical Magazine*, LXXII (1977), 165–225.

81. Gwyn, *Enterprising Admiral*, passim.

82. For Colebrooke see L.S. Sutherland, 'Sir George Colebrooke's world corner in alum, 1771–3', *Economic History*, III (1936), 237–58.

83. Shy, *Toward Lexington*, pp. 335–6.

84. Hancock, '"Domestic bubbling"', p. 683. As Hancock has observed about these men (p. 681, n.7), they might not have been representative of the merchant community in general, but 'they were, rather, "state of-the-art" entrepreneurs, opportunistic and alert, who quickly adopted new practices and ideas.'

85. For the important place of the small entrepreneur and producer in the world of international trade see Brewer, *Sinews of power*, p. 186.

CHAPTER 5   IMPERIAL TIES AND THE ANGLICIZATION OF THE OVERSEAS EMPIRE

1. Jack P. Greene, *Peripheries and center. Constitutional development in the extended polities of the British Empire and the United States, 1607–1788* (Athens, Ga., 1986), pp. xi, 44–7.

2. Speech of 3 February 1766, Simmons and Thomas, *Proceedings and debates*, Vol. II, p. 150.

3. Webb, 'Army and empire', p. 23.

4. In 1749 the size of the Company's army had stood at 3000 men.

5. For the parliamentary estimates for 1755 see Simmons and Thomas, *Proceedings and debates*, Vol. I, p. 24. These figures relate to troops voted by Parliament. The actual numbers on the ground were probably less than this. For the situation in India see G.J. Bryant, 'Officers of the East India Company's army in the days of Clive and Hastings', *JICH*, VI (1978), 203, and C.T. Atkinson, 'In the days of John Company: the early service of the king's troops in India', *Journal of Society for Army Historical Research*, XXXII (1954), 111–17. For an overview of British army strength in peace and war see H.C.B. Rogers, *The British army of the eighteenth century* (1977), pp. 17–31.

6. For the occasional use of garrisons to keep law and order see Shy, *Toward Lexington*, p. 39.

7. There are plenty of examples of those from the colonies marrying into titled metropolitan families. There are also a very small number of examples of individuals such as William Johnson, an Irish immigrant,

landowner and government superintendent for Indian affairs in North America, who became members of the baronetcy.

8.   Quotations from Bridenbaugh, *Cities in revolt*, p. 137.

9.   Nash, 'The early merchants of Philadelphia', 337. This was not always the case, though, and a detailed study of South Carolina reveals that the families of the founding elite were able to survive and were not displaced by immigrants. Instead, wealthy incomers were absorbed into the elite. See Richard Waterhouse, *A new world gentry. The making of a merchant and planter class in South Carolina, 1670–1770* (New York, 1989).

10. For a general discussion of the word 'creole' and a definition of creole society see Brathwaite, *The development of creole society*, pp. xiv–xvi. I use the word in the context of an individual being born in, and committed to, a particular region. For case studies of this process and the changes and tensions it produced see David W. Jordan, 'Political stability and the emergence of a native elite in Maryland', in Thad W. Tate and David L. Ammerman (eds), *The Chesapeake in the seventeenth century. Essays on Anglo-American society* (Chapel Hill, 1979), pp. 243–73, and Carole Shammas, 'English-born and creole elites in turn-of-the-century Virginia', in ibid., pp. 274–96.

11. This important point is made with reference to North America and the West Indies by Steele, *The English Atlantic*, p. 267.

12. For general comments on this see Greene, *Pursuits of happiness*, pp. 162–4.

13. Craton, 'Reluctant creoles', pp. 346–9.

14. For general comments on the place of remigration within the study of movements of people in the eighteenth century see Alan L. Karras, *Sojourners in the sun. Scottish migrants in Jamaica and the Chesapeake, 1740–1800* (Ithaca, 1992), pp. 1–8.

15. For group profiles of transient Scots in Jamaica and the Chesapeake see ibid., pp. 10–13, 45. For Bristol merchants serving apprenticeships in the West Indies before returning home see Morgan, *Bristol and the Atlantic trade*, p. 185, and idem, 'Bristol West India merchants', pp. 191–2.

16. Clive and Bailyn, 'England's cultural province', pp. 207–8.

17. These issues are considered in Shy, *Toward Lexington*, pp. 343–58. For the development of a type of court society by royal officials in Boston in the early eighteenth century see Bridenbaugh, *Cities in the wilderness*, p. 252.

18. For one particular extended family connection that did embrace both east and west see Price, 'One family's empire'.

19. Solow, 'Slavery and colonization', pp. 41–2. Solow has attacked the historiographical trend which promotes a 'continuing homogenization of colonial history that ignores the social, political, economic, legal, and ideological differences between free and slave colonies' (p. 42). For the broad differences between British colonies in the West Indies and those in North America see McFarlane, *The British in the Americas*, pp. 127–87.

20. Greene, *Pursuits of happiness*, p. 175.

21. G.V. Scammell, *The first imperial age. European overseas expansion, c.1400–1715* (1989), pp. 174–5. For the general development of European colonial societies, and the emergence of elites within those societies, before 1715 see ibid., pp. 169–212.

22. Arthur Meier Schlesinger, *The colonial merchants and the American Revolution, 1763–1776* (1917, reprinted 1957), p. 31.

23. For examples of shipowning see Virginia B. Harrington, *The New York merchant on the eve of the Revolution* (1935; reprinted, Gloucester, Mass., 1964), pp. 184–5, and for an extensive list of the individuals connected with the establishment of the Grand Ohio Company in 1769, see Abernethy, *Western lands and the American Revolution*, p. 45.

24. For detailed case studies which stress the broad range of such connections between core and periphery see D.W. Thoms, 'The Mills family. London sugar merchants of the eighteenth century', *BH*, XI (1969), 3–10, and Richard B. Sheridan, 'Planters and merchants. The Oliver family of Antigua and London, 1716–1784', ibid., XIII (1971), 104–13.

25. Shy, *Toward Lexington*, pp. 332–4. The general range of transatlantic connections, several of which were based on family links, involved in the military supply operation is outlined in ibid., pp. 332–7. More generally on the range of business associations and connections in the Atlantic world see Sosin, *Agents and merchants*, pp. 3–5.

26. Bridenbaugh, *Cities in the wilderness*, pp. 187, 339–40; idem, *Cities in revolt*, p. 346; Sosin, *Agents and merchants*, pp. 5–6; Richard Pares, *Yankees and creoles. The trade between North America and the West Indies before the American Revolution* (1956), pp. 8, 16.

27. See, for example, Harrington, *New York merchant*, pp. 116, 127–9. From a metropolitan perspective, the use of agents and attornies in London makes it difficult to determine the full extent of colonial investment in British funds. For one detailed case study see Jacob M. Price, 'The Maryland Bank stock case: British-American financial and political relations before and after the American Revolution', in Aubrey C. Land, Lois Green Carr and Edward C. Papenfuse (eds), *Law, society, and politics in early Maryland* (Baltimore, 1977), 3–40 (esp. 3–8).

28. See, for example, Harrington, *New York merchant*, pp. 185–6.

29. On these issues see, for example, Morgan, 'Bristol West India merchants in the eighteenth century', pp. 191–2, 196–200.

30. Quoted in Schlesinger, *Colonial merchants and the American Revolution*, p. 31.

31. Bridenbaugh and Bridenbaugh, *No peace beyond the line*, p. 133.

32. Gwyn, *Enterprising admiral*, pp. 29–31, 198. For examples of British army officers marrying 'socially prominent American wives' see Shy, *Toward, Lexington*, pp. 355–7.

33. The following paragraph is based upon W.L. Schase, *The colonial American in Britain* (Madison, 1956), esp. pp. 36–44, 121–3.

34. See, for example, ibid., pp. 48–50 and Edmund S. Morgan, *Virginians at home. Family life in the eighteenth century* (Williamsburg, 1952), pp. 10–11.

35. Quoted in Schase, *Colonial American*, p. 61.

36. Quoted in ibid., p. 202.
37. Greene makes this important point about American colonists in *Peripheries and center*, pp. 164–5.
38. Langford, *Polite and commercial people*, p. 701; Greene, *Peripheries and center*, pp. 162–3.
39. Anthony Pagden and Nicholas Canny, 'Afterword. From identity to independence', in Canny and Pagden (eds), *Colonial identity in the Atlantic world, 1500–1800* (Princeton, 1987), pp. 267–8.
40. See, for example, in a North American context Shammas, 'English-born and creole elites', pp. 282–3.
41. Michael Craton and James Walvin, *A Jamaican Plantation. The history of Worthy Park, 1670–1970* (1970), pp. 66–7.
42. See, for example, the report of the speech made by William Beckford on 30 April 1766, Simmons and Thomas, *Proceedings and debates*, Vol. II, p. 376.
43. Quoted in Schase, *Colonial American*, p. 4.
44. Speech of 8 May 1770 (Simmons and Thomas, *Proceedings and debates*, Vol. III, p. 285).
45. Ibid., Vol. II, p. 86.
46. This general point is made by Philip D. Morgan, 'General introduction', in idem (ed.), *Diversity and unity in early North America* (1993), pp. 1–8.
47. For India and the West Indies see pp. 140–46.
48. Richard Middleton, *Colonial America. A history, 1607–1760* (Oxford, 1992), pp. 267–71. It has been been argued (without the deployment of any supporting evidence) that the words 'to Anglicise' or 'to Anglify' came into the English language around 1760. See J. Sturgis, 'Anglicisation at the Cape of Good Hope in the early nineteenth century', *JICH*, XI (1982), 5.
49. Greene , *Pursuits of happiness*, p. 174.
50. For a concise discussion of these issues see idem, *Peripheries and center*, pp. 157–165.
51. Idem, *Pursuits of happiness*, esp. pp. 7–54.
52. This and the following paragraph are based upon A.G. Roeber, '"The origin of whatever is not English among us". The Dutch and German-speaking peoples of colonial British America', in Bailyn and Morgan (eds), *Strangers within the realm*, pp. 220–83.
53. For a concise account of events in New York in the 1670s and 1680s see Middleton, *Colonial America*, pp. 95–103, 148–53.
54. Cornelius Van Horne quoted in Bridenbaugh, *Cities in the wilderness*, p. 461.
55. Quoted in Egnal, *Mighty empire*, p. 71.
56. J.M. Bumsted, 'The cultural landscape of early Canada', in Bailyn and Morgan (eds), *Strangers in the realm*, p. 379. The expulsion of the Acadians from Nova Scotia is examined on pp. 367, 376–8.
57. Bailyn and Morgan (eds), *Strangers within the realm*, pp. 22–3.
58. T.H. Breen, 'An empire of goods. The anglicization of colonial America, 1690–1776', *Journal of British Studies*, XXV (1986); idem, ' "Baubles of

Britain". The American and consumer revolutions of the eighteenth century', *Past and Present,* CXIX (1988), 77–87.

59. Breen, 'Empire of goods', pp. 480–1; Ian K. Steele, 'The empire and provincial elites. An interpretation of some recent writings on the English Atlantic, 1675–1740', *JICH,* VIII (1980), 18.

60. Carole Shammas, 'How self-sufficient was early America?', *Journal of Interdisciplinary History,* XIII (1982), 247–72.

61. These figures have been derived from Shammas, *The pre-industrial consumer in England and America,* pp. 62–8. For the colonial consumer market as it stood at the end of the seventeenth century see Zahedieh, 'London and the colonial consumer'. See also Morgan, *Bristol and the Atlantic trade,* pp. 89–93.

62. W. Schlote, *British overseas trade from 1700 to 1939* (Oxford, 1952), p. 52; Brinley Thomas, *The industrial revolution and the Atlantic economy. Selected essays* (1993), pp. 36–9; D.A. Farnie, 'The commercial empire of the Atlantic, 1607–1783', *Econ. Hist. Rev.,* second series, XV (1962), 214.

63. John Oldmixon cited in Steele, 'Empire and provincial elites', p. 18.

64. Thomas, *The industrial revolution and the Atlantic economy,* p. 34.

65. This paragraph is based on the detailed study of Atlantic communications in Steele, *English Atlantic,* pp. 1–92. See also Morgan, *Bristol and the Atlantic trade,* pp. 66–7.

66. Steele, *English Atlantic,* pp. 6, 209.

67. The tedious and uncomfortable nature of transatlantic journeys is described in ibid., pp. 7–15.

68. Bailyn, *Peopling of British North America,* p. 26.

69. Russell R. Menard, 'Transport costs and long-range trade, 1300–1800. Was there a European "Transport Revolution" in the early modern era?', in Tracy (ed.), *The political economy of modern merchant empires,* p. 252.

70. Steele, *English Atlantic,* pp. 138–67. For the press in the West Indies see p. 141.

71. Clark, *Language of liberty,* pp. 1–6.

72. Greene, *Peripheries and center,* pp. 24–6.

73. Brooke, *House of Commons,* pp. 230–9; Namier, *England in the age of the American Revolution,* pp. 229–73. Namier calculated that in 1761 there were 13 MPs who had been born in the West Indies or had lived there (p. 235).

74. Bowen, *Revenue and reform,* pp. 30–3, 43–4; Brooke, *House of Commons,* pp. 220–30. Brooke identifies broad but overlapping groups in the Commons who had Company connections (p. 221), and he points out that a small number of members were charged with representing in the House the views of individuals, both Indian and British, from the periphery (pp. 229–30).

75. For the colonial agents see Kammen, *A rope of sand,* and Sosin, *Agents and merchants.* The following remarks on American merchant and religious interest groups are based upon Olson, *Making the empire work.*

76. Olson, *Making the empire work,* p. 1. For the American lobby in the

1760s see Thomas, *Stamp Act crisis*, pp. 28–33. For the transatlantic dimension of colonial politics during the early part of the century see Johnson, *Adjustment to empire.*

77. Price, 'Who cared about the colonies?', p. 422. For the central importance of religion in North American colonial life see Patricia U. Bonomi, *Under the cope of heaven. Religion, society, and politics in colonial America* (New York, 1986).

78. For the often fierce debate, both in Britain and the colonies, about the need for an Anglican Bishop in North America see Carl Bridenbaugh, *Mitre and sceptre. Transatlantic faiths, ideas, personalities, and politics, 1689–1775* (New York, 1962), passim; Bonomi, *Under the cope of heaven*, pp. 199–209.

79. Brathwaite, *The development of creole society*, p. 23. The early development of religious activity in the British West Indies is outlined in Bridenbaugh, *No peace beyond the line*, pp. 144–8, 377–93.

80. Schase, *Colonial American*, pp. 70–3.

81. Bridenbaugh, *Mitre and sceptre.*

82. The development of transatlantic religious networks and organizations is traced in Olson, *Making the empire work.*

83. Steele, *English Atlantic*, pp. 228–250.

84. For a recent exploration of this theme see Clark, *Language of liberty.*

CHAPTER 6   MERCHANTS, PLANTERS AND THE GENTLEMANLY IDEAL

1. Bushman, 'American high-style and vernacular cultures', p. 359.

2. These issues are addressed in Craton, 'Reluctant creoles', pp. 314–62. For the refusal of British colonists to accept the realities of life in the West Indies see the examples described in Richard S. Dunn, 'The English sugar islands and the founding of South Carolina' reprinted in T.H. Breen (ed.), *Shaping southern society. The colonial experience* (New York, 1976), pp. 56–7.

3. Isaac, *Transformation of Virginia*, pp. 118, 132; Kulikoff, *Tobacco and slaves*, pp. 276–7.

4. For a discussion of these problems in a Virginian context see Brown and Brown, *Virginia, 1705–1786*, pp. 34–42.

5. Greene, *Pursuits of happiness*, pp. 197–8.

6. Some caution is needed here. A recent analysis of Philadelphia has focused attention on small and middling traders and, by stressing geographical specialization in particular, has challenged the long-standing general view that all merchants operated in a wide variety of different regions and products. Nevertheless, it still appears to be the case that many wealthier merchants, either through choice or in some cases necessity, simultaneously traded with different parts of the world and developed a broad range of different types of activity (Thomas M. Doerflinger, 'Commercial specialization in Philadelphia's merchant community, 1750–1791', *Business History Review*, LVII (1983), 20–49).

7. Greene, *Peripheries and center*, pp. 30–1.

8. Craton, 'Reluctant Creoles', pp. 351, 353–4.
9. Fischer, *Albion's seed*, pp. 573–83.
10. Brathwaite, *The development of creole society*, pp. 5–7; Bridenbaugh, *No peace beyond the line*, pp. 165–94; idem, *Cities in the wilderness*, passim; idem, *Cities in revolt*, passim.
11. Percival Spear, *The nabobs. The social life of the English in eighteenth-century India* (Oxford, 1932, new impression 1980), pp. 68, 100–4.
12. In 1768 the black to white ratio in the population of Jamaica was about 10:1, although the situation was quite different in other colonies with slave populations. In Virginia the ratio stood at 1.3:1 while in Maryland it was around 2:1 (Karras, *Sojourners in the sun*, p. 174). For case studies of life, relationships and regimes on Jamaican plantations see Craton and Walvin, *Jamaican plantation*, pp. 125–54, and J.R. Ward, 'A planter and his slaves in eighteenth-century Jamaica', in T.C. Smout (ed.), *The search for wealth and stability. Essays in economic and social history presented to M.W. Flinn* (1979), pp. 1–20.
13. For the origin and implementation of slave codes in the West Indies and North America see McFarlane, *The British in the Americas*, pp. 138–41, 177–9.
14. Gerald W. Mullin, *Flight and rebellion. Slave resistance in eighteenth-century Virginia* (New York, 1972), pp. 64–7. Morgan, *Virginians at home*, pp. 58–9. For an overview of relations between whites and the slave community of the Chesapeake see Kulikoff, *Tobacco and slaves*, pp. 381–420.
15. See, for example, the observation on the situation in Jamaica in Brathwaite, *The development of creole society*, pp. 179–80.
16. Gallay, *Formation of a planter elite*, p. 38.
17. Ibid., pp. 41–2, 50–1.
18. For the North American context see Darrett B. Rutman, 'Assessing the little communities of early America', *WMQ*, third series, XLIII (1986). For the separation of whites and blacks in Jamaica see Brathwaite, *Development of creole society*, pp. 185–8.
19. Scammell, *First imperial age*, p. 182. Gallay, *Formation of a planter elite*, pp. 1–2. For a detailed elaboration of this theme in relation to temperate zones see Alfred W. Crosby, *Ecological imperialism. The biological expansion of Europe, 900–1900* (Cambridge, 1986).
20. See, for example, details of the moving frontier of the Chesapeake in Kulikoff, *Tobacco and slaves*, pp. 18–19, 92–9.
21. Greene, *Pursuits of happiness*, p. 172.
22. Bridenbaugh, *Cities in the wilderness*, passim; Bushman, *Refinement of America*, pp. 139–69. New York, however, retained many features of its Dutch architectural heritage. For a good brief description of colonial New York see Harrington, *The New York merchant on the eve of the revolution*, pp. 21–3.
23. For a detailed case study of this process see Bushman, *Refinement of America*, pp. 3–29, 100–38.
24. Bailyn and Morgan (eds), *Strangers within the realm*, p. 14.
25. For this general 'developmental framework' see Jack P. Greene and J.R. Pole, 'Reconstructing British-American colonial history' in idem

(eds), *Colonial British America*, pp. 14–15. For a detailed exploration of these themes see Bushman, 'American high-style and vernacular cultures'.

26.   For just one example, see the accounts of the various social activities that took place at the fashionable resorts and spas that developed in the colonies after 1760 (Carl Bridenbaugh, 'Baths and watering places of colonial America', *WMQ*, third series, III (1946), 152–81). For the central importance of good manners, politeness, and social ritual in elite lifestyles see Bushman, *Refinement of America*, pp. 30–60.

27.   Bushman, 'American high-style and vernacular cultures', pp. 366–7.

28.   In addition to the fashionable staples of the elite reading diet, a few men of letters also took a close interest in the learned journals that were beginning to find their way across the Atlantic (Norman S. Fiering, 'The transatlantic republic of letters: a note on the circulation of learned periodicals to early eighteenth-century America', *WMQ*, third series, XXXIII (1976), 642–60).

29.   Bonomi, *Under the cope of heaven*, pp. 97–105.

30.   Steele, *English Atlantic*, p. 268.

31.   Bushman, 'American high-style and vernacular culture', p. 359.

32.   Steele, 'The empire and provincial elites'.

33.   Ibid., p. 18. For similar comments with regard to the Irish ruling elite see Canny, *Kingdom and colony*, p. 133.

34.   Rhys Isaac makes the important point that in the immediate pre-revolution period the Virginia gentry began to identify with the 'heroic' backwoodsmen from the western frontier of the province. Previously, when enthusiastically embracing metropolitan ideals, the gentry had tended to despise these roughnecks (*Transformation of Virginia*, p. 258).

35.   For the case of the Chesapeake and the Middle colonies see Greene, *Pursuits of happiness*, pp. 91–2 and 136–7.

36.   Simmons and Thomas, *Proceedings and debates*, Vol. II, p. 234.

37.   T.H. Breen, 'The meaning of things. Interpreting the consumer in the eighteenth century', in Brewer and Porter (eds), *Consumption and the world of goods*, pp. 252–3. For a large number of examples of shops in the major towns specializing in imported goods from Britain see Bridenbaugh, *Cities in the wilderness*, pp. 341–5.

38.   R. Roth, 'Tea-drinking in eighteenth-century America. Its etiquette and equipage', in R.B. St George (ed.), *Material life in America, 1600–1860* (Boston, 1988), pp. 439–62.

39.   Quoted in ibid., pp. 441–2.

40.   Quotations from F. Thistlethwaite, 'The Atlantic migration of the pottery industry', *Economic History Review*, second series, XI (1958), 266.

41.   See, for example, the case of Ann Lee Russell the American-born wife of the London merchant James Russell in Price, 'One family's empire', p. 177, and the similar case of the wife of the Virginia merchant, John Norton in F.N. Mason (ed.), *John Norton & Sons, merchants of London and Virginia. Being the papers from their counting house for the years 1750 to 1795* (1937; reprinted Newton Abbot, 1968), p. 124. See also Schase, *Colonial American*, p. 127. For the role of women in the trade

of colonial towns see Bridenbaugh, *Cities in the wilderness*, pp. 340–1.

42. Schase, *Colonial American*, pp. 119–20.

43. Breen, 'Empire of goods', p. 497. For examples of purchasing patterns among the Virginia gentry see Louis B. Wright, *The first gentlemen of Virginia. Intellectual qualities of the early colonial ruling class* (Charlottesville, 1940; reprinted, 1964), pp. 73–6.

44. Mason (ed.), *John Norton & sons*, pp. 210–12. Problems such as these are referred to in Price (ed.), *Joshua Johnson's letterbook*, passim.

45. Rev. Hugh Jones, cited in Isaac, *Transformation of Virginia*, p. 15.

46. Quoted in Clive and Bailyn, 'England's cultural provinces', p. 209. For similar contemporary comments made about Boston in the 1720s see Bridenbaugh, *Cities in the wilderness*, pp. 252–3.

47. Much of what follows is based upon Isaac, *Transformation of Virginia*, pp. 11–138. See also Greene, *Pursuits of happiness*, pp. 92–100; Kulikoff, *Tobacco and slaves*, pp. 261–313; Paul G.E. Clemens, *The Atlantic economy and colonial Maryland's eastern shore. From tobacco to grain* (Ithaca, 1980), pp. 120–67.

48. Kulikoff, *Tobacco and slaves*, p. 263.

49. For the relationships within families and the lifestyles of the Virginia and Maryland gentry see D.B. Smith, *Inside the great house. Planter life in eighteenth-century Chesapeake society* (Ithaca, 1980). For some basic details see also Morgan, *Virginians at home*. For details of the general improvement of living standards in the Chesapeake see Lois Green Carr and Lorena S. Walsh, 'The standard of living in the colonial Chesapeake', *WMQ*, third series, XLX (1988), 135–59.

50. Jack P. Greene, 'Foundations of political power in the Virginia House of Burgesses, 1720–1776', *WMQ*, third series, XVI (1959), pp. 485–506. For the attachment of southern gentlemen to the Anglican faith see Bonomi, *Under the cope of heaven*, pp. 97–202.

51. Aubrey C. Land, 'Economic base and social structure. The northern Chesapeake in the eighteenth century', *Journal of Economic History*, XXV (1965), 639–54; idem, 'Economic behavior in a planting society. The eighteenth-century Chesapeake', *Journal of Southern History*, XXXIII (1967), 469–85.

52. Bernard Bailyn, 'Politics and social structure in Virginia', reprinted in Breen (ed.), *Shaping southern society*, pp. 207–8.

53. Breen, *Tobacco culture*, pp. 40–1. This tobacco mentality is explored on pp. 17–23, 40–83.

54. Clemens, *Atlantic economy*, pp. 134–5. For the development of varying patterns of diversification evident among the elite of Maryland see Gloria L. Main, *Tobacco colony. Life in early Maryland, 1650–1720* (Princeton, 1982), pp. 79–91.

55. Selfa, 'Planter industrialists and iron oligarchs', pp. 66–7. For a review essay which stresses the extent to which this sort of entrepreneurial dimension was to be found within all areas of colonial economic activity see Edwin J. Perkins, 'The entrepreneurial spirit in colonial America: the foundations of modern business history', *Business History Review*, LXIII (1989), 160–86. For the relationship between gentility and capitalism see Bushman, *Refinement of America*, pp. xvii–xviii.

56. For details of these and the following trends see Isaac, *Transformation of Virginia*, pp. 34–101.
57. T.H. Breen, 'Horses and gentlemen. The cultural significance of gambling among the gentry of Virginia', *WMQ*, third series, XXXIV (1977), 239–57. Breen emphasizes the extent to which horse-racing contained several of the core elements of gentry values – competition, individualism and materialism – and he argues that this helped to make it an exclusive activity which reinforced the elite's position.
58. For this point about religion see Kulikoff, *Tobacco and slaves*, pp. 237–40.
59. Wright, *The first gentlemen of Virginia.*
60. Quoted in ibid., p. 61.
61. Isaac, *Transformation of Virginia*, esp. pp. 135–8; Breen, *Tobacco culture*, pp. 27–30, 124–59. Breen has questioned the validity of Isaac's view that the gentry were challenged by smaller planters who held quite different views and assumptions that were rooted in the evangelical Protestantism unleashed by the Great Awakening of the 1740s and 1750s. He does not deny that the planters experienced a loss of nerve, and he does not deny that the religious revival posed some very difficult questions for the elite, but he is at pains to stress the central importance of changes in the core experiences of their everyday lives, that is in the world of debt and tobacco production in general.
62. Bernard Bailyn, *The New England merchants in the seventeenth century* (Cambridge, Mass., 1955), pp. 101–2, 134–42, 192–7. For intermingling of land and trade among the elite of Boston and Newport see Bridenbaugh, *Cities in the wilderness*, p. 255, 339; idem, *Cities in revolt*, pp. 144–5.
63. For some comparisons that underscore this point see Thomas M. Doerflinger, *A vigorous spirit of enterprise. Merchants and economic development in revolutionary Philadelphia* (Chapel Hill, 1986), pp. 139, 158–61.
64. Quoted in Bridenbaugh, *Cities in the wilderness*, p. 253. See also p. 290.
65. Greene, *Pursuits of happiness*, pp. 56–80 (quotation on p. 79). For a detailed study of political and social life between 1675 and 1715 see Johnson, *Adjustment to empire.*
66. Harrington, *The New York merchant on the eve of the revolution*, pp. 11–37, 126–63; Bridenbaugh, *Cities in the wilderness*, pp. 186, 254, 339; idem, *Cities in revolt*, p. 145. See also Sung Bok Kim, 'A new look at the great landlords of eighteenth-century New York', *WMQ*, third series, XXVII (1970), 579–614 (esp. 595–600).
67. For a detailed study of the Philadelphia merchants between 1750 and 1775 see Doerflinger, *Vigorous spirit of enterprise*, pp. 11–164. Doerflinger is at pains to point out (pp. 15, 32) that it is misleading to refer to a homogeneous 'merchant aristocracy', as was the case with older generations of historians, because the social elite of Philadelphia contained around 15 per cent of the entire merchant community. The wealth and lifestyle of the majority of merchants was such that it took them a long way from any definition of an aristocracy. For various aspects of the merchant community see also Nash, 'Early merchants',

p. 344; Bridenbaugh, *Cities in the wilderness*, pp. 253–4, 306, 339; idem, *Cities in revolt*, p. 145; Selfa, 'Planter industrialists and iron oligarchs', 63.

68. Greene, *Pursuits of happiness*, pp. 141–51.
69. Gallay, *Formation of a planter elite*, p. 107.
70. Quoted in Dunn, 'English sugar islands', p. 58.
71. This paragraph is based on Richard Waterhouse, 'The development of elite culture in the colonial American South: a study of Charles Town, 1670–1770', *Australian Journal of Politics and History*, XXVIII (1982), 391–404.
72. Gallay, *Formation of a planter elite*, p. 37.
73. Ibid., p. 165.
74. For the traditional view see L.G. Ragatz, *The rise and fall of the planter class in the British Caribbean, 1763–1833* (New York, 1928; reprinted, 1963).
75. Greene, *Pursuits of happiness*, pp. 156, 162–4.
76. Brathwaite, *The development of creole society*, pp. 126–8.
77. Steele, *English Atlantic*, pp. 153, 163. For the shipping arrangements that allowed those in the Caribbean to be kept in touch with news from home see ibid., pp. 21–40.
78. Bridenbaugh, *No peace beyond the line*, pp. 267–305.
79. Richard S. Dunn, *Sugar and slaves: the rise of the planter class in the English West Indies, 1624–1713* (1973), pp. 58, 170–1. For a profile of planter communities in the eighteenth century see Sheridan, *Sugar and slavery*, pp. 360–88.
80. Dunn, *Sugar and slaves*, pp. 46–7.
81. Bridenbaugh, *No peace beyond the line*, pp. 171–2.
82. Zahedieh, 'London and the colonial consumer', 248–53. For the importation of luxury goods and inappropriate fashionable clothing into Barbados in the mid-seventeenth century see, Bridenbaugh, *No peace beyond the line*, pp. 136–7.
83. Zahedieh, 'London and the colonial consumer', p. 257.
84. Dunn, *Sugar and slaves*, pp. 263–300.
85. Craton and Walvin, *Jamaican plantation*, p. 56.
86. Quotation from the historian Bryan Edwards in Brathwaite, *The development of creole society*, p. 123.
87. Craton and Walvin, *Jamaican plantation*, pp. 85, 93. For the emergence of 'creole style' see Brathwaite, pp. 122–6.
88. See, for example, Charles Leslie, *History of Jamaica* (1740), pp. 28–39, cited in Craton and Walvin, *Jamaican Plantation*, p. 84. For similar contemporary observations on town-life in Jamaica during the late-seventeenth century see Zahedieh, 'London and the colonial consumer', pp. 252–3. For urban social activities in general see Bridenbaugh, *No peace beyond the line*, pp. 375–6.
89. For a detailed exploration of this theme see Jack P. Greene, 'Changing identity in the British Caribbean: Barbados as a case study', in N. Canny and A. Pagden (eds), *Colonial identity in the Atlantic world 1500–1800* (Princeton, 1987), pp. 213–66.
90. Marshall, *East Indian fortunes*, pp. 5–28; Spear, *The nabobs*, pp. 23–41.

91. P.J. Marshall, 'Taming the exotic. The British and India in the seventeenth and eighteenth centuries', in G.S. Rousseau and Roy Porter (eds), *Exoticism in the Enlightenment* (Manchester, 1990), p. 49.
92. Marshall, *East Indian fortunes*, pp. 23–5.
93. Quoted in C. Rowell, 'Clive of India and his family. The formation of the collection', in M. Archer, C. Rowell and R. Skelton, *Treasures from India. The Clive collection at Powis Castle* (1987), p. 24.
94. Spear, *The nabobs*, pp. 175–91.
95. M. Archer, 'The British as collectors and patrons in India, 1760–1830', in Archer, Rowell and Skelton, *Treasures from India*, pp. 9–16. For Hastings as a patron and scholar see P.J. Marshall, 'Warren Hastings as scholar and patron', in A. Whiteman, J.S. Bromley and P.G.M. Dickson (eds), *Statesmen, scholars, and merchants: essays in eighteenth-century history presented to Dame Lucy Sutherland* (Oxford, 1973), pp. 242–62, and J.L. Brockington, 'Warren Hastings and Orientalism', in Geoffrey Carnall and Colin Nicholson (eds), *The impeachment of Warren Hastings. Papers from a bicentenary commemoration* (Edinburgh, 1989), pp. 91–108.
96. Marshall, 'British private investment in eighteenth-century Bengal'.
97. Bowen, *Revenue and reform*, p. 87.

CHAPTER 7   THE END OF THE ENGLISH EMPIRE

1. For numerous examples of the way in which contemporary debate was conducted in these different terms see Greene, *Peripheries and center*, pp. 19–42.
2. For foreign investment in the National Debt see Dickson, *Financial revolution*, pp. 304–337; for Irish officers in the Royal Navy see Gwyn, *Enterprising admiral*, p. 198; and for Scottish officers in the army see James Hayes, 'Scottish officers in the British army, 1714–63', *Scottish History Review*, XXXVI (1957), 24–33.
3. Chapman, *Merchant enterprise*, p. 23. It has also been noted that a 'growing minority' of Bristol's merchants were born or trained overseas (Morgan, *Bristol and the Atlantic trade*, p. 10).
4. Jones, *War and economy*, pp. 253–8.
5. Quoted in David Kynaston, *The City of London. Volume 1: A world of its own 1815–1890* (1994), p. 5.
6. De Krey, *Fractured society*, pp. 74–120.
7. Ibid., p. 125. Only 30 per cent of Tory City leaders were merchants.
8. For examples see ibid., p. 76. See also Chapman, *Merchant enterprise*, p. 46; Price, *Joshua Johnson's Letterbook*, xi–xii; and W.E. Minchinton, 'The merchants of England in the eighteenth century', *Explorations in entrepreneurial history*, X (1957), 68.
9. Sosin, *Agents and merchants*, pp. 3–6.
10. G. Yogev, *Diamonds and corals. Anglo-Dutch Jews and eighteenth-century trade* (Leicester, 1978), pp. 20–1.
11. De Krey, *Fractured society*, pp. 101–6.
12. David Ormrod, 'The "Protestant Capitalist International", 1651–1775',

Historical Research, LXVI (1993), 197–208. See the detailed case studies
of fourteen Quaker families of London in Jacob M. Price, 'The great
Quaker business families of eighteenth-century London. The rise and
fall of a sectarian patriciate', in Dunn and Dunn (eds), *The world of
William Penn,* pp. 363–99.
13. These developments are summarized in Ned C. Landsman, *Scotland
and its first American colony, 1683–1765* (Princeton, 1985), pp. 72–7.
14. Morgan, *Bristol and the Atlantic trade,* pp. 133, 155. For the rise of the
outports see above, p. 58.
15. See pp. 88–9.
16. See, for example, Devine, 'An eighteenth-century business elite', p. 52.
17. Chapman, *Merchant enterprise,* p. 46.
18. Nash, 'Early merchants', pp. 338–9, 341.
19. The classic formulation of this view is to be found in Clive and Bailyn,
'England's cultural provinces'.
20. As Richard B. Sher has pointed out, Clive and Bailyn's article did
much to point to similarities in the way in which both Scotland and
America stood in relation to England, but it said very little about
'interprovincial connexions' and the 'direct interaction' between Scotland and America (Richard B. Sher, 'Introduction. Scottish-American
cultural studies, past and present', in Richard B. Sher and Jeffrey B.
Smitten (eds), *Scotland and America in the age of the Enlightenment* (Edinburgh, 1990), p. 4).
21. This point is made in ibid., pp. 4–5 with regard to intellectual and
cultural connections, but the same argument applies to any other
form of relationship between Britain and her overseas possessions.
22. Ned C. Landsman, 'The provinces and the empire. Scotland, the
American colonies and the development of British provincial identity',
in Stone (ed.), *Imperial state at war,* pp. 258–87 (quotations from p.
263). Many of the complexities of the interactive cultural connections
between Scotland and America are explored in the essays in Sher and
Smitten (eds), *Scotland and America.*
23. See, for example, Andrew Hook, 'Philadelphia, Edinburgh and the
Scottish Enlightenment', in Sher and Smitten (eds), *Scotland and
America,* pp. 227–41.
24. Colley, *Britons,* pp. 131–2.
25. Ibid., pp. 117–32, 155–64 (quotation on p. 156). For a large number
of examples of Scottish immigrants doing well and establishing themselves in the upper echelons of colonial American society see Brock,
Scotus Americanus, pp. 24–34.
26. P.J. Marshall, 'Nation defined by empire 1755–1783' (unpublished
typescript), pp. 1–2. This paper was read to the Anglo-American Conference of Historians in 1994. I am grateful to Professor Marshall for
allowing me to read his paper in typescript form.
27. Greene, *Pursuits of happiness,* pp. 47–52. The pattern of emigration
during the seventeenth century is examined in detail in H.A. Gemery,
'Emigration from the British Isles to the New World, 1630–1700',
Research in Economic History, V (1980), 179–231.
28. McCusker and Menard, *The economy of British America,* pp. 211–35.

29. The figures in this paragraph are derived from A. Fogelman, 'Migrations to the thirteen North American colonies. New estimates', *Journal of Interdisciplinary History*, XXII (1992), 691–710.

30. The general context for Irish migration is provided in L.M. Cullen, 'The Irish diaspora of the seventeenth and eighteenth centuries', Nicholas Canny (ed.), *Europeans on the move. Studies on European migration, 1500–1800* (Oxford, 1994), pp. 113–49. For a detailed study of migration from northern Ireland see R.J. Dickson, *Ulster emigration to colonial America, 1718–1775* (1966).

31. Bailyn, *Peopling of British North America*, p. 59.

32. Bailyn, *Peopling of British North America*; idem, *Voyagers to the west*; Fischer, *Albion's seed*; Greene, *Pursuits of happiness*.

33. For detailed discussion and criticism of Fischer's work by a number of historians see 'Albion's seed. Four British folkways in America – a symposium', *WMQ*, third series, XLVIII (1991), 223–308.

34. See, for example, Nash, 'Early merchants'.

35. Doerflinger, *Vigorous spirit of enterprise*, pp. 55–6; Bridenbaugh, *Cities in revolt*, p. 333.

36. Kulikoff, *Tobacco and slaves*, pp. 263–5. For examples of rapid upward mobility to the highest levels of society in the northern Chesapeake see Land, 'Economic base and social structure'. For the entry of Huguenots into the Boston elite in the early eighteenth century see Bridenbaugh, *Cities in the wilderness*, pp. 251–2. For the part played by West Indian, notably Barbadian, planters in the establishment of South Carolina and their subsequent development of economic and political influence in the colony see Dunn, 'The English sugar islands and the founding of South Carolina', pp. 48–58.

37. For the challenges posed to American elites by Irish Protestant migrants see Canny, *Kingdom and colony*, pp. 130–1. Similar challenges were posed by Scottish and Welsh settlers.

38. Lenman, *Integration, enlightenment, and industrialization*, pp. 32–40, 58–9.

39. Colley, *Britons*, pp. 117–32.

40. For discussions of the wide range of economic factors which prompted emigration from Scotland see the contributions in R.A. Cage (ed.), *The Scots abroad, labour, capital, enterprise, 1750–1914* (1985), passim. See also E. Richards, 'Scotland and the uses of the Atlantic empire', in Bailyn and Morgan (eds), *Strangers within the realm*, pp. 67–114. For emigration as only one element within a broader pattern of social mobility see T.C. Smout, N.C. Landsman, and T.M. Devine, 'Scottish emigration in the seventeenth and eighteenth centuries', in Canny (ed.), *Europeans on the move*, pp. 76–112.

41. Daniel Defoe, *A tour through the whole island of Great Britain* (1724–6), ed. Pat Rogers (1971), p. 609.

42. Karras, *Sojourners in the sun*, passim. For examples of the opportunities that North America offered to those excluded from the upper echelons of Scottish society see Landsman, *Scotland's first colony*, pp. 99–101.

43. For examples of the entry of wealthy immigrants into established Chesapeake gentry families via marriage see Kulikoff, *Tobacco and slaves*, p. 266. For the entry of John White (a Welshman) and Hugh Wallace

(an Irishman) by similar means into the merchant elite of New York
see Harrington, *New York merchant*, pp. 16–17. For the integration of
Scottish newcomers into New Jersey society through family and commercial connections see Landsman, *Scotland's first colony*, pp. 159–60,
208–11.

44. See, for example, the cases of Cadwallader Colden, the Scottish-born
acting governor of New York, and William Johnson, the Irish-born
superintendent for Indian affairs who was awarded a baronetcy in
1755 (Egnal, *Mighty empire*, pp. 54–5). For numerous examples of Scottish immigrants rising to the top of American society see Brock, *Scotus
Americanus*, pp. 24–34.

45. Ronald Hoffman, '"Marylando-Hibernus". Charles Carroll the settler,
1660–1720', *WMQ*, third series, XLV (1988), 207–36.

46. Bridenbaugh, *No peace beyond the line*, pp. 195–229.

47. For this process in its Jamaican context, see Karras, *Sojourners in the
sun*, pp. 46–79.

48. Sheridan, *Sugar and slavery*, pp. 197–200. Good examples of marriage
playing an important part in the increase of plantation size may be
seen in the cases of Thomas Meade of Montserrat and Henry Dawkins
of Jamaica, ibid., pp. 177–8, 224–5.

49. Richard B. Sheridan, 'The rise of a colonial gentry. A case study of
Antigua, 1730–75', *Econ. Hist. Rev.*, second series, XIII (1960–1), 345,
349.

50. Sheridan, *Sugar and Slavery*, pp. 158, 369–70.

51. Ibid., 370. Karras, *Sojourners in the sun*, pp. 53, 55.

52. The following two paragraphs are based upon G.J. Bryant, 'Scots in
India in the eighteenth century', *Scottish History Review*, LXIV (1985),
22–41, and J. Riddy, 'Warren Hastings: Scotland's benefactor?', in
Carnall and Nicholson (eds), *The impeachment of Warren Hastings*, pp.
30–57.

53. See, for example, Riddy, 'Warren Hastings', p. 40.

54. Landsman, *Scotland and its first American colony*, p. 101. Landsman's
book is a detailed elaboration of these themes.

55. Karras, *Sojourners in the sun*, pp. 123–31.

56. Landsman, *Scotland and its first American colony*, pp. 3–13, 163–91.

57. Ibid., p. 258. For the caution necessary when applying such a model
to the development of all colonial ethnic groups see pp. 258–9.

58. D.S. Macmillan, 'Scottish enterprise and influences in Canada', in
Cage (ed.), *The Scots abroad*, pp. 46, 56, and 65; J.G. Parker, 'Scottish
Enterprise in India, 1750–1914', ibid., pp. 195–6.

59. Quoted in Egnal, *Mighty empire*, p. 116. The wearing of Highland dress
was not prohibited in the colonies as it was in Scotland itself after the
Jacobite rising of 1745 (Brock, *Scotus Americanus*, p. 70).

60. Karras, *Sojourners in the sun*, pp. 131–7.

61. William Lee quoted in Soltow, 'Scottish traders in Virginia', p. 83. For
the general resentment and hostility directed against the Scots see
Richards, 'Scotland and the uses of the Atlantic empire', pp. 98–101.

62. Quoted in Karras, *Sojourners in the sun*, p. 93.

63. Landsman, *Scotland and its first American colony*, pp. 108–12.

64. Ibid., pp. 262–3. The diverse range of cultural connections between Scotland and America are explored in Sher and Smitten (eds), *Scotland and America in the age of Enlightenment*. The distinct organizational characteristics of Scottish trade with the Chesapeake and the West Indies are summarized above on pp. 88–90.

65. For brief comments on Welsh emigration to North America in the late seventeenth and early eighteenth centuries see H.M. Davies, ' "Very different springs of uneasiness". Emigration from Wales to the United States of America during the 1790s', *Welsh History Review*, XV (1991), 370–1.

66. Quotations from A.H. Dodd, *The character of the early Welsh emigration to the United States* (2nd edn, Cardiff, 1957), p. 15.

67. Ibid., pp. 13–15.

68. Bridenbaugh, *Cities in the wilderness*, pp. 431, 440. Philip Jenkins, *A history of modern Wales, 1536–1990* (1992), p. 71. Gwyn A. Williams, *When was Wales? A history of the Welsh* (1985), p. 157.

69. Quoted in Marshall, 'Nation defined by empire 1755–1783', p. 4.

70. For Scots in the Chesapeake see Karras, *Sojourners in the sun*, pp. 188–202, and for the situation in Scotland itself see Lenman, *Integration, enlightenment, and industrialization*, p. 61.

CHAPTER 8   ENTERPRISE AND EXPANSION: DRAWING A LINE

1. Greene, *Peripheries and center*, p. 136.

2. Marshall, 'Empire and authority in the later eighteenth century', p. 108. For a detailed examination of the ways in which a commercial or mercantilist vision of empire was fused with libertarian political thought see Wilson, 'Empire of virtue'.

3. Greene, *Peripheries and center*, p. 61.

4. McCusker and Menard, *The economy of British America*, pp. 331–44.

5. Greene, *Peripheries and center*, esp. pp. 55–76.

6. Harris, *A patriot press*, pp. 251–3 (quotation on p. 251).

7. Koehn, *Power of commerce*, passim.

8. Speech of 10 December 1755, Simmons and Thomas, *Proceedings and debates*, Vol. I, p. 115.

9. Brewer, *Sinews of power*, p. 114.

10. Simmons and Thomas, *Proceedings and debates*, Vol. II, p. 194.

11. Harris, *Patriot press*, pp. 221–7. Cape Breton was in fact handed back to France three years later in exchange for Madras.

12. Baugh, 'Maritime strength and Atlantic commerce', pp. 210–11.

13. Ibid., pp. 211–12; Wilson, 'Empire of virtue', p. 144.

14. Jack P. Greene, 'The Seven Years' War and the American Revolution. The causal relationship reconsidered', *JICH*, VIII (1980), 85.

15. See, for example, the comments of William Beckford made during a debate on America on 15 November 1768 (Simmons and Thomas, *Proceedings and debates*, Vol. III, p. 15).

16. Greene, 'The Seven Years' War and the American Revolution', pp.

85–105. Several contemporary observations on the colonies are to be found on pp. 85–6.

17. P.J. Marshall, '"Cornwallis triumphant". War in India and the British public in the late eighteenth century', in Lawrence Freedman, Paul Hayes and Robert O'Neill (eds), *War, strategy, and international politics. Essays in honour of Sir Michael Howard* (Oxford, 1992), pp. 57–74.

18. Bowen, *Revenue and reform*, pp. 16–17.

19. The important Pratt-Yorke opinion of 1757 addressed the question of the East India Company's right to retain territory gained in India. The opinion was later used to provide the basis of the arguments of those contesting the Crown's claim to land granted to settlers by North American Indians. For the opinion in its Indian context see H.V. Bowen, 'A question of sovereignty? The Bengal land revenue issue, 1765–67', *JICH*, XVI (1988), 162–3. For its later application in a North American context see Sosin, *Whitehall and the wilderness*, pp. 229–35, 259–67.

20. Bowen, *Revenue and reform*, pp. 25–8 (quotation on p. 25). See also Koehn, *The power of commerce*, pp. 206–7.

21. Baugh, 'Maritime strength and Atlantic commerce', pp. 201–3. Wilson, 'Empire, trade and popular politics', p. 97; idem, 'Empire of virtue', pp. 144–8.

22. Baugh, 'Maritime strength and Atlantic commerce', p. 203.

23. Namier, *England in the age of the American Revolution*, pp. 273–82; Lawson, 'Irishman's prize'; Koehn, *Power of commerce*, pp. 149–84.

24. For the Indian context see Bowen, 'A question of sovereignty?', pp. 155–76, and idem, *Revenue and reform*, pp. 12–15, 103–18.

25. Bowen, *Revenue and reform*, pp. 68–9.

26. Marshall, 'Empire and authority', p. 114; Wilson, 'Empire of virtue', p. 150.

27. Quoted in Bowen, *Revenue and reform*, p. 69.

28. Marshall, 'Empire and authority', pp. 106–7.

29. Paul Langford, 'Old Whigs, Old Tories, and the American Revolution', *JICH*, VIII (1980), 127; Marshall, 'Empire and authority', pp. 108–16.

30. Koehn, *Power of commerce*, pp. 62–3; Greene, *Peripheries and center*, pp. 7–18, 49–53.

31. For a detailed account of the making of the Regulating Act see Bowen, *Revenue and reform*, pp. 133–86.

32. The next two paragraphs are based upon ibid., pp. 67–83. For the 'Borneo enterprise' see Harlow, *Founding of the second British empire*, Vol. I, pp. 70–97.

33. For background and details of the crisis see Das, *British reactions*, pp. 42–9, and Tracy, 'Parry of a threat to India'.

34. Egnal, *A mighty empire*, p. 12.

35. Bailyn, *Peopling of British North America*, p. 74.

36. For the background to, and formulation of, the Proclamation see Sosin, *Whitehall and the wilderness*, pp. 39–64, and Thomas, *Stamp Act crisis*, pp. 41–4.

37. Thomas, *Townshend duties crisis*, pp. 53–9.
38. Ibid., pp. 60–3.
39. For full detail on the Vandalia project and its progress as a political issue see ibid., pp. 66–74.
40. On the general issue of the influence of commercial and manufacturing groups on imperial policy-making see Koehn, *Power of commerce*, pp. 27–30, 54–60, 108–9.
41. Bailyn, *Voyagers to the west*, pp. 30–66.
42. Egnal, *Mighty empire*, pp. 123–5.
43. For the views of consolidators such as Clive see Bowen, *Revenue and reform*, pp. 14–15, 69.
44. For the regulation of private trade in Bengal see Marshall, *East Indian fortunes*, pp. 129–57.
45. Egnal, *Mighty empire*, p. 264.
46. Alan Gallay, 'Jonathan Bryan's plantation empire. Land, politics and the formation of a ruling class in colonial Georgia', *WMQ*, third series, XLV (1988), 253–79; idem, *The formation of a planter elite*, pp. 84–108.
47. For detailed accounts of the developing political and constitutional crisis after 1763 see the three studies by Thomas, *British politics and the Stamp Act crisis*; *The Townshend duities crisis*; and *Tea party to independence*.

AFTERWORD

1. Bayly, *Imperial meridian*, p. 108.
2. For the background to, and details of, these measures see ibid., pp. 100–32.
3. The phrase is Bayly's and is used as the title of Chapter 4 in ibid.
4. Stephen Conway, *The War of American Independence, 1775–1783* (1995), pp. 236–8.

Bibliography

T.P. Abernethy, *Western lands and the American Revolution* (New York, 1937).
'Albion's seed. Four British folkways in America – a symposium', *WMQ*, third series, XLVIII (1991).
B.L. Anderson, 'Provincial aspects of the financial revolution of the eighteenth century', *BH*, XI (1970).
M. Archer, 'The British as collectors and patrons in India, 1760–1830', in Archer, Rowell and Skelton, *Treasures from India*.
M. Archer, C. Rowell and R. Skelton, *Treasures from India. The Clive collection at Powis Castle* (1987).
C.T. Atkinson, 'In the days of John Company. The early service of the king's troops in India', *Journal of the Society for Army Historical Research*, XXXII (1954).
M. Atkinson and C. Baber, *The growth and decline of the South Wales iron industry, 1760–1880* (Cardiff, 1987).
Bernard Bailyn, *The New England merchants in the seventeenth century* (Cambridge, Mass., 1955).
Bernard Bailyn, *The peopling of British North America. An Introduction* (1987).
Bernard Bailyn, 'Politics and social structure in Virginia', reprinted in Breen (ed.), *Shaping southern society*.
Bernard Bailyn with the assistance of Barbara De Wolfe, *Voyagers to the west. Emigration from Britain to America on the eve of the Revolution* (1986).
Bernard Bailyn and Philip D. Morgan (eds), *Strangers within the realm: cultural margins of the first British empire* (Chapel Hill, 1991).
Daniel A. Baugh, *British naval administration in the age of Walpole* (Princeton, 1965).
Daniel A. Baugh, 'Maritime strength and Atlantic commerce. The uses of a "grand marine empire"', in Stone (ed.), *Imperial state at war*.
C.A. Bayly, *Imperial meridian. The British empire and the world, 1780–1830* (1989).
Wyndham Beawes, *Lex mercatoria rediviva. Or the merchants' directory* (1752; 4th edn, 1783).
J.V. Beckett, *The aristocracy in England, 1660–1914* (Oxford, 1986).
J.V. Beckett, *Coal and tobacco. The Lowthers and the economic development of West Cumberland, 1660–1760* (Cambridge, 1981).
J.V. Beckett, *The rise and fall of the Grenvilles, Dukes of Buckingham and Chandos, 1710–1921* (Manchester, 1994).
J.V. Beckett and Michael Turner, 'Taxation and economic growth in eighteenth-century England', *Econ. Hist. Rev.*, second series, XLIII (1990).
A.L. Beier, David Cannadine and James M. Rosenheim (eds), *The first modern society. Essays in honour of Lawrence Stone* (Cambridge, 1992).
Maxine Berg and Pat Hudson, 'Rehabilitating the industrial revolution', *Econ. Hist. Rev.*, second series, XLV (1992).
Jeremy Black, *The English press in the eighteenth century* (1987).
Jeremy Black (ed.), *British politics and society from Walpole to Pitt, 1742–1789* (1990).

Patricia U. Bonomi, *Under the cope of heaven. Religion, society, and politics in colonial America* (New York, 1986).

H.V. Bowen, 'The Bank of England during the long eighteenth century, 1694–1820', in Roberts and Kynaston (eds), *The Bank of England.*

H.V. Bowen, 'Investment and empire in the later eighteenth century. East India stockholding, 1756–1791', *Econ. Hist. Rev.*, second series, XLII (1989).

H.V. Bowen, 'The "little parliament". The General Court of the East India Company, 1750–1784', *HJ*, XXXIV (1991).

H.V. Bowen, 'Lord Clive and speculation in East India Company stock, 1766', *HJ*, XXX (1987).

H.V. Bowen, '"The pests of human society". Stockbrokers, jobbers, and speculators in mid-eighteenth-century Britain', *History*, LXXVIII (1993).

H.V. Bowen, 'A question of sovereignty? The Bengal land revenue issue, 1765–67', *JICH*, XVI (1988).

H.V. Bowen, *Revenue and reform. The Indian problem in British politics 1757–1773* (Cambridge, 1991).

Edward Brathwaite, *The development of creole society in Jamaica, 1770–1820* (Oxford, 1971).

T.H. Breen, '"Baubles of Britain". The American and consumer revolutions of the eighteenth century', *Past and Present*, CXIX (1988), 73–104.

T.H. Breen, 'An empire of goods. The anglicization of colonial America, 1690–1776', *Journal of British Studies*, XXV (1986).

T.H. Breen, 'Horses and gentlemen: the cultural significance of gambling among the gentry of Virginia', *WMQ*, third series, XXXIV (1977).

T.H. Breen, 'The meaning of things. Interpreting the consumer in the eighteenth century', in Brewer and Porter (eds), *Consumption and the world of goods.*

T.H. Breen, (ed.), *Shaping southern society. The colonial experience* (New York, 1976).

T.H. Breen, *Tobacco culture. The mentality of the great tidewater planters on the eve of the revolution* (Princeton, 1986).

John Brewer, *The sinews of power. War, money and the English state, 1688–1783* (1989).

John Brewer and Roy Porter (eds), *Consumption and the world of goods in the seventeenth and eighteenth centuries* (1993).

Carl Bridenbaugh, 'Baths and watering places of colonial America', *WMQ*, third series, III (1946).

Carl Bridenbaugh, *Cities in revolt. Urban life in America, 1743–1775* (New York, 1955).

Carl Bridenbaugh, *Cities in the wilderness. The first century of urban life in America, 1625–1742* (second edition, New York, 1955).

Carl Bridenbaugh, *Mitre and sceptre. Transatlantic faiths, ideas, personalities, and politics, 1689–1775* (New York, 1962).

Carl Bridenbaugh and Roberta Bridenbaugh, *No peace beyond the line. The English in the Caribbean, 1629–1690* (New York, 1971).

W.R. Brock, *Scotus Americanus. A survey of the sources for the links between Scotland and America in the eighteenth century* (Edinburgh, 1982).

J.L. Brockington, 'Warren Hastings and Orientalism', in Carnall and Nicholson (eds), *The impeachment of Warren Hastings.*

John Brooke, *History of Parliament. The House of Commons, 1754–1790. Introductory survey* (Oxford, 1964).

Robert E. Brown and B. Katherine Brown, *Virginia, 1705–1786. Democracy or aristocracy?* (East Lansing, 1956).

G.J. Bryant, 'Officers of the East India Company's army in the days of Clive and Hastings', *JICH*, VI (1978).

G.J. Bryant, 'Pacification in the early British raj, 1755–85', *JICH*, XIII (1985).

G.J. Bryant, 'Scots in India in the eighteenth century', *Scottish History Review*, LXIV (1985), 22–41.

J.M. Bumsted, 'The cultural landscape of early Canada', in Bailyn and Morgan (eds), *Strangers within the realm.*

Richard L. Bushman, 'American high-style and vernacular cultures', in Greene and Pole (eds), *Colonial British America.*

Richard L. Bushman, *The refinement of America. Persons, houses, cities* (New York, 1992).

R.A. Cage (ed.), *The Scots abroad. Labour, capital, enterprise, 1750–1914* (1985).

P.J. Cain and A.G. Hopkins, *British imperialism. Crisis and deconstruction, 1914–1990* (1993).

P.J. Cain and A.G. Hopkins, *British imperialism. Innovation and expansion, 1688–1914* (1993).

P.J. Cain and A.G. Hopkins, 'Gentlemanly capitalism and British expansion overseas I. The old colonial system, 1688–1850', *Econ. Hist. Rev.*, second series, XXXIX (1986), 501–25.

P.J. Cain and A.G. Hopkins, 'Gentlemanly capitalism and British expansion overseas II. New imperialism, 1850–1945', *Econ. Hist. Rev.*, second series, XL (1987), 1–26.

P.J. Cain and A.G. Hopkins, 'The political economy of British expansion overseas, 1750–1914', *Econ. Hist. Rev.*, second series, XXXIII (1980), 463–90.

Rondo Cameron, *Banking in the early stages of industrialization. A study of comparative economic history* (New York, 1967).

J.A. Cannon, *Aristocratic century. The peerage of eighteenth-century England* (Cambridge, 1984).

Nicholas Canny (ed.), *Europeans on the move. Studies on European migration, 1500–1800* (Oxford, 1994).

Nicholas Canny, *Kingdom and colony. Ireland in the Atlantic world, 1560–1800* (Baltimore, 1988).

Nicholas Canny and Anthony Pagden (eds), *Colonial identity in the Atlantic world, 1500–1800* (Princeton, 1987).

Geoffrey Carnall and Colin Nicholson (eds), *The impeachment of Warren Hastings. Papers from a bicentenary commemoration* (Edinburgh, 1989).

Lois Green Carr and Lorena S. Walsh, 'The standard of living in the colonial Chesapeake', *WMQ*, third series, XLX (1988).

Nancy G. Cassels (ed.), *Orientalism, evangelicalism, and the military cantonment in early nineteenth-century India. An historiographical overview* (Lampeter, 1991).

Stanley Chapman, *Merchant enterprise in Britain from the industrial revolution to World War I* (Cambridge, 1991).

K.N. Chaudhuri, *The trading world of Asia and the East India Company, 1660–1760* (Cambridge, 1978).

S.G. Checkland, *Scottish banking. A history, 1695–1973* (Glasgow, 1975).

J.H. Clapham, *The Bank of England. A history*, two vols (Cambridge, 1944).

Charles E. Clark, *The eastern frontier. The settlement of northern New England, 1610–1763* (New York, 1970).

J.C.D. Clark, *The language of liberty 1660–1832. Political discourse and social dynamics in the Anglo-American world* (Cambridge, 1994).

Paul G.E. Clemens, *The Atlantic economy and colonial Maryland's eastern shore. From tobacco to grain* (Ithaca, 1980).

Paul G.E. Clemens, 'The rise of Liverpool, 1665–1750', *Econ. Hist. Rev.*, second series, XXIX (1976).

John Clive and Bernard Bailyn, 'England's cultural provinces: Scotland and America', *WMQ*, third series, XI (1954), 200–13.

Linda Colley, *Britons: forging the nation 1707–1837* (New Haven, 1992).

Stephen Conway, *The War of American Independence*, 1775–1783 (1995).

P.J. Corfield, 'Class by name and number in eighteenth-century Britain', *History*, LXXII (1987).

P.J. Corfield, 'The democratic history of the English gentleman', *History Today*, (December 1992).

N.F.R. Crafts, *British economic growth during the Industrial Revolution* (Oxford, 1985).

G.A. Cranfield, *The development of the provincial newspaper, 1700–1760* (Oxford, 1962).

Michael Craton, 'Reluctant creoles. The planters' world in the British West Indies', in Bailyn and Morgan (eds), *Strangers within the realm.*

Michael Craton and James Walvin, *A Jamaican plantation. The history of Worthy Park, 1670–1970* (1970).

Alfred W. Crosby, *Ecological imperialism. The biological expansion of Europe, 900–1900* (Cambridge, 1986).

D. Crossley and R. Saville (eds), *The Fuller letters, 1728–1755. Guns, slaves, and finance* (Lewes, 1991).

P. Crowhurst, *The defence of British trade, 1689–1815* (Folkestone, 1977).

L.M. Cullen, 'The Irish diaspora of the seventeenth and eighteenth centuries', in Canny (ed.), *Europeans on the move.*

S. Das, 'British reactions to the French bugbear in India, 1763–83', *European History Quarterly*, 22 (1992).

Ashin Das Gupta and M.N. Pearson (eds), *India and the Indian Ocean 1500–1800* (Calcutta, 1987).

H.M. Davies, '"Very different springs of uneasiness". Emigration from Wales to the United States of America during the 1790s', *Welsh History Review*, XV (1991).

K.G. Davies, *The Royal African Company* (1957).

M.G. Davies, 'Country gentry and payments to London, 1650–1714', *Econ. Hist. Rev.*, second series, XXIV (1971).

Lance E. Davis and Robert A. Huttenback, *Mammon and the pursuit of empire. The political economy of British imperialism, 1860–1912* (Cambridge, 1987).

Ralph Davis, 'English foreign trade, 1700–1774', *Econ. Hist. Rev.*, second series, XV (1962).

Ralph Davis, *The industrial revolution and British overseas trade* (Leicester, 1979).

Ralph Davis, *The rise of the Atlantic economies* (Ithaca, 1973).

Ralph Davis, *The rise of the English shipping industry in the seventeenth and eighteenth centuries* (1962).

Daniel Defoe, *A tour through the whole island of Great Britain* (1724–6), ed. Pat Rogers (1971).

Gary Stuart De Krey, *A fractured society. The politics of London in the first age of party, 1688–1715* (Oxford, 1985).

T.M. Devine, 'The colonial trades and industrial investment in Scotland, *c.*1700–1815', *Econ. Hist. Rev.*, second series, XXIX (1976).

T.M. Devine, 'An eighteenth-century business elite. Glasgow–West India merchants, *c.*1750–1815', *Scottish History Review*, LVII (1978).

T.M. Devine, 'Glasgow colonial merchants and land, 1700–1815', in Ward and Wilson (eds), *Land and industry*.

T.M. Devine, 'Sources of capital for the Glasgow tobacco trade, *c.*1740–1780', *BH*, XVI (1974).

T.M. Devine, *The tobacco lords. A study of the tobacco merchants of Glasgow and their trading activities, c.1740–1790* (Edinburgh, 1975).

H.T. Dickinson, *Liberty and property. Political ideology in eighteenth-century Britain* (1977).

P.G.M. Dickson, *The financial revolution in England. A study in the development of public credit, 1688–1756* (1967).

R.J. Dickson, *Ulster emigration to colonial America, 1718–1775* (1966).

A.H. Dodd, *The character of the early Welsh emigration to the United States*, 2nd edn (Cardiff, 1957).

Thomas M. Doerflinger, 'Commercial specialization in Philadelphia's merchant community, 1750–1791', *Business History Review*, LVII (1983).

Thomas M. Doerflinger, *A vigorous spirit of enterprise. Merchants and economic development in revolutionary Philadelphia* (Chapel Hill, 1986).

Richard S. Dunn, 'The English sugar islands and the founding of South Carolina', reprinted in Breen (ed.), *Shaping southern society.*

Richard S. Dunn, 'Penny wise and pound foolish. Penn as a businessman', in Dunn and Dunn (eds), *The world of William Penn.*

Richard S. Dunn, *Sugar and slaves. The rise of the planter class in the English West Indies, 1624–1713* (1973).

Richard S. Dunn and Mary Maples Dunn (eds), *The world of William Penn* (Philadelphia, 1986).

Peter Earle, *The making of the English middle class. Business, society, and family life, 1660–1730* (1989).

W.J. Eccles, 'The fur trade and eighteenth-century imperialism', *WMQ*, third series, XL (1983).

Marc Egnal, *A mighty empire. The origins of the American Revolution* (Ithaca, 1988).

Emory G. Evans, 'Planter indebtedness and the coming of the Revolution in Virginia', *WMQ*, third series, XIX (1962).

Patrick Eyres, 'Fleets, forests, and follies. Supremacy of the sea and of the eye', *New Arcadian Journal*, 35/6 (1994).

Patrick Eyres, 'Neoclassicism on active service. Commemoration of the Seven Years' War in the English landscape garden', *New Arcadian Journal*, 35/6 (1994).

D.A. Farnie, 'The commercial empire of the Atlantic, 1607–1783', *Econ. Hist. Rev.*, second series, XV (1962).

D.K. Fieldhouse, 'Gentlemen, capitalists, and the British Empire', *JICH*, XXII (1994).

Norman S. Fiering, 'The transatlantic republic of letters: a note on the circulation of learned periodicals to eighteenth-century America', *WMQ*, third series, XXXIII (1976), 642–60.

David Hackett Fischer, *Albion's seed. Four British folkways in America* (Oxford, 1989).

Roderick Floud and Donald McCloskey (eds), *The economic history of Britain since 1700. Volume 1: 1700–1860* (Cambridge, 1981).

A. Fogelman, 'Migrations to the thirteen North American colonies. New estimates', *Journal of Interdisciplinary History*, XXII (1992).

Lawrence Freedman, Paul Hayes and Robert O'Neill (eds), *War, strategy, and international politics. Essays in honour of Sir Michael Howard* (Oxford, 1992).

Christopher J. French, '"Crowded with traders and a great commerce". London's domination of English overseas trade, 1700–1775', *London Journal*, XVII (1992).

Alan Gallay, *The formation of a planter elite. Jonathan Bryan and the southern colonial frontier* (Athens, Ga., 1989).

Alan Gallay, 'Jonathan Bryan's plantation empire. Land, politics, and the formation of a ruling class in colonial Georgia', *WMQ*, third series, XLV (1980).

H.A. Gemery, 'Emigration from the British Isles to the new world, 1630–1700', *Research in Economic History*, V (1980).

Conrad Gill, *Merchants and mariners of the eighteenth century* (1961).

Richard Grassby, '*The English gentleman in trade. The life and works of Sir Dudley North, 1641–1691* (Oxford, 1994).

Jack P. Greene, 'Changing identity in the British Caribbean. Barbados as a case study', in Canny and Pagden (eds), *Colonial identity in the Atlantic World*.

Jack P. Greene, 'Foundations of political power in the Virginia House of Burgesses, 1720–1776', *WMQ*, third series, XVI (1959).

Jack P. Greene, *Peripheries and center. Constitutional development in the extended polities of the British empire and the United States, 1607–1788* (Athens, Ga., 1986).

Jack P. Greene, *Pursuits of happiness. The social development of early modern British colonies and the formation of American culture* (Chapel Hill, 1988).

Jack P. Greene, 'The Seven Years' War and the American Revolution. The causal relationship reconsidered', *JICH*, VIII (1980).

Jack P. Greene and J.R. Pole (eds), *Colonial British America. Essays in the new history of the early modern era* (Baltimore, 1984).

Jack P. Greene and J.R. Pole, 'Reconstructing British-American colonial history', in idem (eds), *Colonial British America*.

Julian Gwyn, 'British government spending and the North American colonies, 1740–1775', *JICH*, VIII (1980).

Julian Gwyn, *The enterprising admiral. The personal fortune of Admiral Sir Peter Warren* (Montreal, 1974).

David Hancock, '"Capital and credit with approved security". Financial markets in Montserrat and South Carolina 1748–1775', *Business and Economic History*, XXIII (1994).

David Hancock, ' "Domestic bubbling". Eighteenth-century London merchants and individual investment in the Funds', *Econ. Hist. Rev.*, second series, XLVII (1994).

Richard Harding, *Amphibious warfare in the eighteenth century. The British expedition to the West Indies, 1740–1742* (Woodbridge, 1991).

Vincent T. Harlow, *The founding of the second British empire, 1763–1793*, 2 vols (1952 and 1964).

Virginia B. Harrington, *The New York merchant on the eve of the Revolution* (1935; reprinted, Gloucester, Mass., 1964).

Robert Harris, *A patriot press. National politics and the London press in the 1740s* (Oxford, 1993).

James Hayes, 'Scottish officers in the British army, 1714–63', *Scottish History Review*, XXXVI (1957).

Ronald Hoffman, ' "Marylando-Hibernus". Charles Carroll the settler, 1660–1720', *WMQ*, third series, XLV (1988).

Geoffrey Holmes (ed.), *Britain after the Glorious Revolution, 1689–1714* (1969).

Andrew Hook, 'Philadelphia, Edinburgh, and the Scottish Enlightenment', in Sher and Smitten (eds), *Scotland and America.*

J. Hoppit, *Risk and failure in English business, 1700–1800* (Cambridge, 1987).

D.W. Howell, *Patriarchs and parasites. The gentry of south-west Wales in the eighteenth century* (Cardiff, 1986).

R. Hyam, 'British imperial expansion in the late-eighteenth century', *HJ*, X (1967).

Rhys Isaac, *The transformation of Virginia, 1740–1790* (Chapel Hill, 1982).

Geraint H. Jenkins, *The foundations of modern Wales. Wales 1642–1780* (Oxford, 1987).

Philip Jenkins, *A history of modern Wales, 1536–1990* (1992).

Philip Jenkins, *The making of a ruling class. The Glamorgan gentry, 1640–1790* (Cambridge, 1983).

A.H. John, *The industrial development of South Wales, 1750–1850* (Cardiff, 1950).

Richard R. Johnson, *Adjustment to empire. The New England colonies, 1675–1715* (Leicester, 1981).

Richard R. Johnson, 'The imperial Webb: the thesis of garrison government in early America considered', *WMQ*, third series, XLIII (1986).

D.W. Jones, *War and economy in the age of William III and Marlborough* (Oxford, 1988).

David W. Jordan, 'Political stability and the emergence of a native elite in Maryland', in Tate and Ammerman (eds), *The Chesapeake in the seventeenth century.*

D.M. Joslin, 'London private bankers, 1720–1785', *Econ. Hist. Rev.*, second series, VII (1954).

Michael G. Kammen, *A rope of sand. The colonial agents, British politics, and the American Revolution* (Ithaca, 1968).

Alan L. Karras, *Sojourners in the sun. Scottish migrants in Jamaica and the Chesapeake, 1740–1800* (Ithaca, 1992).

John Keay, *The honourable Company. A history of the East India Company* (1991).

Katherine A. Kellock, 'London merchants and the pre-1776 American debts', *Guildhall Studies in London History*, I (1974).

Eric Kerridge, *Trade and banking in early modern England* (Manchester, 1988).

Sung Bok Kim, 'A new look at the great landlords of eighteenth-century New York', *WMQ*, third series, XXVII (1970).

B.B. King and M.N. Pearson (eds), *The age of partnership. Europeans in Asia before dominion* (Honolulu, 1979).

Nancy F. Koehn, *The power of commerce. Economy and governance in the first British empire* (Ithaca, 1994).

Allan Kulikoff, *Tobacco and slaves. The development of southern cultures in the Chesapeake, 1680–1800* (Chapel Hill, 1986).

David Kynaston, *The City of London. Volume 1: A world of its own, 1815–1890* (1994).

B.W. Labaree, *The Boston Tea Party* (Oxford, 1964).

Aubrey C. Land, 'Economic base and social structure. The northern Chesapeake in the eighteenth century', *Journal of Economic History*, XXV (1965).

Aubrey C. Land, 'Economic behavior in a planting society. The eighteenth-century Chesapeake', *Journal of Southern History*, XXXIII (1967).

Aubrey C. Land, Lois Green Carr and Edward C. Papenfuse (eds), *Law, society, and politics in early Maryland* (Baltimore, 1977).

Ned C. Landsman, 'The provinces and the empire. Scotland, the American colonies, and the development of British provincial identity', in Stone (ed.), *An imperial state at war*.

Ned C. Landsman, *Scotland and its first American colony, 1683–1765* (Princeton, 1985).

Paul Langford, 'Old Whigs, Old Tories, and the American Revolution', *JICH*, VIII (1980).

Paul Langford, *A polite and commercial people. England, 1727–1783* (Oxford, 1989).

Paul Langford, *Public life and the propertied Englishman, 1689–1798* (Oxford, 1991).

Philip Lawson, ' "Arts and empire equally extend". Tradition, prejudice, and assumption in the eighteenth-century press coverage of empire', *Studies in History and Politics*, VII (1989).

Philip Lawson, *The East India Company. A history* (1994).

Philip Lawson, *The imperial challenge. Quebec and Britain in the age of the American Revolution* (Montreal, 1989).

Philip Lawson, ' "The Irishman's prize". Views of Canada from the British press, 1760–1774', *HJ*, XXVIII (1985).

Philip Lawson and Jim Phillips, ' "Our execrable banditti". Perceptions of nabobs in mid-eighteenth-century Britain', *Albion*, XVI (1984).

Bruce Lenman, *Integration, enlightenment, and industrialization. Scotland, 1746–1832* (1981).

Brian Levy, 'From "dark corners" to American domesticity. The British social context of the Welsh and Cheshire Quakers' familial revolution in Pennsylvania, 1657–85', in Dunn and Dunn (eds), *The world of William Penn*.

P.H. Lindert and Jeffrey G. Williamson, 'Revising England's social tables, 1688–1812', *Explorations in Economic History*, XIX (1982).

J. Jefferson Looney, 'Cultural life in the provinces. Leeds and York, 1720–1820', in Beier, Cannadine and Rosenheim (eds), *The first modern society*.

John J. McCusker and Russell R. Menard, *The economy of British America, 1607–1789* (Chapel Hill, 1985).

Anthony McFarlane, *The British in the Americas, 1480–1815* (1994).

D.S. Macmillan, 'Scottish enterprise and influences in Canada', in Cage (ed.), *The Scots abroad.*

John Robert McNeill, *Atlantic empires of France and Spain. Louisbourg and Havana, 1700–1763* (Chapel Hill, 1985).

Frederick Madden with David Fieldhouse (eds), *Select documents on the constitutional history of the British empire and commonwealth,* Vol. III: *Imperial reconstruction, 1763–1840. The evolution of alternative systems of colonial government* (Westport, Conn., 1987).

Gloria L. Main, *Tobacco colony. Life in early Maryland, 1650–1720* (Princeton, 1982).

P. Marshall, 'The first and second British empire. A question of demarcation', *History,* XLIX (1964).

P.J. Marshall, 'British expansion in India in the eighteenth century. A historical revision', *History,* LX (1975).

P.J. Marshall, 'The Company and coolies. Labour in early Calcutta', in Pradip Sinha (ed.), *The urban experience: Calcutta. Essays in honour of Nisith R. Ray* (Calcutta, 1987).

P.J. Marshall, ' "Cornwallis triumphant". War in India and the British public in the late eighteenth century', in Freedman, Hayes and O'Neill (eds), *War, strategy, and international politics.*

P.J. Marshall, *East Indian fortunes. The British in Bengal in the eighteenth century* (Oxford, 1976).

P.J. Marshall, 'Economic and political expansion. The case of Oudh', *Modern Asian Studies,* IX (1975).

P.J. Marshall, 'The eighteenth-century empire', in Black (ed.), *British politics and society.*

P.J. Marshall, 'Empire and authority in the later eighteenth century', *JICH,* XV (1987).

P.J. Marshall, 'Masters and banians in eighteenth-century Calcutta', in King and Pearson (eds), *The age of partnership.*

P.J. Marshall, 'Private British investment in eighteenth-century Bengal', *Bengal Past and Present,* LXXXVI (1967).

P.J. Marshall, 'Private British traders in the Indian Ocean before 1800', in Das Gupta and Pearson (eds), *India and the Indian Ocean.*

P.J. Marshall, 'Taming the exotic. The British and India in the seventeenth and eighteenth centuries', in Rousseau and Porter (eds), *Exoticism in the Enlightenment.*

P.J. Marshall, 'Warren Hastings as scholar and patron', in Whiteman, Bromley and Dickson (eds), *Statesmen, scholars, and merchants.*

P.J. Marshall, 'Western arms in maritime Asia in the early phases of expansion', *Modern Asian Studies,* XIV (1980).

P.J. Marshall and Glyndwr Williams, *The great map of mankind. British perceptions of the world in the age of enlightenment* (1982).

F.N. Mason (ed.), *John Norton & sons, merchants of London and Virginia. Being the papers from their counting house for the years 1750 to 1795* (1937; reprinted, Newton Abbot, 1968).

P. Mathias, 'The social structure in the eighteenth century. A calculation by Joseph Massie', *Econ. Hist. Rev.,* second series, X (1957).

F.T. Melton, 'Deposit banking in London, 1700–1790', *BH,* XXVIII (1986).

F.T. Melton, *Sir Robert Clayton and the origins of English deposit banking, 1658–1685* (Cambridge, 1986).

Russell R. Menard, 'Transport costs and long-range trade, 1300–1800. Was there a European "transport revolution" in the early modern era?', in Tracy (ed.), *The political economy of merchant empires.*

Richard Middleton, *Colonial America. A history, 1607–1760* (Oxford, 1992).

W.E. Minchinton, 'The merchants of England in the eighteenth century', *Explorations in Economic History*, X (1957).

G.E. Mingay, *English landed society in the eighteenth century* (1963).

G.E. Mingay, *The gentry. The rise and fall of a ruling class* (1976).

Robert D. Mitchell, *Commercialism and frontier. Perspectives on the early Shenandoah Valley* (Charlottesville, 1977).

Edmund S. Morgan, *Virginians at home. Family life in the eighteenth century* (Williamsburg, 1952).

Kenneth Morgan, *Bristol and the Atlantic trade in the eighteenth century* (Cambridge, 1993).

Kenneth Morgan, 'Bristol West India merchants in the eighteenth century', *Transactions of the Royal Historical Society*, sixth series, III (1993).

Philip D. Morgan (ed.), *Diversity and unity in early North America* (1993).

Hoh-Cheung Mui and Lorna H. Mui, *The management of monopoly. A study of the English East India Company's conduct of its tea trade, 1784–1833* (Vancouver, 1984).

Gerald W. Mullin, *Flight and rebellion. Slave resistance in eighteenth-century Virginia* (New York, 1972).

C.W. Munn, *The Scottish provincial banking companies, 1747–1864* (Edinburgh, 1981).

D.H. Murdoch, 'Land policy in the eighteenth-century British empire. The sale of crown lands in the Ceded Islands, 1763–1783', *HJ*, XXVII (1984).

Lewis Namier, *England in the age of the American Revolution* (2nd edn, 1961).

Gary B. Nash, 'The early merchants of Philadelphia. The formation and disintegration of a founding elite', in Dunn and Dunn (eds), *The world of William Penn.*

Pamela Nightingale, *Trade and empire in western India, 1784–1806* (Cambridge, 1970).

Patrick O'Brien, 'The political economy of British taxation, 1660–1815', *Econ. Hist. Rev.*, second series, XLI (1988).

P.K. O'Brien and S.L. Engerman, 'Exports and the growth of the British economy from the Glorious Revolution to the Peace of Amiens', in Solow (ed.), *Slavery and the rise of the Atlantic system.*

Alison Gilbert Olson, *Making the empire work. London and American interest groups, 1690–1790* (Cambridge, Mass., 1992).

David Ormrod, 'The "Protestant capitalist international", 1651–1775', *Historical Research*, LXVI (1993).

Anthony Pagden and Nicholas Canny, 'Afterword. From identity to independence', in Canny and Pagden (eds), *Colonial identity in the Atlantic world.*

Richard Pares, 'The economic factors in the history of the empire', *Econ.Hist.Rev.*, first series, VII (1937).

Richard Pares, *Merchants and planters* (Cambridge, 1960).

Richard Pares, *Yankees and creoles. The trade between North America and the West Indies before the American Revolution* (1956).

J.G. Parker, 'Scottish enterprise in India, 1750–1914', in Cage (ed.), *The Scots abroad.*

R.A.C. Parker, *Coke of Norfolk. A financial and agricultural study, 1717–1842* (Oxford, 1975).

J.H. Parry, *Trade and dominion. The European overseas empires in the eighteenth century* (1971).

M.N. Pearson, 'Merchants and states', in Tracy (ed.), *The political economy of merchant empires.*

Douglas M. Peers, 'Contours of the garrison state. The army and the historiography of early nineteenth-century India', in Cassels (ed.), *Orientalism, evangelicalism, and the military cantonment.*

Edwin J. Perkins, 'The entrepreneurial spirit in colonial America. The foundations of modern business history', *Business History Review*, LXIII (1989).

Andrew Porter, ' "Gentlemanly capitalism" and empire. The British experience since 1750?', *JICH*, XVIII (1990).

L.S. Pressnell, *Country banking in the industrial revolution* (Oxford, 1956).

Jacob M. Price, 'Buchanan & Simson, 1759–1763. A different kind of Glasgow firm trading to the Chesapeake', *WMQ*, third series, XL (1983).

Jacob M. Price, *Capital and credit in British overseas trade: the view from the Chesapeake, 1700–1776* (Cambridge, Mass., 1980).

Jacob M. Price, 'Credit in the slave trade and plantation economies', in Solow (ed.), *Slavery and the rise of the Atlantic system.*

Jacob M. Price, 'The great Quaker business families of eighteenth-century London. The rise and fall of a sectarian patriciate', in Dunn and Dunn (eds), *The world of William Penn.*

Jacob M. Price (ed.), *Joshua Johnson's letterbook, 1771–1774. Letters from a merchant in London to his partners in Maryland* (1979).

Jacob M. Price, 'The Maryland Bank stock case. British-American financial and political relations before and after the American Revolution', in Land, Carr and Papenfuse (eds), *Law, society, and politics in early Maryland.*

Jacob M. Price, 'New time series for Scotland's and Britain's trade with the thirteen colonies and states, 1740–1791', *WMQ*, third series, XXXII (1975).

Jacob M. Price, 'One family's empire. The Russell–Lee–Clerk connection in Maryland, Britain, and India, 1707–1857', *Maryland Historical Magazine*, LXXII (1977).

Jacob M. Price, 'The rise of Glasgow in the Chesapeake tobacco trade, 1707–1775', *WMQ*, third series, XI (1954).

Jacob M. Price, 'Sheffield v. Starke, Institutional experimentation in the London–Maryland trade, *c.*1696–1706', *Business History*, XVIII (1986).

Jacob M. Price, 'What did merchants do? Reflections on British overseas trade, 1660–1760', *Journal of European Economic History*, LXIX (1989).

Jacob M. Price, 'Who cared about the colonies? The impact of the thirteen colonies on British society and politics, circa 1714–1775', in Bailyn and Morgan (eds), *Strangers within the realm.*

Jacob M. Price and Paul G.E. Clemens, 'A revolution of scale in overseas trade. British firms in the Chesapeake, 1675–1775', *Journal of Economic History*, XLVII (1987).

L.G. Ragatz, *The rise and fall of the planter class in the British Caribbean, 1763–1833* (New York, 1928; reprinted, 1963).

J. Raven, *Judging new wealth. Popular publishing and responses to commerce in England, 1750–1800* (Oxford, 1992).

Marcus Rediker, *Between the devil and the deep blue sea. Merchant seamen, pirates, and the Anglo-American maritime world, 1700–1750* (Cambridge, 1987).

E. Richards, 'Scotland and the uses of the Atlantic empire', in Bailyn and Morgan (eds), *Strangers within the realm.*

J. Riddy, 'Warren Hastings. Scotland's benefactor?', in Carnall and Nicholson (eds), *The impeachment of Warren Hastings.*

Robert C. Ritchie, *Captain Kidd and the war against the pirates* (Cambridge, Mass., 1986).

R.O. Roberts, 'Financial developments in early modern Wales and the emergence of the first banks', *Welsh History Review*, XVI (1993).

Richard Roberts and David Kynaston (eds), *The Bank of England. Money, power, and influence, 1694–1994* (Oxford, 1995).

John Robertson, 'Union, state, and empire. The Britain of 1707 in its European setting', in Stone (ed.), *Imperial state at war.*

E. Robinson, 'Matthew Boulton and Josiah Wedgewood, apostles of fashion', *BH*, XXXVIII (1986).

A.G. Roeber, '"The origin of whatever is not English among us". The Dutch and German-speaking peoples of colonial British America', in Bailyn and Morgan (eds), *Strangers within the realm.*

H.C.B. Rogers, *The British army of the eighteenth century* (1977).

Nicholas Rogers, *Whigs and cities. Popular politics in the age of Walpole and Pitt* (Oxford, 1989).

Henry Roseveare, *The financial revolution, 1660–1760* (1991).

R. Roth, 'Tea-drinking in eighteenth-century America. Its etiquette and equipage', in St George (ed.), *Material life in America.*

G.S. Rousseau and Roy Porter (eds), *Exoticism in the Enlightenment* (Manchester, 1990).

C. Rowell, 'Clive of India and his family. The formation of the collection', in Archer, Rowell and Skelton, *Treasures from India.*

Darrett B. Rutman, 'Assessing the little communities of early America', *WMQ*, third series, XLIII (1986).

R.B. St George (ed.), *Material life in America, 1600–1800* (Boston, 1988).

G.V. Scammell, *The first imperial age. European overseas expansion, c.1400–1715* (1989).

W.L. Schase, *The colonial American in Britain* (Madison, 1956).

Arthur Meier Schlesinger, *The colonial merchants and the American Revolution, 1763–1776* (1917; reprinted, 1957).

W.R. Schlote, *British overseas trade from 1700 to 1939* (Oxford, 1952).

J.R. Seeley, *The expansion of empire. Two courses of lectures* (1883).

John Bezis Selfa, 'Planter industrialists and iron oligarchs. A comparative prosopography of early Anglo-American ironmasters', *Business and Economic History*, XXIII (1994).

Bernard Semmel, *The liberal ideal and the demons of empire. Theories of imperialism from Adam Smith to Lenin* (Baltimore, 1993).

Carole Shammas, 'English-born and creole elites in turn-of-the-century

Virginia', in Tate and Ammerman (eds), *The Chesapeake in the seventeenth century*.

Carole Shammas, 'How self-sufficient was early America?', *Journal of Interdisciplinary History*, XIII (1982).

Carole Shammas, *The pre-industrial consumer in England and America* (Oxford, 1990).

Richard B. Sher and Jeffrey R. Smitten (eds), *Scotland and America in the age of the Enlightenment* (Edinburgh, 1990).

Richard B. Sheridan, The British credit crisis of 1772 and the American colonies', *Journal of Economic History*, XX (1960).

Richard B. Sheridan, 'The commercial and financial organization of the British slave trade, 1750–1807', *Econ. Hist. Rev.*, second series, XI (1958).

Richard B. Sheridan, 'Planters and merchants. The Oliver family of Antigua and London 1716–1784', *BH*, XIII (1971).

Richard B. Sheridan, 'The rise of a colonial gentry. A case study of Antigua, 1730–1775', *Econ. Hist. Rev.*, second series, XIII (1960).

Richard B. Sheridan, *Sugar and slavery. An economic history of the British West Indies 1623–1775* (Baltimore, 1973).

John Shy, *A people numerous and armed. Reflections on the military struggle for American independence* (Oxford, 1976).

John Shy, *Toward Lexington. The role of the British army in the coming of the American Revolution* (Princeton, 1965).

Gill Simmons, 'Buckler's Hard. Warship building on the Montagu estate at Beaulieu', *New Arcadian Journal*, 35/6 (1993).

R.C. Simmons and P.D.G. Thomas (eds), *Proceedings and debates of the British Parliament respecting North America, 1754–1783* (6 vols, New York, 1982–6).

D.B. Smith, *Inside the great house. Planter family life in eighteenth century Virginia* (Ithaca, 1980).

T.C. Smout (ed.), *The search for wealth and stability. Essays in economic and social history presented to M.W. Flinn* (1979).

T.C. Smout, N.C. Landsman, and T.M. Devine, 'Scottish emigration in the seventeenth and eighteenth centuries', in Canny (ed.), *Europeans on the move*.

Barbara L. Solow, 'Slavery and colonization', in Solow (ed.), *Slavery and the rise of the Atlantic system*.

Barbara L. Solow (ed.), *Slavery and the rise of the Atlantic system* (Cambridge, 1991).

J.H. Soltow, 'Scottish traders in Virginia, 1750–1775', *Econ. Hist. Rev.*, second series, XII (1959).

Jack M. Sosin, *Agents and merchants. British colonial policy and the origins of the American Revolution, 1763–1775* (Lincoln, Nebr., 1965).

Jack M. Sosin, *Whitehall and the wilderness. The middle west in British colonial policy, 1760–1775* (Lincoln, Nebr., 1961).

Percival Spear, *The nabobs. The social life of the English in eighteenth-century India* (Oxford, 1932; new impression, 1980).

W.A. Speck, 'Conflict in society', in Holmes (ed.), *Britain after the Glorious Revolution*.

Ian K. Steele, 'The empire and provincial elites. An interpretation of some recent writings on the English Atlantic, 1675–1740', *JICH*, VIII (1980).

Ian K. Steele, *The English Atlantic, 1675–1740. An exploration of communication and community* (New York, 1986).

Ian K. Steele, 'A London trader and the Atlantic empire. Joseph Cruttenden, apothecary, 1710–1717', *WMQ*, third series, XXXIV (1977).

Lawrence Stone (ed.), *An imperial state at war. Britain from 1689 to 1815* (1994).

J.E. Sturgis, 'Anglicisation at the Cape of Good Hope in the early nineteenth century', *JICH*, XI (1982).

John Styles, 'Manufacturing, consumption, and design in eighteenth-century England', in Brewer and Porter (eds), *Consumption and the world of goods.*

L.S. Sutherland, *The East India Company in eighteenth-century politics* (Oxford, 1952).

L.S. Sutherland, *A London merchant, 1695–1774* (Oxford, 1933).

L.S. Sutherland, 'Sir George Colebrooke's world corner in alum, 1771–3', *Economic History*, III (1936).

Carl E. Swanson, 'American privateering and imperial warfare, 1739–1748', *WMQ*, third series, XLII (1985).

Thad W. Tate and David L. Ammerman (eds), *The Chesapeake in the seventeenth century. Essays on Anglo-American society* (Chapel Hill, 1979).

F. Thistlethwaite, The Atlantic migration of the pottery industry', *Econ. Hist. Rev.*, second series, XI (1958).

Brinley Thomas, *The industrial revolution and the Atlantic economy. Selected essays* (1993).

P.D.G. Thomas, *British politics and the Stamp Act crisis. The first phase of the American Revolution, 1763–1767* (Oxford, 1975).

P.D.G. Thomas, 'The cost of the British army in North America, 1763–1775', *WMQ*, third series, XLV (1988).

P.D.G. Thomas, *Tea Party to Independence. The third phase of the American Revolution, 1773–1776* (Oxford, 1991).

P.D.G. Thomas, *The Townshend duties crisis. The second phase of the American Revolution, 1767–1773* (Oxford, 1987).

R.P. Thomas and D.N. McCloskey, 'Overseas trade and empire, 1700–1860', in Floud and McCloskey (eds), *The economic history of Britain since 1700.*

D.W. Thoms, 'The Mills family. London sugar merchants of the eighteenth century', *BH*, XI (1969).

J.D. Tracy (ed.), *The political economy of merchant empires* (Cambridge, 1991).

Nicholas Tracy, 'Parry of a threat to India, 1768–1774', *Mariner's Mirror*, LIX (1973).

Alison Vickery, 'Golden age to separate spheres? A review of the categories and chronologies of English women's history', *HJ*, XXXVI (1993).

J.R. Ward, 'The industrial revolution and British imperialism, 1750–1850', *Econ. Hist. Rev.*, second series, XLVII (1994).

J.R. Ward, 'A planter and his slaves in eighteenth-century Jamaica', in Smout (ed.), *The search for wealth and stability.*

J.T. Ward and R.G. Wilson (eds), *Land and industry. The landed estate and the industrial revolution* (1971).

Richard Waterhouse, 'The development of elite culture in the colonial American South. A study of Charles Town, 1670–1770', *Australian Journal of Politics and History*, XXVIII (1982).

Richard Waterhouse, *A new world gentry. The making of a merchant and planter class in South Carolina, 1670–1770* (New York, 1989).

I.B. Watson, *Foundations for empire. English private trade in India, 1659–1760* (New Delhi, 1980).

Stephen Saunders Webb, 'Army and empire: English garrison government in Britain and America', *WMQ*, third series, XXXIV (1977).

Stephen Saunders Webb, 'The data and theory of Restoration empire', *WMQ*, third series, XLIII (1986).

A. Whiteman, J.S. Bromley and P.G.M. Dickson (eds), *Statesmen, scholars, and merchants. Essays in eighteenth-century history presented to Dame Lucy Sutherland* (Oxford, 1973).

Franklin B. Wickwire, *British subministers and colonial America, 1763–1793* (Princeton, 1966).

Glyndwr Williams, '"The inexhaustible fountain of gold": English projects and ventures in the South Seas, 1670–1750', in Flint and Williams (eds), *Perspectives of empire.*

Gwyn A. Williams, *When was Wales? A history of the Welsh* (1985).

J.E. Williams, 'Whitehaven in the eighteenth century', *Econ. Hist. Rev.*, second series, VIII (1956).

John E. Wills, Jr, 'European consumption and Asian production in the seventeenth and eighteenth centuries', in Brewer and Porter (eds), *Consumption and the world of goods.*

Kathleen Wilson, 'Empire, trade, and popular politics in mid-Hanoverian Britain. The case of Admiral Vernon', *Past and Present*, CXXI (1988).

Kathleen Wilson, 'Empire of virtue. The imperial project and Hanoverian culture, c.1720–1785', in Stone (ed.), *An imperial state at war.*

R.G. Wilson, *The merchant community in Leeds, 1700–1830* (Manchester, 1971).

Louis B. Wright, *The first gentlemen of Virginia. Intellectual qualities of the early ruling class* (Charlottesville, 1940; reprinted, 1964).

M.E. Yapp, *Strategies of British India. Britain, Iran, and Afghanistan, 1798–1850* (Oxford, 1980).

G. Yogev, *Diamonds and corals. Anglo-Dutch Jews and eighteenth-century trade* (Leicester, 1978).

Nuala Zahedieh, 'London and the colonial consumer in the late seventeenth century', *Econ. Hist. Rev.*, second series, XLVII (1994).

Nuala Zahedieh, 'Trade, plunder, and economic development in early English Jamaica, 1655–89', *Econ. Hist. Rev.*, second series, XXXIX (1986).

Index

Acadia, *see* Nova Scotia
Acadians, 116
Act of Union (1707), xiii, 99, 149, 161
Addison, Joseph, 151
Africa, trade with, 34, 59, 96
Aix-la-Chappelle, Treaty of, 23
Allahabad, Treaty of, 24
America, British *see* North America, British
American Iron Company, 88
anglicization, 6; of British elite, 52; of British India, 143–6; of empire, 113–14, 125; of North America, 107, 114–19, 130–40; of West Indian elite, 140–3
Anglo-Dutch War, third, 114
Anson family, 77
Anson, George, 77
Antigua, 22; elite in, 163; militia of, 29; Scots in, 163
aristocracy, attacks on, 66; in colonies, 104–5; *see also* landed society
armed force, 4; and empire, 23–6, 103–4; and trade, 24–5
Asia, private trade in, 43; trade with, 34–5, 59
Asiatic Society of Bengal, 168
Atlantic empire, British, 3, 7, 9; communications in, 118–19; merchant networks in, 108–9; and Navigation Acts, 33, 36; trade with, 32–5, 59, 70
Austrian Succession, War of, 23
Awadh, 180
Awadh, Wazir of, 23

Backwell, Edward, 55
Bagg, Stephen, 59
Bailyn, Bernard, 6, 90, 118, 158, 159
Baird, Hay, & Co., 94
Balambangan, 184
Baltimore, Lord, 162
Bank of England, 61–2
bankers, attitudes to, 62; *see also* financial elite, British
banks, English, 95; development of, 60, 62; in London, 55, 62; provincial banks, 62; structure of, 61–2

banks, Indian, 97
banks, Scottish, 61, 95
Barbados, 22, 162; elite in, 141, 142
Baugh, Daniel A., 179
Beaulieu, 54
Beawes, Wyndham, 56
Bengal, British control over, 30; credit system in, 96–7; Nawab of, 23, 44; revenues of, 30, 38; Scots in, 164; trade with, 38
Bennett, Joseph, 132
Birmingham, 93
Board of Trade, 121, 122, 182, 187
Bombay, 22, 29, 97–8
Boston, 132
Braddock, General, 104
Branson, William, 42
Braund, William, 61
Brewer, John, 84
Bristol, colonial debts to, 93, 94; growth of, 58, 153; merchants in, 56, 57, 58, 59, 88–9, 154
British Empire, *see* empire
Browne, Arthur, 105
Bryan, Jonathan, 191–2
Burke, Edmund, 164
Bushman, Richard L., 131
Buxar, battle of, 24
Byrd II, William, 129

Cain, P.J., 12, 16–21
Calcutta, 22, 29, 143
Canada, 27, 59, 116, 179, 180; Scots in, 165, 166; views of, 75
Cannon, John, 66
Canton, 38
Cape Breton, 176
Carroll, Charles, 162
Cartagena, 25
Carteret, John, Earl of Granville, 90
Cary, John, 72
Celts, in armed forces, 157; in empire, 149, 160–70; in metropolitan society, 20–1, 149, 150, 156
Chandos, Duke of, 54
Charles II, King, 42
Charles Town, 115; elite of, 140
Charter Act (1813), 196

Chesapeake, the, elite of, 133–7, 160; and tobacco trade, 88–9; *see also* Maryland, Virginia
Child, Sir Josiah, 67
Childs Bank, 55
China, 180; trade with, 38, 98
City, the, 20, 48; attitudes within, 66; bankers in, 55; colonial debt and, 92–5; criticism of, 65; domestic economy and, 96; and funding the state, 83–4; investment in, 53, 54–6, 83–4; and overseas expansion, 84; private banks in, 62–3; stock market in, 62, 175
Clapham, Sir John, 61
Clark, J.C.D., 8
Clayton and Morris, 87
Clive, John, 6
Clive, Robert, 30, 87, 177, 184, 190, 191
Codrington, Edward, 99
Codrington, Sir William, 99
coffee, consumption of, 39, 74; trade in, 39
Colebrooke, Sir George, 99, 178, 181
Colley, Linda, 6, 8, 66, 156, 161
colonies, economic development of, 80–1, 92, 172; importance of trade with, 32, 72; indebtedness of, 93–5
Colquhoun, Patrick, 50
Commons, House of, Americans in, 120; East India interest in, 121; membership of, 51; West Indians in, 120
consumer goods, in Britain, 72–3; in colonies, 116–18
Coode's Rebellion, 162
credit, 68–9; in British India, 96–8; and colonial development, 80, 82, 92; in North America, 93–4; and trade, 95–6; in the West Indies, 94–5
creolization, 126, 141
Cruger, Henry Jr, 94
Cruttenden, Joseph, 59
Cumbria, 67
Cunninghame group, 89, 94
Cymmrodorion Society, 169

Darien Company, 153
Darnall, Colonel Henry, 162
Dartmouth, Lord, 91, 189
Davies, K.G., 85
Davis, Lance E., 79
Defoe, Daniel, 161

De Lancey family, 110
Devine, Thomas M., 95
Dickson, P.G.M., 83
diwani, the, 30, 87
Dominica, 74
Drayton, William Henry, 191
Dunbar, William, 163
Dundas, Henry, 164

East Florida, 91
East India Company, 10, 22, 33, 48, 79, 81, 97, 144, 176; army of, 29, 30–1, 71; conduct of servants, 144–6, 183–4, 190–1; foreign investment in, 86; and gentlemanly ideal, 144–6; investment in, 86–7, 175; military assistance from Crown, 26; monopoly of, 195–6; politics of, 76, 121; reform of, 144–6, 184; revenue collection by, 29, 38; Scots in, 164–5; and the state, 15, 36, 121, 172–3, 184–5, 192; and tea trade, 38–9, 177–8; as a territorial power, 15, 30, 75, 180; territorial revenues of, 30–1, 73, 87; *see also* Indian empire, British
East Jersey, 165, 168
Economic History Review, 16
Eddis, William, 133
Egmont, Earl of, 90–1
empire, anglicization of, 113–19; attitudes to, 69–78, 172–92, 193–6; benefits derived from, 70–4; and British society, 48, 72–3; Celts in, 156–70; constitution of, 173; core–periphery relationships, 7–8, 16–21, 103–4, 154–6, 167–8, 172–4; crisis within, 171, 178; and domestic economy, 71–2; elites in, 104–11, 125–6, 146, 160–70, 172, 192, 196; Englishness of, 149; finances of, 79–82; gentlemanly ideal in, 126–30, 192; government of, 123–4; historians' views of, 9–10, 11–13, 69–70; identities within, 11–13, 149, 165–70, 171; and ideology, 70, 174–5; and industrialization, 36–9, 71; informal, 34, 44; and landscape architecture, 77–8; and the press, 74–6, 177; and religion, 120, 122–3; and the theatre, 75; and trade, 32–6, 43–4; and war, 23–4; *see also* Atlantic empire, British; expansion (of empire); Indian empire, British; North America, British; West Indies, British

English Harbour, Antigua, 26
Europe, British trade with, 34–5, 152–3
expansion (of empire), 179–81; curbs on, 180–1, 183, 186–8; and domestic investment, 84–5, 100; dynamics of, 26–8, 40, 42–4; fears about, 33–4, 178–82, 183; and industrialization, 37; and land speculation, 41; political framework for, 172–3; and trade, 33, 36, 43–4

Fairfax, Lord, 90
financial elite, British, 47, 60–4; bankers within, 60–3; and 'financial revolution', 83–4; and gentlemanly ideal, 68; and government, 84; in House of Commons, 51, 84; investments of, 86; stock brokers in, 63–4; *see also* monied interest
'financial revolution', the, 14, 81, 95
'fiscal-military state', 81; Britain as, 14; finances of, 82–5
Fischer, David Hackett, 158, 159
Fitzwilliam family, 55
Florida, 23, 192
Fort Stanwix, Treaty of, 187
Fort William (Calcutta), 29, 31
France, threat from, 4, 15, 25, 26–8, 176, 185
Franklin, Benjamin, 115, 132
Franks family, 98–9, 108
Freame-Barclay Bank, 62
French and Indian War, *see* Seven Years' War
Fuller, John, 54
Fuller, Rose, 54

Gale, John, 89
'garrison government', 7, 28–30
'gentlemanly capitalism', critiques of, 18–21; definition of, 17, 64; elements within, 17, 64, 69; overseas expansion of, 17–18
gentlemanly ideal, in Britain, 64, 65, 68–9; in British India, 143–6; in North America, 130–40; in overseas empire, 125–30, 146, 192; in West Indies, 140–3
Georgia, 191
Glasgow, banks in, 61; colonial debts to, 93–4; growth of, 58, 153; merchants in, 58, 61, 68; tobacco trade and, 88–9, 153; trade with West Indies, 57

Gordon Town, 141
Goslings Bank, 55
Grand Ohio Company, 187
Grant, Alexander, 99
Grant, Sir Archibald, 91
Greene, Jack P., 130, 158, 173
Grenada, 94
Grenville, Thomas, 77
Grote, Andrew, 62
Guadeloupe, 180

Haidar Ali, 175
Halifax, Lord, 175
Halifax, Nova Scotia, 166
Hall, Thomas, 59
Hare, Francis, 97
Harlow, Vincent, 11, 98
Hastings, Warren, 144, 164
Heathcote family, 59
Heathcote, Sir Gilbert, 59
Hillsborough, Lord, 187, 189
Hoares Bank, 55
Holwell, John, 31
Hopkins, A.G., 12, 16–21
Hopkinson, Francis, 113
Hudson Bay, 23
Hudson Bay Company, 22, 87
Humphries, Miss, 144
Hutchinson, Thomas, 185
Huttenback, Robert A., 80

identities, 6; of Britons, 8, 157; in overseas empire, 111–13, 146, 165–70, 171; in North America, 111–13; in West Indies, 112, 140–1, 143
imperialism, *see* empire
'improvement', in Britain, 52, 68; in the colonies, 127
Indian empire, British, 3, 9, 22; Crown troops in, 104, 143–6; elite in, 105–6; expansion of, 23–4, 27–8, 31, 43–4, 86, 180, 193; and French, 27–8, 175, 185; as garrison state, 30; metropolitan attitudes to, 176–7, 183–5; political crisis in, 171; private trade in, 43–4; Scots in, 164–5; views of, 75; *see also* East India Company
industrial revolution, and overseas expansion, 18, 36, 71
industrialization, and empire, 36–9
Ireland, xii, 6, 20; emigration from, 158, 159, 162, 189; trade with, 34, 35

Jagat Seths, House of, 97
Jamaica, 22; debts of, 95; economic
  development of, 43, 80; elite in,
  141-2, 163; militia of, 29; public
  buildings in, 141; Scots in, 163,
  166
Jefferson, Thomas, 93
Jenkins' Ear, War of, 23, 25
Johnson, Samuel, 188
Johnson, Sir William, 187
Jones, Rev. Hugh, 133, 136
Jones, Sir William, 168

Kidd, Captain, 43
King, Gregory, 50, 58
Kingston, Jamaica, 141

Lancashire, 67
Lancaster, 93
Land Tax, 74, 82, 83
landed elite, British, 47, 49-56;
  divisions within, 52; economic
  interests of, 52-6; education of, 52;
  and 'financial revolution', 83; and
  gentlemanly capitalism, 17, 20; and
  industry, 53-4; influence of London
  upon, 52; investment in City by,
  53-6, 83; and landscape architecture,
  77-8; and monied interest, 17, 64-9,
  82, 91; overseas investments of, 90-1;
  political influence of, 51; religion of,
  52; size of, 50; wealth of, 50; *see also*
  aristocracy
landed society, entry to, 67-8; *see also,*
  landed elite, British
Landsman, Ned C., 155
Langford, Paul, 67
Leeds, 93
Leeward Islands, the, 141
Leisler, Joseph, 115
Lindsay, Sir John, 175
Liverpool, 93; growth of, 58; merchants
  in, 154; slave traders in, 96, 153
Logan Gilmour & Co., 94
London, 7; colonial debts to, 93, 94;
  commercial position of, 153;
  emigration from, 189; influence of,
  48, 52, 69, 110-11, 133, 154;
  merchant community of, 57, 58,
  150-3; politics in, 151-2; religion in,
  151-2; trade with Chesapeake, 57, 88;
  see also City, the
Lords of Trade, 124, 182
Louisbourg, 23, 71, 176

Madras, 22, 23, 29, 144
Maine, 22
Manchester, 93
Maroon War, 25
Marshall, P.J., 157
Marshall, Peter, 98
Maryland, 162; elite of, 135; and
  tobacco trade, 89; *see also* Chesapeake
Massie, Joseph, 50, 58
merchant fleet, 71
merchants, American, and British
  Merchants, 108-9
merchants, British, and American
  merchants, 108-9; attitudes to, 56,
  66; and banking, 60; borrowing by,
  95; colonial debts to, 93-4; and
  consignment system, 88-9;
  cosmopolitan nature of, 150-3;
  definition of, 56, 57-8; diversification
  of activities, 59-61, 98-100; elite in,
  47, 56-60; firms of, 57, 58, 88-9;
  numbers of, 57-8; political influence
  of, 66-7; resources of, 56-7, 58;
  specialization of, 58; and 'store'
  system, 88-9
Middleton, Samuel, 97
migration, 106, 157-8, 160-4, 188-9
Mingay, G.E., 50, 53
monied interest, definition of, 61;
  hostility towards, 65, 83-4; and
  landed society, 17, 64-9, 82, 91;
  see also financial elite
Montagu, John, Duke of Beaulieu,
  54
Montgomery, Sir James, 91, 165
Montserrat, 22, 92
Mortimer, Thomas, 150

'nabobs', 76, 183
Namier, Sir Lewis, 32
National Debt, 73, 82-3, 150, 152,
  175
naval bases, 25-6
naval stores, 35
Navigation Acts, 24, 32-3, 117, 172
Nevis, 22, 162
New England, 59, 71; elite of, 138
'new' imperial history, 5-10
New Jersey, 88, 166
New York, 24, 88, 114-15; elite of,
  138
Newfoundland, 23, 24
Nine Years' War, 23
Norfolk, 67

North America, British, 4, 22;
    anglicization of, 107, 114–19; armed
    forces of, 25, 71; British army in, 26,
    40, 41, 104; consumer goods in,
    117–18, 132–3; crisis in, 171, 192;
    debts of, 93–4; development of,
    130–1; diversity in, 157–60; Dutch in,
    114–15; elites in, 105, 110–11, 125,
    128, 130–40, 159–60, 160–1, 162,
    192; garrisons in, 7, 24; Germans in,
    115–16; government of, 121–2,
    123–4, 173; government spending in,
    80; identity in, 112, 113; immigration
    into, 157–9; Irish in, 158; land
    grants in, 41; land purchase and
    speculation, 40, 41, 90–1, 138–9,
    185–6, 187–9; lobbying by, 121;
    metropolitan attitudes to, 69–70, 175,
    176, 182; militia in, 28; population
    of, 34, 157–8; press in, 119; religion
    in, 122–3, 192; Scots in, 153, 155,
    158, 159, 161–2, 165–8, 170;
    territorial expansion of, 27, 43; and
    tobacco trade, 88–9; towns, 130;
    trade with, 34–5, 117; Welsh in, 158,
    159, 168–9
North British Society, 168
North Carolina, 90
Norton & Son, John, 93, 133
Nova Scotia, 23, 24, 91, 116

Ohio Company, 27, 90
Oswald, Richard, 99

Pares, Richard, 47, 81
Paris, Treaty of (1763), 23, 74, 179–80
Parliament, colonial representation in,
    120; and East India Company, 120–1;
    imperial issues in, 14, 15, 67, 122,
    172; press coverage of, 76
Penn, William, 42
Pennsylvania, Germans in, 115; land
    distribution in, 42; Welsh in, 168,
    169
Philadelphia, 115; elite of, 139, 155,
    160; land grants in, 42; merchants,
    109, 139, 160; Quakers in, 154; and
    Scotland, 155; Welsh in, 169
piracy, 26, 42–3
Pitt, William, 103, 113
Plassey, Battle of, 177
Pontiac Rising, 186
Port Antonio, 25
Port Royal, 26

Porto Bello, 25
Pownall, Thomas, 113
Prescotts, Grote, Culverden and
    Hollingworth Bank, 62
Price, Charles, 112, 143
Price, Jacob M., 69, 70, 95
Prince Edward Island, 165
Proclamation Line (1763), 27, 186
Progressive historians, 178
Pym, Francis, 97

Quakers, and banking, 62; elite of
    Delaware Valley, 159; as merchants,
    154; as settlers, 42, 159, 169
Queen Anne's War, *see* Spanish
    Succession, War of

Rathell, Catherine, 133
Reeve, William, 94
Regulating Act, 184
Rolle, Denys, 91
Royal African Company, 85, 87
Rush, Benjamin, 111
Russell, James, 99

St Andrew, 141
St Christopher, *see* St Kitts
St John, 91
St Kitts, 22, 23, 162, 163; debts of, 94;
    land sales in, 74
St Vincent, 74
Sargent, John, 99
Schlesinger, Arthur, 108
Scotland, 6, 7, 20; and American
    Revolution, 170; and Atlantic empire,
    153, 155, 167–8; banking in, 61; and
    colonization, 153; emigration from,
    158, 161–2, 189; entry into landed
    society in, 68; and India, 164–5;
    landed elite in, 52, 53; merchants in,
    153; newspapers in, 76; settlers in
    America from, 159, 161–2, 165–8;
    settlers in West Indies from, 163–4;
    and tobacco trade, 88–9; *see also*
    Glasgow
Scottish American Company, 91
Seeley, Sir John, 16
Selkirk, 165
Seven Years' War, 15, 23, 176, 179
Shah Alam II, Mughal Emperor, 23, 30,
    87
Sheffield, 93
shipping, 32, 72, 118–19
Shugborough, 77

slave trade, 71, 96, 153
slavery, 129, 157
Society of Ancient Britons
 (Philadelphia), 169
Society for the Propagation of the
 Gospel in Foreign Parts, 123
Society for the Promotion of Arts,
 Manufactures and Commerce, 77
South Carolina, 191; economy of, 92;
 elite of, 139
South Sea Bubble crisis, 56, 87
Southern Department, 15
Spain, 67; threat to Britain from, 15,
 25, 26–7; empire of, 25
Spanish Succession, War of, 23
Spanish Town, 141
Spectator, The, 131
Steele, Ian K., 131
Stock Exchange, the, 62
stockjobbing, hostility towards, 63
Stowe, 77, 78
Stuart, James, 77
Stuart, John, 191
sugar, trade in, 39, 58
Surat, 22
Swallow, Frances, 133

Tatler, the, 131
taxation, 82–3; *see also* Land Tax
tea, consumption of, 38–9, 73; trade in,
 38–9
Third Mysore War, 176
Thompson, Maurice, 59
Tipu Sultan, 176
tobacco, consumption of, 39, 73;
 economy of Chesapeake, 134–5;
 trade in, 38, 58, 88–90
Tobago, 74
trade, and armed force, 24, 29, 33, 44;
 and convoys, 26; and empire, 32–6,
 117–18; on global scale, 59–60;
 growth of, 34–5; and kinship ties,
 62–3, 108–9, 152; and national
 strength, 32; organization of, 88–90;
 private, 43–4; and territorial
 expansion, 33, 36, 43–4

Treasury, the, 15, 74, 121
Trecothick, Barlow, 175
Tullideph, Walter, 163
Tyrone, Earl of, 91

Utrecht, Treaty of, 23, 74

Vandalia, 91, 187, 188
Verney family, 55
Vernon, Admiral, 25
Virginia, 59, 90; debts of, 93; expansion
 of, 27; gentry of, 134–7; Scots in,
 161, 167; and tobacco trade, 89
Virginia Bristol ironworks, 88
Vyner, Sir Richard, 55

Wales, 6, 20, 54; landed elite in, 52, 53;
 and North America, 168–9; Quakers
 from, 42, 169; settlers in America
 from, 158, 159, 168–9
Walpole, Sir Robert, 25
Ward, J.R., 37, 38
Warren, Admiral Sir Peter, 43, 92, 99,
 110
Washington, George, 41
Wedgwood, Josiah, 132
Wells, Robert, 167
West Indies, British, 4; British troops
 in, 26, 104; consumer goods in, 132,
 142; debts of, 94–5; economic growth
 of, 81, 141; elites in, 106, 109–10,
 128, 140–3, 162–4; identity in, 112,
 140–1, 143; lobbying by, 121; militia
 in, 28–9, 142; press in, 141; religion
 in, 122–3; Scots in, 162–3, 166; *see
 also* Barbados, Jamaica etc.
Westminster, Treaty of, 114
Weymouth, Lord, 175
Wharton, Samuel, 187
Whitefield, George, 129, 140
Whitehaven, colonial debts to, 93;
 growth of, 58; merchants in, 89
Wilkins family, 54
Wilson, Kathleen, 70, 74

Yorkshire, 67